LITERARY LEGACIES

FOLKLORE FOUNDATIONS

LITERARY LEGACIES

FOLKLORE FOUNDATIONS

*Selfhood and Cultural Tradition
in Nineteenth- and Twentieth-Century
American Literature*

KAREN E. BEARDSLEE

The University of Tennessee Press — Knoxville

Selection from *The Minister's Wooing* by Harriet Beecher Stowe. 1896. Reprinted courtesy of Houghton Mifflin.

Selection from *American Indian Stories* by Zitkala-Sǎ. Published 1921 by University of Nebraska Press. Reprinted courtesy of University of Nebraska Press

Selection from *How to Make an American Quilt* by Whitney Otto. Copyright © 1991 by Whitney Otto. Reprinted by permission of Villard Books, a Division of Random House Inc. Published in the United States by Random House. Published in the United Kingdom by Macmillan Publishers, London, 1991.

Selection from *The Conjure Woman* by Charles Chesnutt. Published 1969 by The University of Michigan Press. Reprinted courtesy of The University of Michigan Press.

Selection from *The Chaneysville Incident* by David Bradley. Copyright © 1981 by David H. Bradley, Jr. Reprinted by permission of HarperCollins Publishers, Inc.

Selection from *Ceremony* by Leslie Marmon Silko, copyright © 1977 by Leslie Silko. Used by permission of Viking Penguin, a division of Penguin Putnam Inc.

Selection from *The Study of American Folklore: An Introduction,* Third Edition by Jan Harold Brunvand. Copyright © 1986, 1978, 1968 by W. W. Norton & Company, Inc. Used by permission of W. W. Norton & Company, Inc.

Selection from *The Sacred Hoop* by Paula Gunn Allen. Copyright © 1986, 1992 by Paula Gunn Allen. Reprinted by permission of Beacon Press.

Selection from *Studies in American Indian Literature* by Paula Gunn Allen. Reprinted by permission of the Modern Language Association of America, copyright © 1983 by Modern Language Association of America.

Selection from *Intaglio, A Novel in Six Stories* by Roberta Fernández is reprinted with permission from the publisher (Houston: Arte Público Press—University of Houston, 1990).

Library of Congress Cataloging-in-Publication Data

Beardslee, Karen E., 1965–
    Literary legacies, folklore foundations : selfhood and cultural tradition in nineteenth- and twentieth-century American literature / Karen E. Beardslee.— 1st ed.
    p. cm.
    Includes bibliographical references and index.
    ISBN 1-57233-152-6 (cl.: alk. paper)
    1. American fiction—History and criticism. 2. Literature and folklore—United States. 3. Group identity in literature. 4. Ethnic groups in literature. 5. Folklore in literature. 6. Culture in literature. 7. Self in literature. I. Title.

PS374.F62 B43 2001
813'.309355—dc21   2001002741

I would like to thank my family, especially my grandparents. This project is a result of my experiences with them, the stories they have shared . . . the gift of myself.

CONTENTS

Introduction   ix

1. With This Needle . . . : Harriet Beecher Stowe's
   The Minister's Wooing and Whitney Otto's *How
   to Make an American Quilt*   1

2. Everybody Loves a Good Story: Charles Chesnutt's
   The Conjure Woman and David Bradley's *The
   Chaneysville Incident*   59

3. New Footing on Ancient Ground: Zitkala-Ša's
   American Indian Stories and Leslie Marmon
   Silko's *Ceremony*   99

4. What I Learn from You Goes with Me on the
   Journey: María Cristina Mena's "The Birth of the
   God of War" and Roberta Fernández's *Intaglio:
   A Novel in Six Stories*   129

   Conclusion   159
   Notes   167
   Works Cited   193
   Index   199

INTRODUCTION

Studies in Contemporary Literature:
The Search for Self—as It Was, as It Is

In the summer of 1993, I was asked to take over the Contemporary American Novel course offered by the community college where I teach. Although I had taught other literature courses for the college, I had not taught this course. The contemporary is my main area of specialization, so I was thrilled with the offer to finally get my hands wet. However, because the course had been given up just two short weeks before the class was to begin, the books to be used for it had already been ordered, and the course objectives and concerns already established. We would be reading the works of early contemporary authors—John Updike's *Rabbit, Run;* Ralph Ellison's *Invisible Man;* Philip Roth's *Goodbye, Columbus;* and Saul Bellow's *Seize the Day.* We would be studying the texts with a focus on the search for self, or, more accurately, the impossibility of such a thing. I say this because, as I and my students came to find, by and large, these texts posit self-understanding as an impossibility, something yearned for but fated to remain looming large on the unreachable horizon. Hardly culturally diverse, the text list supported *The Heath Anthology of American Literature*'s suggestion that apparent in many works of the 1950s is an anxiety over being different from mainstream culture, a culture existing through and maintained by a constant reiteration of its own monomyth. In literature courses of the early 1950s, this reiteration was accomplished, in part, by the almost exclusive teaching of "male experience theme" literature. The "Search for Self" delineated in such works resided outside the individual's family or community—"in business, the natural world, or war" (Lauter 1975 vol. 2). It was assumed, almost without question, that this search for self somehow spoke for all and not any group's particular experience. As the literary scene began to diversify culturally, however, a shift in the writing from a reflection of a monoculture—which renders individual lives and particularities of culture invisible or nebulous at best—to a reflection of cultural multiplicity occurred. And as our view of the literary landscape changed, so did our understanding of the "search for self," including both its outcome and its location.

When we look at the early contemporary works studied prior to multiculturalism's influence, we see that most rely upon the notion that a sense of self is not only virtually unattainable but also pursued in isolation, outside one's cultural community. When literature is studied through a multicultural lens, however, we find this notion is quite often refuted: a sense of self is attainable, but only if the individual situates the search within his/her cultural community. Ubiquitous today are multicultural literature studies that focus on the elucidation of a new place where a sense of self *can* be established. For instance, through a close reading of texts by authors of differing backgrounds, Bonnie TuSmith's *All My Relatives* and Missy Kubitschek's *Claiming the Heritage*,[1] illustrate that the literary search for self no longer occurs outside one's cultural community, but within it, and that a sense of self *is* achievable via a *return to roots,* so to speak. Studies such as these are important beginnings in changing our thinking about contemporary literature's portrayal of the search for self. However, while it is comforting to think that if we go home, there we are, surely something more is required: not only what the return home is like, but, once there, what the search for self actually entails for the individual.

The Search for Self: Literature and Life

> As long as one keeps searching, the answers come.
>
> JOAN BAEZ

Be it in literature or in life, the search for self begins with a series of questions the individual poses to him- or herself, questions best put by Ralph Ellison, a noted African American scholar and author of the contemporary masterpiece *Invisible Man.* In his seminal work *Shadow and Act,* a collection of essays about literature, art, and the relationship between creativity, culture, and personal identity, Ellison relates the queries involved when he embarked on his own search: "Who am I, what am I, how did I come to be? What shall I make of the life around me, what celebrate, what reject, how confront the snarl of good and evil which is inevitable? What does American society *mean* when regarded out of my *own* eyes, when informed by my *own* sense of the past and viewed by my *own* complex sense of the present?" (xxii) And then, as Ellison also suggests, the search for self requires an agency through which these questions can be answered. For Ellison, this agency was and is writing, writing that invariably draws on and celebrates the folk traditions of his community:

> I use folklore in my work not because I am Negro, but because writers like Eliot and Joyce made me conscious of the literary value of my folk inheritance. [. . .] For me, at least, in this discontinuous, swiftly changing and diverse American culture, the stability of the Negro American folk tradition became precious as a result of an act of literary discovery. Taken as a whole, its spirituals along with its blues, jazz and folk tales, it has [. . .] much to tell us of the faith, humor and adaptability to reality necessary to live in a world which has taken on much of the insecurity and blues-like absurdity known to those who brought it into being. For those who are able to translate its meanings into wider, more precise vocabularies it has much to offer indeed. (58–59)

Here Ellison confirms that although writing is his means to self, it is informed by what may be someone else's means entirely—folklore.

Folklore in Context

Definitions of folklore are abundant and ever changing. Barre Toelken writes the following in *The Dynamics of Folklore:*

> [t]hese wars, the struggles over definition, and the seemingly dizzy variety of approaches may initially put off the person newly interested in folklore. They need not be the occasion for fear, however, if put in a proper perspective. [. . .] One needs in any field to determine what one is studying, and to outline at least in general those approaches to the subject that have been considered fruitful by those who have spent a considerable amount of time trying to understand the materials. (6, 9)

Essential to my own definition of folklore is the relevance of cultural context to the significance or meaning of the folklore in question. As I have come to understand it, folklore is "[. . .] the traditional, unofficial, noninstitutional part of culture. It encompasses all knowledge, understandings, values, attitudes, assumptions, feelings, and beliefs transmitted in traditional forms by word of mouth or by customary examples." Moreover, it is a habit of thought or behavior that always interacts with and is influenced by the whole cultural context that surrounds it (Brunvand 4).[2] It is tied to and shaped by the cultural milieu from which it springs; we can discuss commonalties, but we should not forget that a folklore element's full meaning and purpose are directly related to the group(s) engaged in its transmission. Because of this, we may say, to know the folklore one must know the group, and vice versa. In Alan Dundes's essay "Defining Identity through Folklore," he urges us to consider the relationship between folklore and identity. Dundes sees folklore as a group-defining mechanism: through folklore we show others who we are and to which group we belong (7–13). And, surely, if folklore is a way of illustrating who we are to others as a group, it can be a way through which we define who we are to ourselves as individuals.

The significant role folklore plays in the lives of individuals is discussed at length by Robert A. Georges and Michael Owen Jones in the chapter entitled "Folklore as Personal Resource," found in their work *Folkloristics: An Introduction.* Here we learn that while an individual shares folklore with the members of a group, individuals also have their own vast repertoire of personal folklore; unique to each member is the perception, recall, and transmission of, for example, traditional stories. Of particular import here is the recognition that the folklore of the group is used by individuals—in a variety of ways—both to identify and to define themselves. That is, on the one hand, individuals make themselves recognizable to others through, say, the type and shape of the stories they tell. On the other hand, they engage in a tradition to come to terms with their world, using folklore as a "personal resource" to negotiate their lives (269–312). I well know how valuable folklore can be when put to this task.

Folklore and the Search for Self

Early in Ralph Ellison's life, he found that engaging in folk traditions provided an "unselfconscious affirmation" that could not be experienced in the more structured settings one becomes a part of outside the community (*Shadow and Act* 7–9).[3] In my own life, this has also been the case. Six years ago, shortly before my twenty-eighth birthday, a sense of who I was seemed to elude me. I could not find my own presence in the graduate classrooms I was so much a part of, in the New Jersey home I was making with my husband, in the long runs I took every morning to start my day. Seeking answers to the same questions Ellison asked of himself, I embarked on my own search. Influenced by the literary criticism I was reading at the time, I felt if I could only go "home," there I would be—me—in all my glory.[4] Unfortunately, as a member of a family dispersed across the eastern seaboard, there was not one place I could, in all honesty, call home, a community per se I would call my own. Or so I thought, until I went to visit my grandparents, who have lived in the same small town of Chambersburg, Pennsylvania, since my father was seven. During this visit I found myself listening to my grandparents, mainly my grandfather, tell the same family stories I had heard as a child. My grandfather has always been a storyteller, and in me he has always found a captive audience. But it wasn't until this visit, a visit that has now become a yearly tradition, that I realized his stories had meaning beyond entertaining a grandchild on a winter's night. His stories linked me to people both known and unknown. And in his stories of distant family members, some living, some dead, I found lessons for living this life; I found new—although ancient in many respects—ways to negotiate this world. My grandfather recognized my need—he recognized the journey I was beginning. There have been many visits like this since, the lengthiest storytelling sessions being held each Christmas Eve after the rest of the family has gone and my grandfather and I, often with my father and grandmother present, sit around the battered kitchen table weaving generations together through words. During these times, the stories pour forth, the lessons, sometimes hard to decipher, always a part of the lore passed between us. Yet, most important, because I am the only one my grandfather shares the stories with in this way—person to person, voice to ear to heart—I know he has chosen me as the person to pass them on. And in this act of choosing, he has given me the vehicle I needed to reach myself. Like Ellison's writing, my family's oral lore is my means to self. Over and over again, my experience with my grandfather illustrates to me that folklore is one of the most important ways we give life meaning beyond the immediate present.[5] The process of listening to and learning to tell my grandfather's stories connects me to the past, situates me in the present, and prepares me for the future. It is an ongoing and sometimes arduous process, but when it comes to the current questions I have about myself, I am finding the answers through folklore. I am not alone in this discovery.

The Search for Self: Folklore and Literature

It is my conviction that many writers of differing ethnic origins, both women and men, make an engagement in folk tradition, designed and designated to facilitate the individual's achievement of self, a necessary part of their characters' journeys to wellness. However, connecting folklore and literature, as proving my contention requires me to do, is a difficult task; anyone attempting to do so faces a plethora of tasks relating to definition, demonstration, and judgment. Many theories about the relationships between folklore and literature are available to the scholar who wants to create a methodology that will facilitate such analysis. Hence, the initial challenge comes in extracting "the theories most likely to foster understanding of the complex relationships" between the folk traditions and literary texts under scrutiny (Kirkland 1).[6]

The majority of critics now agree that by identifying a literary text's reliance upon or reference to folklore traditions and conventions, "one can convincingly demonstrate the very great extent to which literature relies upon folk traditions to hook and hold its audience"(Jones xv). Nevertheless, according to Richard Dorson's pivotal essay, "The Identification of Folklore in American Literature," in order to do this while also avoiding the pitfalls often attributed to folklore and literature studies, the scholar must "identify and document as accurately as possible the contact of authors with folk traditions [. . .] prove that authors have directly dipped into the flowing stream of folk tradition, [and] discuss whether or not this folklore contributes to a given literary work in any important way" (199, 209).[7]

Over the years, although elaborated upon and modified to some extent, Dorson's objectives have remained guiding principles in folklore and literature studies.[8] Nevertheless, while folklorists such as Georges, Jones, and Toelken urge us to study folklore in literature with an eye to how writers use it to convey theme or, more important, *as* theme, scholars in this field have continued to limit themselves to pinpointing and describing the way the folk aesthetic structures the literary text. Therefore, my study aims to move beyond "structuring" questions to questions concerning content and theme. That is, it asks the following: (1) What is the relationship between the character(s) and the folk tradition? (2) What statement is being made about the folk tradition through this relationship? (3) How does this statement shape what we are to come away with upon finishing the story?[9]

I will focus my exploration of these issues on the theme of individual wellness and cultural return as dramatized in four contemporary novels centered around folk traditions.[10] My chosen novels—Whitney Otto's *How to Make an American Quilt,* David Bradley's *The Chaneysville Incident,* Leslie Marmon Silko's *Ceremony,* and Roberta Fernández's *Intaglio: A Novel in Six Stories*—all trace an individual's journey to wholeness, a journey intrinsically linked to the individual's return to a specific community and culture. However, Otto, Bradley, Silko, and Fernández make clear that more is required than a simple return. All four novelists show that an understanding of and participation in specific cultural traditions is key to the completion of this journey. Accordingly, I believe those cultural traditions not only structure the texts but also become significant thematic subtexts. In other words, we are talking about more than a mere chronicling of folk traditions as they are a part of a particular community's way of life, more than a delineation of particular traditions in the service of thematic objectives. Rather—or in addition—we are talking about texts that afford "folk traditions" a central role by making the traditions part and parcel of what the character goes through and finally achieves. Moreover, the authors pinpoint a "particular" folk tradition as a means to self-knowledge, indicating that cultural communities design and designate specific traditions to facilitate the *individual's* healing process.[11]

Although this type of folklore and literature study may be fairly new, the American author's use of folklore is not. To illustrate the point, I pair the contemporary authors with their forerunners. Here, following the model provided by Mobley and Kubitschek, I discuss authors of earlier periods in relation to contemporary authors partially in order to break free of the constraints strict periodicity imposes.[12] Implicitly, however, my pairing of texts works as a critique of the progress model of history—a model that maintains there is a greater and greater America to be made and had. Progress, in this model, means to leave behind what is often seen as a simpler way of life, a way of life that has community and cultural tradition at its heart. What we have lost through a "progress model" study of literature is what my study hopes to retrieve—the continuities between authors of different time periods and literary movements whose works suggest a constant, and perhaps oppositional, American folk culture. That is to say, in marking these earlier authors as literary cultural forebears, I hope to show that authors of the late nineteenth and early twentieth centuries laid the foundation for the type of literary folk houses being built today.

Joining nineteenth- and twentieth-century authors with this objective in mind addresses two of my own pedagogical concerns. The first is how to bring students closer to the literature of earlier periods. Because students, I find, are forever trying to tie what they read to the world they are coming to know, the question I pose to myself is this: How do I convey that what has been written in the past contains meanings and messages applicable to contemporary characters? By pairing contemporary authors with authors of earlier periods, I feel I can demonstrate the links hoped for. For if we see our contemporary authors as carrying on a legacy, rather than breaking off to begin anew, we create a bridge to cover the gap that exists for students between the past and present. We enable students to discuss literature both in relation to the world it grew out of and in relation to the world they are living in.

The second pedagogical concern my study addresses has to do with the critical methods we make available to students of literature and the way in which those methods are viewed. Because folklore has been perceived by some as "a bastard field that anthropology begot upon English" (Coffin v), literature's indebtedness to folklore has, until fairly recently, been either deliberately ignored or simply largely overlooked. Whatever the reason, for the scholar wishing to study literature with folklore in mind (even minimally), this has meant running up against a good deal of resistance typically based on issues of responsibility. In addition, studies—whether folklore or literature—founded on the idea of reciprocity between folklore and literature, have suffered from a kind of forced "academic compartmentalization." As Richard Bauman asserts in *Story, Performance, and Event,* "[. . .] the rise of academic differentiation and its concomitant division of intellectual labor have fragmented the unified vision of literature as cultural production that was folklore's birthright." As a result, Bauman proclaims, for both the folklorist and the literary accessor, "much has been lost" (1). I could not agree more. Confined to separate realms, professionals within the fields have been done a disservice. We have been limited in the ways we approach our subjects. What's more, so have our students.

This is what makes opening the critical pathways between folklore and literature imperative. For when I engage my students in multicultural studies, I am asking them to analyze culture. In asking them to look closely at culture, I am requiring them to study tradition, which means I am, at the very least, pointing them in the direction of folklore. And when my students find the great extent to which cultural groups live through their traditions, they should have at their disposal the means to determine whether or not those groups (or individuals within those groups) might be writing through and/or about those traditions as well. I am not placing my students on a slippery slope here. Rather, in opening the road between folklore and literature, I am not only broadening the critical approaches available to my students, but also placing literature and folklore on a level playing field where their work can be seen as reciprocal. That is, we can come to see that folklore and literature work together to suggest the possibility of survival whole, rather than the inevitability of a fluctuating and fragmented American way of life.

A Century Apart: Folk Group vs. Gender and Ethnicity

A superficial survey of my pairings—Harriet Beecher Stowe's *The Minister's Wooing* with Whitney Otto's *How to Make an American Quilt*, Charles Chesnutt's *The Conjure Woman* with David Bradley's *The Chaneysville Incident*, Zitkala-Šá's *American Indian Stories* with Leslie Marmon Silko's *Ceremony*, and María Cristina Mena's stories with Roberta Fernández's *Intaglio*—would lead one to suppose that they are based on the gender and ethnicity of the authors. Yet in truth what structures the pairings I have created are the folk groups to which the characters of the novels belong, as well as the way our concepts of gender and ethnicity affect the characters' sense of self.[13] I pair by "folk group" because groups differentiated by gender and ethnicity fall under this heading; an ethnic group, for instance, is a type of folk group.[14] As Alan Dundes tells us, "the term 'folk' can refer to *any group of people whatsoever* who share at least one common factor. It does not matter what the linking factor is—it could be a common occupation, language or religion—what is important is that a group formed for whatever reason will have some traditions which it calls its own" (*Study of Folklore* 11). Barre Toelken explains it as follows:

> [. . .] in the case of ethnic groups, the question of whether the group is a folk group will rest not on surnames or skin color or genetics but on the existence of a network of dynamic traditional interactions. A black American who does not participate in any Black traditional systems is not a functioning member of any Black folk group. A white American who does participate fully (language, custom, dance, food, etc.) in an American Indian tribe may be said to be a member of that folk group—whether or not his grandmother was a Cherokee princess, while someone who is genetically 100 percent

Native American may not be a member of that folk group if
he does not participate in the folk customs. Thus, we must
look at the nature of the dynamic interaction, not at
superficial details. (72)

Because these principles also apply to the relationship between gender and
folk group, we should understand that although gender *and/or* ethnicity may
be influential in bringing an individual to a group, what binds and defines the
members as a whole goes beyond constructed categorical concepts, such as
gender and ethnicity—concepts that are "both socially and historically contingent and politically charged" (Fox 31).[15] What binds a folk group of any kind is
"the common core of traditions belonging to the group," and it is these "traditions which help the group to have a sense of group identity" (Dundes, *Study
of Folklore* 11). Hence, with the characters' folk groups as the linking factor
between texts, the focus is on the tradition(s) the characters engage in as a
means to self-realization, rather than solely on the gender or ethnicity of the
characters or authors.[16]

   This is not to say that gender and ethnicity do not play a significant
role in the characters' trials with a sense of self, for they do. In the contemporary novels, the characters' achievement of this is threatened, mainly because
they are attempting to define themselves according to one or both of these concepts. The problem is our conceptions of gender and ethnicity are ever changing. Hence, individuals who seek self-definition through these concepts find
their sense of self in a constant state of flux. Moreover, what truly problema-
tizes identity for the contemporary characters is the fact that they have allowed
or are allowing their definitions of self to be determined strictly from the outside in. Seeking a sense of self in this way is a dangerous endeavor, and one
doomed to failure as the characters eventually learn. However, once they identify themselves with a specific folk group and engage in the traditions that
define that group, they find that the group's folklore provides individual members with a means of determining for themselves what is valuable and what dis-
cardable in terms of the externally defined concepts with which they have been
struggling. This layered lesson, however, is not one the characters in the
nineteenth-century novels have to learn. The characters in the nineteenth-
century novels of this study do not define themselves according to concepts;
working from the inside, as part of an established folk group, they learn early
on to define themselves through folk traditions designed with that end in mind.

Any encounters these characters have with socially constructed concepts occur after the traditions have been fully ingrained—a part of who they are. In other words, they already know the way to return to themselves if the need arises.

This study's central concern is the textual illustration of the individual's ability to achieve a positive sense of self and place in the world.[17] Thus, my aim in entering these conceptual debates is to show, *first,* how the contemporary texts I have chosen mark concepts of gender and ethnicity as impediments to the individual's quest for whole survival. And, *second,* as the individual is then in need of an alternate, more direct and personal route to self, I argue that the nineteenth-century authors through their texts provide an answer the contemporary authors take up—a twofold harmonizing course: community return *and* immersion in tradition.

The Life of the Text

What folk traditions an author portrays, of course, depends upon the life to be presented. In the nineteenth-century novel analyzed in my second chapter, *The Minister's Wooing,* Harriet Beecher Stowe creates a community with a female base.[18] The women are the focal point; thus, it is female folk traditions we learn of here. Stowe is very crafty in the way she makes these traditions relevant to the life of the community. She does this by creating characters whose roles and actions actually resemble the folk traditions they perform. Because the primary tradition on which Stowe focuses is needlework, it is Miss Prissy, the community seamstress, who stitches the community of *The Minister's Wooing* together. She is the connecting thread, bringing diverse portions of it into the fold. In *The Minister's Wooing,* Stowe redeems women's folk culture, presenting the tradition of needlework as a self-centering and defining mode of female survival. Stowe's work provides space and model for the contemporary work studied in this chapter: *How to Make an American Quilt* by Whitney Otto.

In her novel, Otto illustrates how the female folk tradition of quilting not only mirrors life processes but also provides life lessons. For the quilting tradition is not only ethic but also aesthetic—the text is pieced together much like a quilt. Like Stowe, by focusing on a female folk tradition, Otto is able to confront accepted notions of what it means to be female and what it means to be an individual and a community member. Yet even more important, Otto's focus serves to pinpoint the female folk tradition of quilting as a means through which the individual can successfully complete a "journey to know."

The idea of a "journey to know" is also embedded in Charles Chesnutt's *The Conjure Woman,* the nineteenth-century text studied in chapter 2. On the one hand, in *The Conjure Woman,* Chesnutt takes his readers on a journey to know the real "plantation story," calling into question the values that give rise to the notions of benevolent master and loyal slave. On the other hand, the series of interrelated tales Uncle Julius imparts both criticize a system *and* celebrate a culture. Hence, Chesnutt also takes his readers on a journey to know a particular aspect of black folk life—the folktale—and a particular role within the black community—the folktale teller. Uncle Julius's tales illustrate the folktale's communal value—for through it one could transmit information, maintain hope, and teach proper modes of behavior. And as Uncle Julius fulfills the role of taleteller, Chesnutt also illustrates the relationship of the tradition to the individual. As taleteller, Uncle Julius is clearly linked to the past, the present, and the future. Hence, the tradition of oral taletelling serves to define and center him. Through Uncle Julius's tales, Chesnutt is able to chronicle other black folk traditions, such as conjuring. But it is through Uncle Julius himself that he is able to pinpoint a tradition as a means to both community and individual survival. This message is not lost on the contemporary author, David Bradley, whose novel *The Chaneysville Incident* applies the lesson to present-day life.

In *The Chaneysville Incident,* the oral tradition as a means of learning about, acting in, and passing on history is at odds with the main character's reliance on written history. Made evident through what John, the main character in the novel, finally learns is that true and meaningful history must be a reconciliation of both traditions. For it is only through this reconciliation that John is able to come to terms with his past and its influence on his present state of being. When he studies the written facts alone he is no more than a passive observer, but when he becomes the storyteller himself, combining the documented facts with his own oral interpretations, he becomes an active participant in past, present, and future realities. Engaged in the tradition of oral storyteller, he is finally able to reconcile those parts of himself fragmented by an isolating contemporary life and a hauntingly enticing past.

The tensions that arise when internalized cultural traditions must be distorted to fit external foreign structure permeate Zitkala-Ša's *American Indian Stories,* the nineteenth-century text that begins chapter 3. Given voice here is a struggle to reconcile new traditions with old—the Anglo-American written tradition with the Native American oral tradition. Maintaining tradition and establishing identity become increasingly difficult in the face of acculturation, as we see in both the autobiographical sketches and the series of connected stories that follow. For the combined parts of the text maintain an air of fragmentation, an underlying fissure that coexists with the affirmation of cultural traditions.

While the first half of the autobiographical text has a distinct coherence, as Zitkala-Să celebrates place and links cultural tradition to self-definition, when we move to the second part of the autobiographical text, fragmentation becomes apparent. No longer can we follow the movement of life according to season or habit; life is depicted as moving through a series of struggles as Zitkala-Să begins oscillating between two distinct worlds—one of ingrained tradition, the other of outward structure. In her attempts to reconcile new traditions with old, Zitkala-Să's sense of self and time clouds and we enter fully the realm of legend.

In this section appears a series of Native American legends, through which Zitkala-Să shows that legends are not strictly myth or fable or truth.[19] They are ambiguities that work to place the essence of truth in the hands of the individual. Moreover, their appearance at the point of fragmentation makes them an offering to coherence. For although the stories may not seem related, connecting them is their articulation of the relationship of individuals to their community and culture, a relationship meant to transcend betrayal, dispersal, loss of land, and even death. Each story contains a version of this lesson and thus works with the first half of the book as an answer: fragmentation need not mean total loss, and neither fragmentation nor loss need be bereft of possibility. Hence, although the work ends with an essay addressing the American Indian's Problem—an essay that rounds out the book, with its enunciation of the issues residing within the body of the text—the theme of the work, the connecting thread, is the idea of possibility, "this vision of wholeness in which the conflicting parts of her existence can be reconciled" (xviii).

However, in the contemporary novel of chapter 3, *Ceremony* by Leslie Marmon Silko, possibility is what the main character, Tayo, fails to see until he returns to his community and engages in a tribal tradition that not only brings him back among others, but also gives him back to himself. Silko's *Ceremony*, in both theme and structure, illustrates the intimate relationship between cultural traditions and individual survival. In blending folk aesthetic and folk ethic, Silko asks that we not only absorb the way the text works on the page, but also the way the mythic ceremony works in tribal communities. The text is structured such that we have the story of Tayo, whose experiences as a half-breed and World War II veteran have nearly destroyed his sense of self, interspersed with ancient stories of recompense and renewal. The stories that interrupt Tayo's are directly related to the trials Tayo must go through and the lessons he must learn along his journey to wholeness. Yet the direct relationship of the stories to Tayo's journey is not made explicit until Tayo comes to an understanding of the structure of tribal traditions, something the tribal healer, Betonie, gives voice to. Betonie tells Tayo that inherent in these traditions is the notion of change and renewal. The traditional ceremonies, rituals, and ways of healing were meant to change over time, but the result was to be the same—restoration and recovery. Betonie's teachings free up Tayo to relate an ancient tribal myth to his own life. His lessons allow and encourage Tayo to interpret the myth according to his own trials, questions, circumstances, and experiences. For the myth, which embodies a ceremony, will not have import for Tayo until he enacts the ceremony the myth lays out and shapes that ceremony to make it his own. He must create his own ceremony in order to arrive, finally, at a place where survival whole is possible. Hence, through structure and content, Silko marks the mythic ceremony as curative for the isolated individual.

The restorative powers of folk traditions are also made apparent in the works of the Mexican American women writers focused on in chapter 4: early-twentieth-century short-story writer María Cristina Mena and contemporary author Roberta Fernández. Until recently, however, the folk work Mena did went virtually unnoticed.[20] For as Tiffany Ana López explains in "María Cristina Mena: Turn-of-the-Century La Malinche and Other Tales of Cultural (Re) Construction," Mena's authorial and character tricksterism created a surface image so large that only a reader aware of the "codes always embedded in trickster narratives for their cultural insiders" could find the valuable cultural work being done (27). Through a reevaluation that reveals the trickster element embedded in Mena's fiction, López shows us how Mena, as creator of the feminist trickster, reconstructs "a mythic tradition that makes women central to cultural production: a movement across a culture that is set up to limit women, and toward a location of empowerment" (40).

Where this study is concerned, López's work is invaluable. For as Mena's tricksterism is revealed, I am able to move below the surface of Mena's texts, where I find an abundance of connections made between other folk traditions and female survival. To expose these connections, I will focus on that part of Mena's work López identifies as her "second stage," a time when Mena "began to signify upon Mexican folklore," and a place where Mena "demonstrates her assertion of Mexican female characters as powerful figures in the community, as matriarchs, storytellers, and heroines" (26). For instance, I will use the story "The Birth of the God of War" to illustrate how Mena makes storytelling an essential aspect of the narrator's youth, and the storyteller (the narrator's *mamagrande*) a model of self-definition.

But López's work is also valuable to me because it points out how Mena's dual engagement with the folk tradition of tricksterism allowed her both to survive as an artist and to create a message of survival for the Mexican American female community. As feminist trickster, Mena cleared a space for later authors to inhabit. And, with the authorial trickster groundwork done, contemporary authors are free to comment outright on the "central role women play in cultural production" without the need to create or become tricksters themselves (López 40).

Such freedom is fully utilized by Roberta Fernández in *Intaglio: A Novel in Six Stories*. In this work, not only does Fernández make female traditions central to cultural communities, but she shows how such traditions serve to define and center the individual women who engage in them. I close chapter 4, and my study, with Fernández because, unlike the other authors, her work identifies a variety of traditions women engage in when seeking or maintaining a sense of self. In other words, this novel moves us to understand that part of the value of such self-defining folk traditions is their variety, which means, as the narrator learns, that the individual has the freedom to choose the tradition that best fits the shape of her journey to know herself.

Finally, I return to the pedagogical concerns fueling this study by further comparing the primary texts to each other, highlighting *both* commonalties and differences. As teachers of literature, we often emphasize commonalties in an effort to make all texts meaningful to all students. My approach, with its focus on the search for self and folklore, is, yes, an effort to show what, as a unit, the authors—through their texts—suggest to their readers about the two: that a sense of self is directly linked to an acknowledgment of and engagement in folk traditions. But, more importantly, my approach seeks to convey the particularities of the folk groups and folk tradition(s) the writers affirm by having them inform their texts so completely. That is to say, I want to stress the inadequacy and incompleteness of a common message if one does not *first* come to an understanding of the folk group the author presents, the particular traditions native to it, the way they are perceived and utilized by the group, and how a return to traditional roots can be or is achieved in each case, *before* deciding why, in general, a return to community *and* tradition must occur: to reintegrate humans with their unique environments.

I begin this final discussion here because I believe discussing similarities between texts, although beneficial, is such safe ground; students as well as teachers enjoy the moment when the unfamiliar becomes familiar by way of analogy. However, the moment of difference, although it is often the most active time, makes us a bit uncomfortable. This may be because the word *different* is, these days, loaded with negative associations. But it is more likely because, to point out differences between texts is to mark off places where much must be learned and studied, where not only the action, but also, on occasion, the writing itself, requires, at the very least, rudimentary research rather than simple relating. This part of my study seeks to emphasize the responsibility of student and teacher alike to acquire a basic knowledge of the lives presented in the texts and through the texts, lives that may not be at all like their own. I stress folklore studies as a means to fulfilling that literary responsibility.[21]

Then, as the value of folklore and literature studies is once again brought to the forefront, and because the literature written over a century ago is sometimes considered by students as removed from their experience as the literature written today by authors of differing cultural backgrounds, I will suggest how this type of folklore and literature approach might be applied in the classroom to other nineteenth-century and contemporary works.

LITERARY LEGACIES

FOLKLORE FOUNDATIONS

CHAPTER 1

With This Needle . . .

Harriet Beecher Stowe's
The Minister's Wooing and
Whitney Otto's *How to
Make an American Quilt*

Needlework as Art, Needlework as Life: Harriet Beecher Stowe's The Minister's Wooing

[. . .] what matters most is that we learn from living.

DORIS LESSING

Numerous critics have suggested that we read women's writing with an eye trained on needlework imagery, an ear tuned to piecing metaphors, so that we may uncover the intimate relationship between women's "piecing" traditions and women's literary creativity.[1] One of the most valuable studies of this relationship appears in Elaine Showalter's *Sister's Choice*. In the chapter "Common Threads," Showalter traces the trajectory of the female author's use of "piecing and patchwork" metaphors, from their heyday in the early nineteenth century, to their decline in mid-century, to their resurgence almost one hundred years later. Women's cultural traditions, she asserts, can be studied as "both theme and form in women's writing [. . .]" (146).[2] Such an analysis focuses not only on how these traditions structure female texts—"on the level of the word, the sentence, the structure of a story or novel, and the images, motifs, or symbols that unify a fictional work"—but on what their relationship is to the lives presented in the text (151).

Although Showalter does not use the term *folklore,* the female cultural traditions her discussion highlights are a part of women's folklore. Furthermore, in asking us to examine the traditional process(es) that went into making a text, as well as the traditional processes depicted therein, Showalter encourages a folklore and literature study that puts to use the more recent performance-centered folklore approach. Performance-centered folklore approaches concern themselves more with process than with product. Linda Pershing explains in "Peace Work out of Piecework":

> With the advent of performance-centered approaches, which
> have as their primary concern the behavior, activity, and creative
> communicative processes of expression, many folklore scholars
> have moved away from analysis of the folk object as an end in

itself and toward the study of people's behavior in interacting
with objects. With this new focus there is a recent concern for
the people who create and use objects and for how they
behave in relation to those objects within a specific sociohis-
torical setting. This newer orientation has as its goal the better understanding of how people relate to and manipulate
objects in order to express themselves, their notions of identity, and their personal and cultural values. (335)

Much can be gained by a performance-centered approach to the folk traditions structuring and informing female texts. Such a folklore and literature
investigation would seek to determine what the literary allusion to and depiction of a tradition's processual aspects has to do with the writing of the text and
the life presented in the text—the very things I want to reveal in my discussion of Harriet Beecher Stowe's *The Minister's Wooing*.

Studied, until recently, mainly for the messages it sends about Calvin-
ist doctrine and slavery issues, the main plot of *The Minister's Wooing* centers
on the choices Mary Scudder, a self-contained young woman, faces in choosing
a mate: either her own first love, James, an unconverted seagoing young man,
or her mother's choice for her, Dr. Hopkins, the town's much respected anti-
slavery-minded minister and Mary's religious mentor. However, neither an
analysis of Stowe's Calvinism critique nor of her marriage plot would expose
what is of interest here and what I believe is *The Minister's Wooing*'s overall
structuring tool and primary focus: women's cultural traditions.

While illustrating her points about the relationship between women's
cultural traditions—specifically piecing and patchwork—and literary expression, Showalter often turns to Stowe's work in general, and *The Minister's Wooing* in particular. *The Minister's Wooing* is indeed replete with needlework
metaphors that relate this set of almost exclusively female cultural traditions
not only to Stowe's writing process, but also to the way women negotiate the
world.[3] That is to say, by way of her own comments in the text, and especially
through the female folk group *The Minister's Wooing* brings to life, Stowe
urges us to consider needlework as both a model for women's writing and a
method for female living.[4]

In Stowe's day, patchworking involved the pulling together of scraps
and fragments into a useful item.[5] Such scraps and fragments, left over from
clothesmaking and the like, and perhaps worthless to the untrained eye, were
saved in the ever-present scrapbag of the needleworker in the family. While the

needleworker's skills were often prized and admired, they were also a necessity for early American families.[6] With the harsh winters and scarcity of goods, the needleworker's ability to combine thrift and craft into useful articles was much needed. Jonathan Holstein tells us, in *American Pieced Quilts* that in eighteenth- and nineteenth-century America

> [. . .] needlework was a highly-prized, indeed, an essential feminine skill.
>
> [. . .] an integral part of every girl's education was the competent production of sewn articles. For the leisured, it was a necessary social grace; for those who depended on the work of their hands to keep their families in clothes and their homes in bed clothing and other necessary cloth articles, it was an absolute necessity. (10)[7]

And because the ability to do needlework was both a social and an economic imperative for women, scholarly discussions of the craft move us to avoid an overly romantic view of needlework and what it provided individual women. Echoing and elaborating on what Holstein tells us, Marilyn Lithgow, in her work *Quiltmaking and Quiltmakers,* explains:

> Needlework was not a pleasant pastime but an economic necessity. Every piece of clothing and all household linens had to be stitched by hand, and only the very wealthy could afford to purchase the quilted bed coverings and curtains that provided a degree of comfort in the days before central heating. Quilts and bed hangings were included in the items listed in old wills as valuable property to be handed down to the next generation. It was not until well after the Civil War that ready-made blankets came into general household use, and the necessity for making quilts and comforters at home began to wane. (3)

Moreover, in her essay "Quilts and Women's Culture," Elaine Hedges tells us that in terms of

> [. . .] women's work and oppression within a patriarchal society [. . .] needlework was not only symbol but actuality. Before the days of machine-made clothing and blankets, little girls

were forced to learn to sew; and learning to sew often took
precedence over, or was the female substitute for learning to
read and write [. . .] Sewing, for instance, of samplers with
moral messages, was intended to inculcate in little girls their
class or gender virtues of neatness, submissiveness, docility
and patience. One learned quilting by working on one small
square, sewing it, ripping out the stitching, sewing it again,
over and over and over, until proficiency had been achieved.
Many women learned to hate the work [. . .] one must ask to
what extent needlework had to substitute, for women, for
what might have been freely chosen work, or for various
forms of political activism. (18)

Nevertheless, whether needlework was an economic necessity or not for the
women of these times, piecing and patchworking fit well into their lives; it
could be done not only from fragments but also *in* fragments. Typically, patchworking was done during those rare moments the needleworker found to herself, when other household tasks were completed for the time being and
husband and children were not under foot. According to art critic Lucy Lippard, "the mixing and matching of fragments is the product of the interrupted
life [. . .] a necessity for those whose time comes in small squares" (32).

A task in itself to be sure, patchwork also provided a welcome "relief
from the real labor of family maintenance" (Holstein 12); it yielded women, on
an individual basis, the time for personal reflection, a few moments to order the
scraps of daily life and the fragments of the American experience into a coherent design of her own choosing.[8] And, as few creative outlets were afforded to
women, this designing also became women's primary mode of artistic expression. Patchwork items, such as quilts, were a composite of aesthetic choices and
personal record. They contained family history and reflected the likes and dislikes, joys and sorrows of their makers. For the most part, each piece that went
into a finished patchwork product was chosen both for its utility and its emotional pertinence. Thus, although the organization of fragments may have
seemed arbitrarily pleasing to the untrained observer, the ordering of pieces
revealed as much about a woman's eye for arrangement as it did the significance
of her memories and experiences.[9]

Like fragments going into the making of a quilt, *The Minister's Wooing* first appeared as installments in the *Atlantic Monthly*, running from

December 1858 to December 1859. Although the text's initial pieced together form might alert one to the role quilting plays in it, it is Stowe herself who calls immediate attention to her writing's relationship to patchwork traditions. After but one line of exposition, Stowe breaks the story off, begins a new paragraph, and launches into a commentary on the task of storytelling, likening beginning a story, quite succinctly, with the way one embarks on a piecing project:

> When one has a story to tell, one is always puzzled which end
> of it to begin at. You have a whole corps of people to intro-
> duce that you know and your reader doesn't; and one thing so
> presupposes another, that, whichever way you turn your
> patchwork, the figures still seem ill arranged. (1)

As suggested here, like the patchwork quilt maker who knows the significance of each piece going into the quilt and, thus, may find it difficult deciding which piece belongs where and with which one to begin, Stowe, too, found it hard deciding which piece (read: character and scene) should take center stage at the outset of her narrative. Moreover, as the quilter knows that although her work may look to the "uninterested observer like a miscellaneous collection of odd bits and ends [. . .]," Stowe realizes that the random nature of her story's beginning belies its systematic narrative structure, which will only reveal a coherent whole after each piece is read and deciphered ("The Patchwork Quilt" 11). In a further allusion to quilting practices, Stowe goes on to tell us that although her choice of beginnings would seem to be random, having cho-sen "a small item which [. . .] will do as well as any other to begin with," she has a method to her piecing choices: this first piece leads to a question that will start her "systematically" on her story (1).

What immediately follows Stowe's aside, however, is not the story of the previously mentioned tea party, nor does what comes next conform to a tradi-tional literary system of linearity. Instead, the remainder of this first chapter and the entire second chapter jump back and forth between detailing New England life and manners and providing a brief history of events prior to the story's present. Only briefly, at the beginning of chapter 2, does Stowe return to the tea party of the story's first line. But this is a crafty design trick, for although it comforts the reader to know Stowe has not lost the guiding thread of her story, it actually permits her to describe the efficiency of the New England woman's kitchen and housekeeping habits and further to introduce main char-acters. Finally, at the end of chapter 2, Stowe comments, "You see, instead of getting our tea ready, as we promised at the beginning of this chapter, we have filled it with descriptions and meditations, and now we foresee that the next chapter will be equally far from the point" (21).

By remarking on the crazy pattern she is creating, Stowe, again, although more covertly in this instance, alludes to her writing's relationship to patchworking. Rather than following the clear line (design) a reader (beholder) presupposes, Stowe's work moves over the thoughts and associations brought to mind by the first pieces she laid out for inclusion in her story (quilt): Mrs. Katy Scudder and the tea party. And, she warns us her design will continue to travel in this seemingly haphazard manner. We can take heart, however, when she tells us, "But have patience with us; for we can write only as we are driven, and never know exactly where we are going to land" (21). For here she once more surreptitiously gives reason for her literary lingering and patchwork meandering: the emotional significance and loaded associations of the pieces.

These metaphorical narrative asides slyly suggest the system dictating the shape of Stowe's story: that of the "pieced" or "patchworked" quilt of her day. In doing so, she points to a way of figuring her focus. We should read her story's pieces and their arrangement as we would the patchwork quilt's, with a concern for determining the overall connecting thread. The pieces reviewed thus far are the foundational squares of Stowe's textual quilt, and like so many of those to follow, these pieces refer us constantly to the surroundings and daily habits of the women in this New England community. Through such faithful references, Stowe makes the female community the element of significance in *The Minister's Wooing,* upon which she wants our eye trained, for much will be revealed there about the relationship between what women do and how women live.

Stowe began establishing the components of this female community in the first line of her text, in which she introduced the members of Mrs. Scudder's tea party: Katy Scudder herself, Mrs. Twitchel, Mrs. Brown, and Mrs. Jones. However, as the text moves and more members are revealed—Mary, Miss Prissy, Candace, Cerinthy Ann—we soon find that what we have is not simply a community of women, but an established female folk group.[10] What sets this group of women apart from the larger community of women are the traditions it lays claim to—needleworking traditions.

Spotlighting women's lives, *The Minister's Wooing* covers, often in depth, the compendium of day-to-day tasks in which women engage: cooking, cleaning, laundering, to name a few. Nevertheless, because the text is focused on the female folk group mentioned above, the most prevalent of women's activities in *The Minister's Wooing* is needlework. This work is constantly being done, and its fruits are frequently displayed. It is the activity engaged in at the tea party; it is what Mary does in her bedroom; it is Miss Prissy's occupation. It is a subject of correspondence and a frequent topic of conversation. It also goes into the most prized aspects of the characters' surroundings. Take, for instance, what holds the women's attention at the tea party—not only their needlework as they do it, but also the needlework enhancing the tea table. From Mrs. Scudder's "snowy damask covering" to Mary's napkins, each piece laid out is carefully scrutinized, briefly historied, and subsequently complimented. In addition, the text returns again and again to the needlework hanging on the walls and windows, covering the bed, filling the closet, and waiting to be set in motion on the spinning wheel. These pieces are highly regarded because, Stowe explains, to the women needlework is not only useful, it is artistic:

> The good wives of New England, impressed with that thrifty orthodoxy of economy which forbids to waste the merest trifle, had a habit of saving every scrap clipped out in the fashioning of household garments, and these they cut into fanciful patterns and contracted of them rainbow shapes and quaint traceries, the arrangement of which became one of their fine arts. Many a maiden, as she sorted and arranged fluttering bits of green, yellow, red, and blue, felt rising in her breast a passion for somewhat vague and unknown, which came out at length in a new pattern of patchwork. Collections of these tiny fragments were always ready to fill an hour when there was nothing else to do; and as the maiden chattered with her beau, her busy flying needle stitched together those pretty bits, which, little in themselves, were destined by gradual unions and accretions to bring about at last substantial beauty, warmth, and comfort,—emblems thus of that household life which is to be brought to stability and beauty be reverent economy in husbanding and tact in arranging the little useful and agreeable morsels of daily existence. (316)

Hence, as necessity, as art, we find needlework everywhere, a core part of everything. Being such, it is exposed as the women's principal method of identifying each other and defining themselves.

We first see how the women are likened to and defined through their needlework during the tea party that finally takes place in chapter 4. Here we find that the knitting habits of Mrs. Twitchel, the tea party's first arrival, mirror her tendency to run at the mouth. As she talks "a steady stream," her knitting needles trot along "contentedly to the mournful tone of her voice." We witness how the affected airs of Mrs. Simeon Brown, the wife of a wealthy ship owner and slave trader, are evidenced as such to others whenever she gives "a nervous twitch to her yarn." And we learn that Katy Scudder's knitting is understood by Mrs. Brown to be indicative of the very person she is, her "[. . .] quiet, positive style [. . .] an implication of independence of her sway" (35). Then, much later in the text, we discover that Mary's work with needle and thread is, according to the others, like Mary herself, "a pattern" the other girls in the community would do well in following (331). In these instances, distinctions are made between women according to their work; because the women see handiwork as either reflection of personality or evidence of true nature, they use it to identify one another. Nowhere is the relationship between needlework and personality more apparent than when we meet Miss Prissy Diamond, the town's seamstress.

Unlike the other women, whose needlework can be found, for the most part, only in their own homes, Miss Prissy's work can be detected everywhere. Her creations complement every conceivable closet, her threads and patches an invisible part of the most important trousseaus.[11] And Miss Prissy herself is similarly ubiquitous, with such a "string of engagements with the women that she never found half an hour to listen to what any man living would say to her, supposing she could stop to hear him" (136). She, like her work, is perhaps the most valued and influential element of this community of women. As Stowe, in a moment of serious humor, tells us: "You may have heard of dignitaries, my good reader; but, I assure you, you know very little of a situation of trust or importance compared to that of *the* dressmaker in a small New England town" (139). But the significance the town's women accord to Miss Prissy's work goes beyond her ability to restore scraps to "pristine splendor"; it has to do with her talent for joining individual lives as well, "mending and preserving the fabric of society" (Marcus 388). It is Miss Prissy who, during her "nomadic" forays, passes information between households. Miss Prissy's propensity for gossip is not the result of an evil nature, it is "innocent gossip, not a bit of malice in it" (139). Her benevolent news-passing has as much to do with her understanding of her patrons' and friends' curiosity and concern for each other as it does their acceptance of Miss Prissy as the rightful intimater of their joys and sorrows. They know her treatment of their intimacies will be like her treatment of their garments. As her needlework, while concealing the rips and stains of old, assures a much cherished garment will not go the way of the trash, so her sharing of their lives protects their secrets while maintaining their connections with each other.

> [. . .] the arrival of Miss Prissy in a family was much like the
> setting up of a domestic showcase, through which you could
> look into all the families of the neighborhood, and see the
> never-ending drama of life,—births, marriages, deaths,—joy
> of newmade mothers, whose babes weighed just eight
> pounds and three quarters, and had hair that would part with
> a comb,—and tears of Rachels who wept for their children
> and would not be comforted because they were not. Was
> there a tragedy, a mystery, in all Newport, whose secret
> closet had not been unlocked by Miss Prissy? She thought
> not; and you always wondered, with an uncertain curiosity,
> what those things might be over which she gravely shook her
> head, declaring, with such a look, "Oh, if you only could
> know!" and ending with a general sigh and lamentation, like
> the confidential chorus of a Greek tragedy. (140–41)

Miss Prissy, like her work, has "great power" in this community, and the articulation of the relationship between her craft and her person imbues needlework with recondite meaning. It also permits discussions concerning the relevance of the materials of that craft, which, as Stowe points out on numerous occasions, should be understood as identifying mechanisms.

These materials—"[. . .] ribbons, cast-off flowers, soiled bits of gauze, trivial, trashy fragments of millinery [. . .]"—are poignant beyond their beauty; through them one can come to know something about the person who has cherished them enough to save them. To this individual, Stowe asserts, such scraps "hold an awful meaning"; they are "memorials" to the people and the events that continue to shape her everyday existence (147–48). Therefore, as I mentioned earlier, we should pay as much attention to the materials a woman chooses to work with as we do to the technique she employs. For where the technique reveals a woman's personality and character traits, the materials she chooses to include in a project disclose what is of importance to her, the people she holds dear, what occurrences have mattered most in her life. Needleworkers' materials are a document of their "inner world—a landscape of their loves, wounds, hopes, wishes, fears and dreams [. . .] their confession in cloth" (Damashek qtd. in Karpinski 6). Stowe makes this passionately clear, first in her description of the hand-made imported textiles filling the "camphor-wood brass bound trunk [. . .] kept solemnly locked in Mrs. Katy Scudder's apartment," and then in her portrayal of the woven articles filling Mary's bedroom.

The contents of Mrs. Scudder's trunk could fill volumes with stories of the past. Mrs. Scudder's wedding gown is kept there,

> [. . .] its stiff ground broidered with heavy knots of flowers; and there were scarfs of wrought India muslin and embroidered crape, each of which had its own history, for each had been brought into the door with beating heart on some return voyage of one who, alas, should return no more! The old trunk stood with its histories, its imprisoned remembrances,—and a thousand tender thoughts seemed to be shaken out of every rustling fold of silk and embroidery, on the few yearly occasions when all were brought out to be aired, their history related, and then solemnly locked up again. (23–24)

Made by others and given as gifts, these articles are repositories of memory, the trunk a strongbox for the past. Still, it is the "plain stuff and homespun" that satisfies the women's "larger portion of existence commonly denominated among them 'every day'" (24). These homemade things we find in Mary's bedroom, some pieces, like the bed cover and window drapes, the "fringes of Mary's own knotting," others the handiwork of female relatives. As useful as they may be, these items, we find, when Stowe fully delineates them in a later, more complete depiction of Mary's room, are no less chronicles of life than the expensive items brought from overseas. Actually, they are even more loaded with meaning and memory. Writing in a manner of loving admiration and a centuries-old wisdom that knows the value differential between a store-bought item and an article stitched by hand, Stowe details Mary's garret boudoir. This room

> [. . .] was formed by blankets and bedspreads which by reason of their antiquity had been pensioned off to an undisturbed old age in the garret,—not common blankets or

bedspreads, either, bought, as you buy yours, out of a shop, spun or woven by machinery, without individuality or history. Every one of these curtains had its story. The one on the right, nearest the window, and already falling into holes, is a Chinese linen, and even now displays unfaded, quaint patterns of sleepy-looking Chinamen in conical hats, standing on the leaves of most singular herbage, and with hands forever raised in act to strike bells which never are struck and never will be till the end of time. These, Mrs. Katy Scudder had often instructed Mary, were brought from the Indies by her great-great grandfather, and were her grandmother's wedding curtains,—the grandmother who had blue eyes like hers and was just about her height.

The next spread was spun and woven by Mrs. Katy's beloved Aunt Eunice, a mythical personage, of whom Mary gathered vague accounts that she was disappointed in love, and that this very article was part of a bridal outfit, prepared in vain, against the return of one from sea who never came back; and she heard of how she sat wearily and patiently at her work, this poor Aunt Eunice, month after month, starting every time she heard the gate shut, every time she heard the tramp of a horse's hoof, every time she heard the news of a sail in sight,—her color, meanwhile, fading and fading as life and hope bled away at an inward wound,—till at last she found comfort and reunion beyond the veil.

Next to this bedquilt pieced in tiny blocks, none of them bigger than a sixpence, containing, as Mrs. Katy said, pieces of the gowns of all her grandmother's, aunts, cousins, and female relatives for years back; and mated to it was one of the blankets which had served Mrs. Scudder's uncle in his bivouac at Valley Forge, when the American soldiers went on the snows with bleeding feet, and had scarce anything for daily bread except a morning message of patriotism and hope from George Washington.

Such were the memories woven into the tapestry of our little boudoir. (181–82)

Such lengthy and specific detailing of the histories behind the materials making up the products the women of this family have created, highlights how important those materials are. Yet, as *The Minister's Wooing* also suggests, paramount to technique *and* material is the very act of engaging in the needlework tradition itself, which Stowe depicts as providing these women with "a socially sanctioned framework for the expression of critical anxiety-producing problems as well as a cherished artistic vehicle for communicating ethos and worldview" (Dundes, *Interpreting Folklore* 9). That is to say, needlework itself is shown as the means through which these women negotiate the world, the method through which they come to an understanding of themselves.

Traditionally, when women have come together to sew, the meetings have been understood as more than a time to stitch together fabrics; they have been viewed as a time to tack a supportive network of friends and confidantes. In fact, the "collective aspect of the art was frequently what endeared it to many women, otherwise isolated on their frontier farms" (Hedges and Wendt 4–5). Although men were often invited to come to the latter parts of these meetings, when the food was served and dancing, courting, or celebrating were indulged in, sewing circles, quilting bees, and the like were especially important events for women, the time they spent alone utilized for making and renewing contacts, sharing personal news, and developing plans for community projects. Moreover, because, for the most part, few public outlets were allotted women, such gatherings gained added significance as they provided women a medium for political and religious discussion.

> For example, Susan B. Anthony's first talk on equal rights for women occurred at a quilting bee in Cleveland, and earlier Sarah Grimke advised women to embroider antislavery slogans and images on domestic articles, urging, "May the point of our needles prick the slave-owner's conscience." (Pershing 338)

And, according to Suzy McLennan Anderson's *Collector's Guide to Quilts*, that such meetings

> [. . .] served as a forum for women to express themselves politically is evidenced by the pattern names on quilts dating from this era. "Drunkards Path," for example, was a popular pattern during the temperance movement of the early 19th century [. . .]; "Radical Rose and the Underground Railroad"

expresses sympathy with the slaves of the Civil War period, just as quilts depicting Lincoln or southern leaders echoed regional political differences. (24)[12]

That a primary objective of needlework meetings was to bring women together is evidenced throughout *The Minister's Wooing,* beginning with the tea party/needlework meeting thrown by Katy Scudder. The fact that this tea party is also a needlework meeting is hinted at in our view of Mrs. Scudder as she waits on her guests, "her company knitting work in her hands," and is then made clear as all but one of the attendant members arrive with needlework in tow and barely sit before busying their hands with some ongoing and transportable sewing project.[13] Take, for instance, the first arrival, Mrs. Twitchel; her day's dress is fully equipped for an afternoon of sewing, for the "large, comfortable pocket, hung upon the side, disclosed her knitting work ready for operation" (33). And we know that Mrs. Brown has brought her needlework as well, for Stowe describes her as jerking at her own handiwork as she joins in the conversation (37). Nevertheless, the needlework, like the tea, is secondary to the real reason these women are present at this gathering—to be in the company of other women, company in which it is safe to voice one's opinions on matters traditionally taken up by men, company interested in the workings of a woman's life.

Each of the women in attendance at Katy Scudder's has made it a point to be there, regardless of the distance or the myriad duties waiting to be done. Mrs. Twitchel, for example, even comes with a subject of particular import in mind for discussion, knowing she will be free, in this company, to expound upon this subject without reserve. As she tells Katy, "I keep goin' and goin' [. . .] I didn't see how I *was* to come here this afternoon; but then I *did* want to see Miss Scudder and talk a little about that precious sermon, Sunday" (33). Talk about the "precious sermon" they do, but they also discuss other things relevant to their lives. Mrs. Twitchel remarks upon her troubles turning her daughter's head from "vanity and dress" to attributes of a higher power. When Mrs. Jones arrives and the tea is ready, the conversation centers on needlework. After this, they compare notes on raising daughters and how best to run a household, which leads them to a discussion of the merits of keeping slaves, as Mrs. Brown does. And, then, finally, just before the men begin arriving, they ponder how one achieves excellence in the culinary arts.

Prior to the men's appearance, the women have the floor, their voices alone filling the house, their opinions and concerns the central focus, the conversation moving from topic to topic amorphously, naturally. But when the men pull in, they take over. And although the women join in the discussion on occasion, it is the men who dictate where it will go, giving it shape according to their own interests. Positioning these parts of the tea party side by side— the women alone together working, then the women *and* the men feasting— highlights the difference in the women's behavior when the men are not around and stresses the significance of those occasions. Hence, as occasions of free expression are so important to the lives of women, they occur quite often in *The Minister's Wooing*, and Stowe lets us peek into them regularly.[14]

One of the most important needlework meetings to which Stowe allows us admittance is the quilting bee that occurs prior to and in preparation for Mary's nuptials. Because the days of early American life forced geographic distance between women, they eagerly anticipated events such as quilting bees. For like other needlework meetings, quilting bees were "one of the rare opportunities when they could share in woman's talk. They would arrive early in the morning at the hostess's home and spend the day, talking as fast as their fingers stitched the quilts" (Lithgow 23). In some regions, Marilyn Lithgow explains in *Quiltmaking and Quiltmakers*,

> [s]ocial gatherings known as friendship quilt parties were held by the young girls not yet of marriageable age. Each girl brought scraps of her old dresses to make a quilt block that was embroidered with her name and date. The finished blocks were set together and presented to one member of the group who in turn gave a quilting bee to finish the friendship quilt, thus providing the opportunity for two parties, which livened the daily routine. (23)

Although quilting bees were not confined to special occasions (Holstein 11), the wedding quilting bee, "considered the most solemn and important recognition of betrothal" (Stowe 315), was perhaps the most commonly expected occurrence in the lives of young women in Stowe's day. And, according to Stowe, it was similarly anticipated and meticulously prepared for by the older women involved in it:

> Grave, elderly matrons [. . .] speculated on bedquilts and tablecloths, and rummaged their own clean, sweet-smelling stores, fragrant with balm and rose leaves, to lay out a bureau

cover, or a pair of sheets, or a dozen napkins for the wedding
quilt. (314)

Such a momentous affair deserves our full attention; thus, in *The Minister's Wooing* we spend quite some time as audience to this one-day event. Providing us with more than a glimpse of this particular type of needlework meeting is especially important, for quilting bees embody and display all the needlework aspects revealed in Stowe's work thus far: time and fragment thrift, fine female artistry, identity determining techniques, memory laden materials, folk group renewal, and general celebration. As Stowe explains, prior to the bee "there was a solemn review of the stores of beauty and utility thus provided and the patchwork-spread best worthy of distinction was chosen for the quilting" (316). Then, after the quilting bee was announced,

> [t]hereto, duly summoned, trooped all intimate female friends
> of the bride, old and young, and the quilt being spread on a
> frame, and wadded with cotton, each vied with the others in the
> delicacy of the quilting she could put upon it. For the quilting
> also was a fine art, and had its delicacies and nice points, which
> grave elderly matrons discussed with judicious care. The quilt-
> ing generally began at an early hour in the afternoon, and ended
> at dark with a great supper and general jubilee [. . .] (316)

Stowe's attention to *The Minister's Wooing's* quilting bee attests to its multi-faceted function. But this mindfulness also works to bring yet another aspect of needlework to the surface: a more individualized form of female bonding, that of woman to woman.

Before and during the bee, we view women meeting one to one for private discussions in which secrets are shared and personal friendships are renewed and strengthened. For instance, the morning of the bee permits Candace and Miss Prissy a private moment among the pantry shelves for "a confidential outpouring" of premonitions, signs, and dreams. Believing in such "heathenish" things as dreams or premonitions is looked down upon by the church in general, and Dr. Hopkins in particular. But the quilting bee provides an occasion for the two women to discuss their, for the most part, mutual belief in such things, as well as their most recent experiences of them, one of which has Candace convinced that Mary's first love, James Marvyn, presumed dead, is actually alive and well. Then, once the quilting bee is underway, we find Mary and Mrs. Marvyn, James's mother, secreted away in "Mary's little room, with their arms around each other, communing in low and gentle tones" about their feelings for James and their love for each other. During this heart-to-heart, Mrs. Marvyn tells Mary that she is "in some respects the dearest friend" she has, and Mary returns the affection by assuring Mrs. Marvyn that, regardless of her marriage to the doctor, instead of to James as Mrs. Marvyn would have liked, Mrs. Marvyn will always be "as a mother" to her (324–32).

These two meetings, Candace and Miss Prissy sharing secrets and Mrs. Marvyn and Mary reaffirming ties, highlight the importance of female friendships. Exhibited here is the fact that unlike women's relationships with men, women's relationships with each other furnish them space and time to explore alternative values and express reciprocal desires.[15] Because distance and obligation make rare the opportunities for the intimate meetings these women so obviously need, the quilting bee is understood as a chance to connect with each other on an individual basis. Other needlework meetings work in much the same manner, especially those in which fewer than the total membership are in attendance.

As should be expected, in a life of so much duty and unexpected occurrence, not all the members of the folk group are present each time a needlework meeting takes place. For instance, a member of this group, Miss Prissy, as we know, was not at the tea party. And the other members are not there when the newly introduced Miss Prissy joins Mrs. Scudder and Mary for needleworking later in the text. Such fluctuating attendance, however, is typical of folk groups in general, who see the occasional absence of members as a given and not a threat to the solidarity of the group.[16] Actually, such absences often work to the advantage of the group; when fewer than the total are present, deeper relationships between individual members are fostered. Stowe illustrates this folk group aspect when she creates needlework meetings in which only two or three members of the total group are in attendance.

One such meeting follows on the heels of the quilting bee. Occurring two weeks before the wedding, this meeting includes only Mary and Cerinthy Ann. Needlework is what Mary is doing when Cerinthy Ann arrives at her door, and bringing Mary a needlework gift is Cerinthy Ann's excuse for a confidential consultation with Mary. In addition, although Mary's needlework is interrupted, when the girls decide to move from indoors to outdoors, Mary takes her needlework with her. Different as these two young women may be, Cerinthy Ann being high spirited and skeptical of religion and Mary being subdued and completely given over to God, they still share a mutual respect and a deep affection for each other. With none of the other folk group members present during this "needlework" meeting, the girls are free to indulge their friendship fully, traversing subjects of particular import to women their age, such as impending marriages and hoped-for engagements. During this interview, the girls exhibit female friendship at its best, for their discussion focuses on their feelings and is noncompetitive, highly expressive, and wholly satisfying. And yet, as important as this meeting is to Stowe's representation of female friendships, the next partial-membership needlework meeting truly demonstrates that women's relationships with each other are the instruments shaping their lives.

This meeting takes place shortly after it is known to all that James is actually alive and has returned home unharmed. The morning following James's reappearance on the scene, Madame de Frontignac tries to contrive time alone with Mary. However, with Mrs. Scudder constantly underfoot, deliberately attempting to prevent a Mary- and-Madame-only rendezvous, such a tryst seems highly improbable. In fact, the interview Madame de Frontignac so desperately wants with Mary seems utterly impossible until a needlework meeting saves the day. That is to say, only when Mary retreats to her room for some spinning does Madame de Frontignac have an excuse to be with her alone. On the pretense of spinning together, Madame de Frontignac (who has taken up temporary membership in the folk group during her visit with the Scudders) and Mary face the issue of James's return. During this discussion, Madame de Frontignac tries to convince Mary of the rightness of breaking off with the doctor so she can be with the man she really loves. Although her efforts to move Mary from spinning the wheel to spinning her own fate come to no avail, the meeting is still significant as far as female friendships go. For as we see here, in this type of relationship women can express themselves fully and honestly. Confident of Mary's lasting friendship, Madame de Frontignac conveys her opinion on the matter of James versus the doctor without restraint or fear of reprisal. And Mary, although she may refuse to be honest with the doctor, as her obligation to her word already given prohibits her, she is not, nor need she be, dishonest with her friend. While it may not alter the situation, this honesty between friends, at the very least, gets Mary thinking about the options available to her and alleviates the burden of carrying her secret alone.

Like the full-group meetings, the partial-membership meetings illustrate how needlework, as it connects strands of yarn, ties women to each other, encouraging relationships that contour lives. But needlework is not always done as a group or in pairs; it is often done in solitude. When a woman engages in needlework alone, the activity works as a self-defining mechanism, as *The Minister's Wooing* also illustrates—a method through which individual women come to terms with the world around them, determine what they want and who they are.

In "The Patchwork Quilt," an excerpt from *The Lowell Offering*, Annette (a pseudonym) remarks on the solace she found in solitary piece-work as she emerged into adolescence. She tells us that, prior to her budding girlhood, "the patchwork joys had been enhanced by the sympathy, praises and assistance of others; but now they were cherished 'in secrecy and silence.'" Moreover, she explains that the work produced during those lone moments "[. . .] bears witness to the [. . .] vanity of youthful hopes—the mutability of earthly wishes" (12–13). This young woman's chronicle of her own experiences with needlework affirms what Joanne Karpinski asserts in "The Shadow Block: Female Bonding in *Quilters*," that "[. . .] the solitary act of 'piecing' [. . .] supported and reconstituted women emotionally" (6). Moreover, it supports Pershing's claim that "sewing their secret language," women worked "through invalidated hopes and fears with needle and thread" (339). In sum, it testifies to the craft's self-actualizing dimension, the aspect of needlework Stowe discloses in *The Minister's Wooing* through a close look at Mary's own unaccompanied encounters with needle and thread.

We see Mary on numerous occasions secreted away in her garret boudoir, spinning alone. Rarely when we view her thus is she simply getting work done. More often than not, she is spinning in order to reflect on her life, turning the wheel as she turns the whole of her world over in her mind. Mary's spinning is so conducive to meditation that she would do it "for hours and hours, with intervals, when, crouched on a low seat in the window, she pored over her book, and then, returning again to her work, thought of what she had read to the lulling burr of the sounding wheel" (183). Mary is lucky to have such a reflective tool in her life; it serves her well, for instance, when she learns of James's supposed death at sea. Unlike James's mother, who, after learning of her son's demise, takes to her bed for days of inactivity, Mary takes to the needle and the spinning wheel, the only things to bear witness to the fact that while she appears calm and entirely accepting of the situation, "through that silent heart were passing tides of thought that measured a universe [. . .] through that one gap of sorrow flowed in the whole awful mystery of existence [. . .]" (261). In a somber explanation of the personal and spiritual discoveries Mary's work provides her with, Stowe writes: "[. . .] silently, as she spun and sewed, she thought over and over again all that she had been taught, and compared and revolved it by the light of a dawning inward revelation" (261). This time Mary's busy hands move her from "infinite sorrow" to "infinite peace," and give her the strength to share her transformation with others in the offering of a prayer that Miss Prissy exclaims, "seemed to take us all right up and put us down in heaven" (267). As Miss Prissy's declaration suggests, Mary's ability to pull herself together through her own work surrounds her with an air of self-containment and makes her a model of self-composure. But it also supplies her with a sense of self-sufficiency and a certain measure of independence.

It is not as though Mary does not need other women, for she does. Nevertheless, unaccompanied engagement with a female tradition gives her the ability to work through life's mysteries herself. The reflective activity permits her time when she, and she alone, dictates what gets done and what topics get taken up, time when her very understanding of self is the chief focus.

We see how this works during the week following James's initial departure, when two important things happen to Mary: she realizes that she loves James and she meets Aaron Burr and Madame de Frontignac. These occurrences are crucial to Mary's emotional well-being; because of them her feelings run the gamut from sorrow to joy to anticipation and back again, leaving her in a rather confused state. To sort through her feelings, she goes to her room to reel yarn while thinking "the whole over by herself" (184). In this isolated place, doing this solitary work, she is free to cogitate without reserve and to determine how she truly feels about those things she would be uncomfortable discussing with her mother. Here her work is her means of dealing with a newly awakened surge of love, loss, and sexual attraction. But as these developments have also made her question her notion of herself, her work is likewise her method of tying together her old understanding of who she is with her new insight into what she wants and how others see her.

With Mary as her example of someone who puts folklore to use for personal reasons, Stowe pushes us to grasp all the individual may receive from working within a tradition. Moreover, Stowe positions Mary's use of the craft as a lesson to others—to Madame de Frontignac in particular.

So enamored with Mary is Madame de Frontignac that shortly after their second meeting she begins engaging in the habits that have gone into shaping such a wonderfully contained young woman. Over the course of

Madame de Frontignac's stay in the town, as Stowe tell us, "[. . .] she blended herself with the quiet pursuits of the family" and "insisted on being taught to spin at the great wheel" (222–23). Madame de Frontignac's dedication to Mary's rituals is not a passing fancy, for although she waxes poetic on them quite often and leaves the community shortly after her tutelage in them begins, when she returns, it is not for a simple visit, but to reconnect with herself through those activities she has seen working like results on Mary.

Madame de Frontignac returns to the Scudder cottage at a crossroads—unhappy and confused as to where to go in life. Because, upon her first visit, she saw in Mary a seemingly "unknown, unattainable peace" (220), she goes to her now in hopes of achieving the same within herself. Mary, however, has had much to deal with during Madame de Frontignac's absence, for in the interim the news of James's death arrived, leading Mary to turn repeatedly to her solitary spinning and sewing (261). And because she is still grieving when Madame de Frontignac reenters the story, this is what the madame finds her doing when she arrives again at the Scudder cottage for what will be a prolonged stay full of lessons about the healing and self-defining power of engagement with tradition.

When Madame de Frontignac arrives at the Scudder cottage, Mary is "spinning in her garret boudoir." Eager to get to her, the madame simply pursues "the sound of Mary's spinning wheel [. . .]," and when she reaches Mary, makes the rather revelatory assertion: "I knew where I should find you, ma blanche! I heard the wheel of my poor little princess! It's a good while since we spun together, mimi!" (279). Madame de Frontignac knows of Mary's recent loss; hence, her claim that Mary would obviously be at the wheel at this time, does more than suggest her unconscious understanding of the role needlework plays in Mary's personal life, it anticipates her later use of it for those same purposes in her own life. Nevertheless, before this happens, Madame de Frontignac explains what has brought her to the point of needing what Mary has to offer. To begin, she has been forced to realize that the woman she is, is not the woman others would have her be. She proclaims to Mary:

> Now don't call me Madame any more. Do you know, do you
> know that there are two me's to this person?—one is Virginie,
> and the other is Madame de Frontignac. Everybody in
> Philadelphia knows Madame de Frontignac; she is very gay,
> very careless, very happy; she never has any serious hours, or

any sad thoughts; she wears powder and diamonds, and
dances all night; and never prays. That is Madame. But Virginie is quite another thing. She is tired of all this,—tired of
the balls, and the dancing, and the diamonds, and the beaux;
and she likes true people, and would like to live very quiet
with somebody that she loved. She is very unhappy; and she
prays, too, sometimes, in a poor way, like the birds in your
nest out there, who don't know much, but chipper and cry
because they are hungry. This is your Virginie. Madame
never comes here,—never call me Madame. (280–81)

Virginie's plea for reprieve from such other-definedness is a request Mary, of
course, is more than willing to grant, but her eyes question what compelled
Virginie to see herself as two incompatible people. Therefore, Virginie goes on
to bare her soul on such topics as her upbringing, her marriage, and her association with Aaron Burr, identifying the interrelatedness of these issues as the
cause of her present pain and confusion. Raised in a convent after her mother's
death, Virginie grew up learning only the powerful love of God. Her upbringing did not explain that an equally powerful love was possible between men
and women. Thus, in the early days of her arranged marriage to Monsieur de
Frontignac, she readily accepted the lack of love between them, becoming
content with the comfort of material things. But when Aaron Burr awakened
in her an idea of love heretofore unknown, her understanding of herself and
the world began to change. As she found herself loving Aaron Burr "with a
religion," she lost all sense of right and wrong, all sense of who she was. She
tells Mary,

I would have died for him; [. . .] I did not know myself; I was
astonished I could feel so; and I did not dream that this could
be wrong. How could I, when it made me feel more religious
than anything in my whole life? Everything in the world
seemed to grow sacred. I thought, if men could be so good and
admirable, life was a holy thing, and not to be trifled with. (283)

Attempting to quell this rising tide of confusion, she turned to her religion and,
for the first time, it did not provide her comfort. What changed her situation
was a large dose of reality, something her years at the convent denied her.
Aaron Burr is a flesh-and-blood man, susceptible to treachery and lies, and

wholly undeserving of the godlike love Virginie was ready to bestow on him. Unfortunately, Virginie's recognition of Burr's betrayal does not push her back to the person she was before he entered her life, a person who, in doing what was expected of her, cared for nothing. On the contrary, her experience outside the realm of social standards makes a return to that time when her heart was "still and quiet" utterly impossible. She exclaims to Mary, "I have tried to do that; I can't; I cannot get back where I was before," and asks that Mary help her find the way back to herself (286).

In response to Virginie's cry for help, Mary insists on the healing power of her religion. However, while Virginie accepts that religion is one source of Mary's peace, as she has already experienced failure in this area and as her religion differs from Mary's, religious comfort must be seen as secondary to what Virginie really turns to Mary for. Contrary to what Mary thinks at the moment, in saying to Mary, "I want you to show me how to find peace where you do; will you let me be your sister?" (289), Virginie is not asking for healing via a religious conversion or revelation. She does not see religion as the exclusive source of Mary's strength and solid sense of self. Rather, what she wants in asking to be Mary's sister, and in begging to be taken in by the Scudders, proclaiming, "[. . .] I shall help you with the spinning—you know I spin beautifully,—and I shall make butter, and milk the cow, and set the table. Oh, I will be so useful, you can't spare me" (289), is to be a part of the folk group to which Mary belongs, to engage in the activities Mary does, the activities that serve Mary in ways her religion does not.

It becomes quite apparent that this is what Virginie sees as most valuable in terms of Mary's sense of self and her own, when we note that during her stay with Mary, very little time is given to religious reflection, but a great deal of time is given to her engagement in the folkloric activities of the women of Newport. The "domesticating of Madame de Frontignac" takes many forms: a change from elaborate dress to simple attire, an engagement in the activities spelled out in her request to stay with Mary, a temporary membership in the folk group during the quilting bee. Although on occasion Mary and Virginie discuss religion and its healing attributes, what really helps Virginie create an inroad to her self is stripping away all artifices of the madame; doing, instead of merely observing, the projects that make the world run smoothly; establishing relationships with women rather than with men. In fact, it is Virginie herself who makes this distinction. In a letter to a friend, she discusses the Newport community, remarking on the religiosity of the people, yes, but pinpointing their folk-traditional way of life as their most valuable attribute and, thus, her primary reason for being there:

> These people in the country here in America have a charac-
> ter quite their own, very different from the life of cities,
> where one sees, for the most part, only a continuation of the
> forms of good society which exist in the Old World.
>
> In the country, these people seem simple, grave, severe,
> always industrious, and, at first, cold and reserved in their
> manners toward each other, but with great warmth of heart
> [. . .] here in New England the people for the most part keep
> no servants, but perform all the household work themselves,
> with no end of spinning and sewing besides. It is the true
> Arcadia, where you find cultivated and refined people busying
> themselves with the simplest toils. For these people are well
> read and well bred, and truly ladies in all things. And so my
> little Marie and I, we feed the hens and chickens together,
> and we search for eggs in the hay in the barn. And they have
> taught me to spin at the great wheel, and at a little one too,
> which makes a noise like the humming of a bee. (353–54)

Virginie's description, in its positioning of country life against the city life, establishes the primacy of the folk, suggesting that a folkloric way of life is more apt to produce happy, well-rounded, centered individuals. Moreover, she underscores the significance of one particular folk tradition—needlework—when she marks it as both the emblem of women's self-defining busy-handedness and her own choice of personal enrichment activities.

What Virginie gains during her stay in Newport is a much needed relationship with another woman, one that withstands time and distance, buttressed by a lesson in traditional engagement that stays with her long after she leaves the Scudder household. She provides the evidence of this in her first letter to Mary following her departure:

> At last, my sweet Marie, you behold us in peace after wan-
> derings. [. . .] Ah, my sweet saint, blessed was the day I first
> learned to know you! [. . .] I am far happier, *ma Marie*, than
> I ever thought I could be. I took your advice, and told my
> husband all I had felt and suffered. [. . .] and he was very

good and noble and helpful to me; [. . .] I should be a very
bad woman, if I did not love him truly and dearly,—as I do.

I must confess that there is still a weak, bleeding place in
my heart that aches yet, but I try to bear it bravely; and when
I am tempted to think myself miserable, I remember how
patiently you used to go about your housework and spinning,
in those sad days when you thought your heart was drowned
in the sea; and I try to do like you. (414)

As we see here, Virginie has successfully incorporated into her own life on the
Mediterranean what she learned from Mary's folklore use while in residence
at the cottage. And this touching testimony to the efficacy of Mary's lesson is
Stowe's most passionate avowal of folklore's (self-)centering power. Through
Madame de Frontignac, Stowe illustrates that once a tradition is fully understood and ingrained, its lessons are not fleeting. The self-sustaining provisions
inherent in it will always be available as long as one continues to recognize the
tradition's value and puts it to use in her life. This is what the folk group women
of *The Minister's Wooing* have always known; this is what Mary teaches
Madame de Frontignac; this is what Stowe passes on to her readers by making
the needlework tradition both pattern and fabric of her story. So meaningful is
this message that it has endured over a hundred years of change in American
life and found its way, once again, into the work of a female author: the contemporary text *How to Make an American Quilt* by Whitney Otto.

Quilted Writing, Quilted Living: Whitney Otto's How to Make an American Quilt

> We learn best to listen to our own voices if we are listening at the
> same time to other women [. . .] whose stories, for all our differ-
> ences, turn out, if we listen well, to be our stories also.
>
> BARBARA DEMING

In the century since Harriet Beecher Stowe pointed to needlework as the way
women write, and the way women live, much has changed. Women's lives have
moved increasingly away from home and hearth, and, likewise, it would seem,
from the traditional cultural forms Stowe identified as aesthetic models and

defining mechanisms. Yet, as the contemporary author Whitney Otto shows us in her novel *How to Make an American Quilt,* women's folklore is alive and well today and is being put to the same uses it was more than one hundred years ago. Otto's work illustrates that the needlework tradition is still indispensable when it comes to women's literary creativity and self-defining impulses; it is still a pattern women follow when they put pen to paper, when they seek self in world. There is only one difference between Stowe's and Otto's representations, and this is due to a bit of fine-tuning on Otto's part. Where Stowe makes needlework in general (although she refers us to patchworking most often) the crux of her parallels, Otto makes one particular type of needlework her structuring tool and symbol: quilting.

Quilting, as discussed earlier in this chapter, is an age-old craft practiced throughout the world.[17] It is a tradition that continues to be passed from generation to generation, furnishing families with much needed articles and women with a mode of expression translatable to other areas of their lives, such as their writing. Although few actually quilt, many women writers today, as Elaine Showalter tells us, adopt "[. . .] quilt imagery in their poems or novels," envisioning quilts as records of women's lives, the quilting process a pattern for how women live (162).[18] For these writers, the quilt is "a communicative expressive form or sign that has a multiplicity of functions in the society that produces it" (Roach 55). But this understanding of the quilt and quilting has resulted in more than literary imagery. It has also moved contemporary female authors to use quilt creation as a method for structuring their texts, interpreting the quilting process as the writing process. Like their literary foremothers, writers such as Whitney Otto put their stories on paper as they would stitch patches on a quilt.

When creating a quilt of any kind, the first thing a quilter does is decide on a design; then the individual pieces are laid out to determine how each piece fits into the whole pattern. While the quilt is worked on, the overall design is no more than a chalk outline, a ghost sketching hardly readable by the untrained eye. But when the quilt is finished, all pieces joined and in place, the original design comes back into focus.[19] This process is similar to the one *How to Make an American Quilt* requires its readers to engage in. The text makes necessary a survey of its individual parts before we can see "how each piece fits into the whole pattern." Once these connections are made, "the reader realizes that the design was there from the very beginning, every stitch in place" (McCorkle 10).

The design of *How to Make an American Quilt* is as complicated as the crazy quilt the women in the novel work on. Similar to the crazy quilt, which is a "hodgepodge of materials, 'laid on' a plain background and stitched down" (Lithgow 2, 26), *How to Make an American Quilt* is a mix-match of seven stories about seven different women, all members of the Grasse Quilting Circle, and seven sets of quilting instruction, sewn loosely onto the blank pages of Finn Bennett-Dodd's undertaking in self-discovery. And just as the crazy quilt displays no hierarchy in the placing of pieces, so *How to Make an American Quilt* displays no center stage in its presentations of instructions and stories. Rather, the organization of the text, in correspondence with the scheme of a crazy quilt, is based on the (similar) scope of instructions (sizing of patches) and the balancing out of the stories' thematic content (combining of colors).

Beyond design, however, Otto's work also incorporates the three structural elements most crazy quilts consist of: a backing or foundation block, a top piece, and a lining. Using the book's cover and back as her quilting frame, Otto arrays these working materials before us. The prologue to the novel, Finn's story, serves as this textual quilt's backing, a foundation for the chapters that follow. Fitting instruction and story together "like a puzzle," these chapters, like fabric patches, become Otto's top piece, contouring but not stretching out the shape of her backing (Lithgow 85). Once the backing and top piece are situated, a lining is inserted—this Otto provides through the combined voice underlying the text, quietly identified only at the end as Anna Neale's—founder of the Grasse Quilting Circle—*and* Finn's—granddaughter of one of the circle's principle members.[20]

With these elements in place, design and materials merge, and but one step remains for the project to be complete: binding top piece to backing (Lithgow 85). Where *How to Make an American Quilt* is concerned, this last step means connecting instructions and stories to Finn's present-day dilemma. This amalgamation, the novel's subtext, Otto makes with barely perceptible thread, left unknotted at the finish as well. It is up to us to find that almost invisible fiber and tie up its loose ends. But how to begin sewing the elements of this text together if we don't know how to quilt? Well, as the title suggests, we learn. As we follow Finn through her quilting lessons, through the stories of the women in this folk group, through her journey to self, we learn how to combine seemingly disconnected parts to form a whole. We learn what the Grasse Quilting Circle members already know—how to live through folklore.

Finn comes to the Grasse Quilting Circle a novice to both quilting and living, a philanderer at this point in time who sees her present life as a series of unfulfilled quests, her current self, a set of unanswered questions. As she tells us in the prologue, she has spent much of the past few years moving from one study interest to another, going from art history to physical anthropology to literature—seeking a comfortable niche for herself. What she finds instead is that her nature resists not only being pigeonholed into one area of study, but also having to study that area in some already prescribed and accepted way, as occurs in the field of history, for instance, Finn's most recently rejected study choice. With history she learned that although one is required to focus mainly on dates and time lines and matters of large significance, what she found interesting and perhaps even more absorbing were "the small, odd details [. . .] discovered here and there when looking into the past." She wanted history to be "the silly and the sublime; [. . .] a whole picture, a grudgingly true past. And out of that past truth a present reality [. . .] vital, alive." At first, her desires in regard to the past perplexed her: She imagined someone saying to her, "Finn, what ever gave you the idea that history was any sort of living thing?" (4). But when she is faced with yet another major life decision—her boyfriend, Sam, asks her to marry him—she realizes there is a connection between what she needed in history and what she now needs in her own life:

> Then Sam asked me to marry him.
>
> It seemed a good idea.
>
> Yet it somehow led me back to my educational concern, which was how to mesh halves into a whole, only in this case it was how to make a successful link of unmarried to married, man to woman, the merging of the roads before us [. . .]. How does one accomplish such a fusion of selves? And, if the affection is that strong, how does one *avoid* it, leaving a little room for the person you once were? (4)

This connection and the questions it leads to leave her "wondering, astonished, and a little put off"; thus she postpones a wedding and a career choice for the time being, opting instead to spend the summer with her grandmother, Hy Dodd, her great aunt, Glady Jo Cleary, and the other women of the Grasse Quilting circle, a firmly rooted female folk group. Her decision to retreat from her world of unsatisfying choices and too many ideas of what it means to be a woman at this point in history, and a married woman at that, to a world of women who "have a lot to say" is important. She has lost track of the sort of girl she is. She tells us, "I cannot fathom who I think I am *at this time.*" In these women—in their craft, in their words—she recognizes something she desperately needs—a way to herself. She is ready to learn, she is "ready to listen" (5–6).

As defined in the prologue, the barriers to Finn's coherent sense of self include her desire to know both the profound and trivial past, her need to find in that whole past meaning for the present, and her inability to determine the shape of her life as a woman today. She works through these hindrances by immersing herself in the Grasse Quilting Circle, learning through the instructions she receives a tradition that naturally reflects and addresses these issues, and finding in the stories she is told a link between quilting and both history and female life. We see Finn coming to these connections in her first set of instructions. For in Instructions No. 1, she makes the quilting process her model for how to sustain the past, the crazy quilt her sign of undisciplined history, a work of the hands that validates the way her eyes view antiquity.

Similar to the past, which she believes should be painstakingly put together and preserved in its entirety for generations to come, here she learns that the quilt requires "finely honed" needles so as not to "break the weave of your fabric [. . .] and plenty of good-quality thread [. . .] to hold the work together for future generations [. . .] generations of people you will never meet" (8). Moreover, just as Finn's idea of history consists of great and small occurrences, so she finds that the crazy quilt the Grasse Circle works on while she apprentices requires diversity—"remnants of material in numerous textures, colors; 'pieces stitched together' of all sizes and shapes." This type of quilt, like her type of history, requires "the least amount of discipline" while providing "the greatest measure of emotion." Hence, she asserts, in a comment on the crazy quilt that surely applies to history *her way* as well, "You will find this work to be the most revealing [. . .] This random piecing together" (8–9). And to back up this conviction, in the following section she uses the quilt to show us how much of our existence is embodied in "excess material."

Speaking directly to the would-be quilter, providing her with "More Instructions," Finn writes the following:

> Take material from clothing that belongs to some family member or friend or lover. [. . .] Bind them together carefully. Wonder at the disparity of your life. Finger the patches representing "lover" and meditate on the meaning of illicit

love in early American society. Failing that, consider the
meaning of the affair in today's time frame. (9)

In this advice, she urges amateur quilters to understand that as you quilt a reality both private and public comes back to you; one single quilt patch has the
ability to elicit speculation about the present, evoke memories of the past, and
call forth snippets from the whole of American life. Thus, you must see your
pieces as a series of interrelated stories, your stitches a link between your experiences and the experiences of the world at large. And as those individual
scraps also connect to others that undoubtedly do the same with different
material and so on and so on, so each part of Finn's own repetitive pattern (of
interpretive quilting instructions matched with related personal histories)
leads (like quilt patches) to other applicable anecdotes and typically ends with
a version of the saying "But that is another story."

Like a quilter connecting fabric and thread to voice her opinions and
express her feelings, to cast her ballot and record her loves and losses (13–14),
in this section Finn joins "mysteries and clues [. . .] things that cannot be fath-
omed" in order to reconstruct American history, to make "a new, useful object"
out of "that which would normally be thrown out, 'waste,' [. . .]" (9). For
instance, while discussing nineteenth-century quilt topics, she is reminded of
the wars fought on American ground, the Civil War in particular. Thinking
about this war, she calls to mind an aspect of it often forgotten: that it was a
struggle between family members, a battle among individuals always already
tenaciously and precariously bound to each other. What Finn values in
history—those seemingly smaller lives and the occurrences significant only
to them—is what Stowe depicted in her novel. In a sense, then, Otto's novel,
like Stowe's, can be seen as historical. Published on the eve of the Civil War,
The Minister's Wooing was also about those parts of the war often forgotten—
the skirmishes that occurred not on the battle fields but also in the homes,
among family members and friends. Such conflicts, Finn asserts, shape the
lives of individuals to a greater extent than do wars of the Civil War sort:

> Your concern might be trying to reduce your chosen quilt
> topic to more manageable dimensions. [. . .] There is the Civil
> War, which is a conflict of the blood tie. No one fights dirtier
> or more brutally than blood; only family knows its own weak-
> ness, the exact placement of the heart. The tragedy is that one
> can still love with the force of hatred. Feel infuriated that

once you are born to another, that kinship lasts through life
and death, immutable, unchanging, no matter how great the
misdeed or betrayal. Blood cannot be denied, and perhaps
that is why we fight tooth and claw, because we cannot, being
human, put asunder what God has joined together. (12–13)

Although typically viewed as a huge and horrible incident in our past, something that happened to other people, when Finn imagines the war as a quilt
theme, it becomes a part of our everyday, a battle representative of us all. For
many this is a new way of understanding our lives—connecting ourselves to
history through its forgotten odds and ends. But as renderings such as this are
intrinsic to the quilting process, for quilters such fittings are customary when
it comes to better knowing themselves and figuring their individual realities
into the grand scheme of things. For the most part denied active involvement
in the larger world, women stitched themselves into their quilts; as their quilts
chronicled what was happening around them and how they felt about it, so
they made themselves a part of the action.

> Women were witness to Abraham Lincoln's assassination.
> Find some quality silk and cotton in red, white, and blue.
> Cut white stars in the evening as you sit on your summer
> porch. Appliqué the letters that spell out your name, your
> country, your grief. Stitch across the quilt a flag held in the
> beak of a dove. Ponder the fact that you could not vote for
> the man but will defy any male citizen who will not allow you
> your measure of sorrow at the president's sudden death. Say
> something in cloth about the Union lasting, preserved. Lis-
> ten to the men expound their personal satisfaction in glory
> of the vote. Listen to them express surprise that you, too,
> would like to vote and be heard. [. . .] Save your opinions for
> the quilt. (13)

This contemplating over how women once negotiated the world, helps Finn
find a way to begin doing so herself. Her words directed inward this time, she
tells herself not to forget her own relationship to the past:

> You may feel that all those things that went before have little
> to do with you, that you are made immune to the past by the
> present day: All those dead people and conflicts and ideas—

why, they are only stories we tell one another. History and
politics and conflict and rebellion and family and betrayal.
Think about it. (14)

Then, having discovered in the quilt and the quilting process affirmation of a
past heretofore denied her, she puts her own advice to task. Using the materials closest at hand, as a quilter would, she moves from instruction to story,
inserting the story of her grandmother and her aunt into her own, illustrating
for herself how the very small slivers of the past impinge upon the present.

Most of the women's stories in *How to Make an American Quilt* center on what amounts to a mere second in the life. Similar to a singular quilt
patch, which often encompasses the whole of a life in the memories it evokes,
these flashes in time work as defining moments, the significance of which is apt
to be known only to those involved, as is the case of Hy and Glady Jo. Their
many neighbors "cannot recall a time when Glady Joe and Hy were not 'old.'"
It is as though "[. . .] they had somehow executed the leap from girlhood to
middle age to senior citizen, lacking any sort of transitional areas in between"
(15). Yet the two sisters share a sliver of middle age that negates the possibility
of their having lived always as they are now, a mutual shred that cancels their
chance of living only in today.

Both their husbands deceased, Hy and Glady Jo live together in the
house where the quilting circle meets. Made different from the other houses
in the neighborhood by its "odd back rooms; [. . .] covered floor to ceiling with
bits of glass, tile, shells, and china. Some beads here and there. All affixed to
the walls [. . .] of the laundry room, back den, and part of the large kitchen—
as if time or materials suddenly ran out," the house, Anna Neale tells Finn, is
haunted by an absence, "a thing lost" (16, 20). That thing is trust.

When Finn's grandfather, James, is in the hospital dying, her grandmother, Hy, and Glady Jo's husband, Arthur, Finn's uncle, spend one empty
afternoon loving each other. Unintentionally betraying Glady Joe and James,
they turn to each other out of a need to be touched, a will to fill a void. Their
coupling, rooted in loss, has little, if anything at all, to do with sex. Yet when
their betrayal reaches Glady Jo, this knowledge does not comfort her, even
though she has not been sexually interested in her husband for years. Screaming at Arthur, "*Friends* don't betray each other" (40), she proceeds to break to
pieces whatever she can get her hands on: "atomizer bottles, makeup jars, an
in-laid rosewood box he had given her for their second Christmas [. . .] a small

porcelain bowl" (39). Then, instead of throwing out the leftover shards, she begins applying the fragments to the walls of her home "in intricate patterns." Arthur believes that what she is doing is strange; he can't understand why she doesn't just toss the pieces in the trash. The quilter in Glady Joe could explain this to him, however; she could tell him *that* part of her refuses to throw anything away simply "because it is broken," to "waste what could still be of use." Moreover, that part of her, the quilter, is what is saving her from going over the edge. For patching her walls with porcelain and glass, "shattered markers of the Cleary marriage, their life together as one [. . .]," fills her with "a sense of purpose and calm, as if this is the only way she can somehow go on with her life—transforming these pieces of junk, swept up from her bedroom and bathroom floors, into art [. . .] it helped to hold her fractured life together" (41–42). It also helped to eventually bring Hy and Glady Jo to some forgiveness and reconciliation—enough that they can live and travel together after both their spouses have passed away.

Still, Hy will always refuse to enter the rooms where these ceramic quilts festoon the walls. Their existence alone is enough to remind her that as the jars and bottles can never regain their original form, so the sisters' lives cannot be restored to what they once were. Because of the story contained in this glass tapestry, the past does not exist behind Hy or Glady Joe, separate from them—it lives with them, influencing their everyday, shaping who they are. It also provides Finn with a folklore lesson in forgiveness: when something shatters your world—or a single relationship in it—to pieces, use what you know of tradition—or, as we see with Hy, the nature of your craft—to re-create it. But what to do when your *whole* life seems a jumble of fragments that refuse to meet, as Finn's does? How can you alone fit and hold all those scraps together? These questions are at the core of Finn's next instruction and story set.

In Instructions No. 2, Finn learns first how to figure a place to start when each quilt piece (life problem) seems as perplexing as any other:

> If you quilt alone, choose your subject carefully. Expect to live with it for approximately two years, depending on the simplicity or complexity of the work. The fairly intricate quilt will contain roughly, thirty-five pieces per block. Perhaps a thousand pieces in the finished quilt. Shake your head at the occasional quilt that boasts *thousands* of pieces. Puzzle out the fact that a single woman could hold all those pieces

together without misplacing, losing, or mistaking a piece. Understand that she must be someone of extraordinary strength and organization and discipline. Someone who is a stranger to the false step in life; someone a mother would admire. Question whether you would share your mother's admiration. (49)

In other words, to begin deciphering the pieces of a life, the fragments of a quilt, Finn, as a quilter, must first make just one of those scraps her whole subject, expecting it will take time to interpret that piece as well as to understand how the others fit to it. Moreover, she should consider that others have done this work before her, contemplate how they accomplished it:

Do a quick calculation of time and cloth pieces. Understand the sum to be breathtaking: hundreds of years of time spent quilting millions of pieces. How to keep it all in order. Under control.

It is not simply the color and design, but the intricate stitchwork involved. Miles of small, perfect stitches, uniform, each as the smallest link in the overall pattern of beauty and grace. All hand-sewn, with the Singer machine idle by the wall. You know quilters. (48)

Then, Finn is warned, no matter how astounded at their method, no matter how much it "boggles the mind. Forces you to sit down at your kitchen table, eyes closed, hand to your forehead, crushed under the weight of all those numbers" (48), she must ask herself whether their way will work for her. She must determine if she can work with a design so old, a pattern she fears may not be her own.

A quilter who cannot, a quilter who feels drawn to resist repeating a pattern even as her nature begs repetition, will probably prefer the pictorial quilt, finding it to be what she would like her life to be, "[. . .] finite, contained." And she will experience discomfort with both the repeating pattern, which is "a nod to reality. Your life. Everyone's life," and the crazy quilt, which is even worse. What with "its lack of order, its randomness, its shrouded personal meanings [. . .] its lack of skill and finesse," the crazy quilt presents a problem when it comes to how this quilter perceives women today. A nineteenth-century fad, it is her emblem of how women lived in the past, it is "not translatable to the twentieth century," to "modern women who control their lives and are not, in

turn, controlled by them" (49). Still, Finn is instructed, all this resistance to repetition on the one hand and aimlessness on the other has mainly to do with the
fact that even as we rebel, even as we express our free will, we follow in others'
footsteps. To prove this to herself, Finn turns from her instructions to one of
the women's stories: Sophia Darling's. For Sophia's life story illustrates the tru-
ism that how we live is handed down to us like quilting skills (50).

Although Sophia Darling's story actually begins much earlier, its text
commences when she meets her soon-to-be husband, Preston Richards, who
falls for Sophia as she falls in one beautiful arch after another from the high
dive at the public swimming pool. Recognizing in her actions that day a kin-
dred free spirit, he tells her after learning her name, "When we are married,
we will break tradition so you can keep your perfect name" (56). However, in
the life the two start together shortly thereafter, Preston's words prove ironically prophetic.

This occurs partly because of the life-instructions Sophia's mother
hands down to her. For instance, in preparation for her first date with Preston,
Sophia's mother tells her:

> [. . .] listen, sweetheart, let him do all the talking. Men love a
> good listener; it makes them feel important and smart. Be
> bright, but not too bright, and let him see that you are a
> young lady, a girl to be respected. [. . .] Follow his lead or, at
> least, give the appearance of following his lead. Just to be on
> the safe side—men are funny that way [. . .] You never know
> if he is The One. [. . .] You know I love you but you are not
> pretty enough to be on your own in this world [. . .] I know
> whereof I speak.

And on other occasions she has said things to the tune of this:

> *Sophia sweetheart, marriage is a difficult undertaking at best
> and the secret is to please your husband and be there for your
> children. Do not wander from the path you have chosen.* Or:
> *Rule the house with a velvet glove that serves to hide your
> will. Make your husband respect you.* And: *All else is failure.*
> (57–58)

Both sets of advice urge Sophia to put her own needs aside in favor of her
man's and her children's. They suggest that the only way to marital success is

through a woman's self-negation. Sophia has two mutually exclusive reactions to her mother's axioms:

> Mrs. Darling's love-advice often left her daughter ill tempered and suspicious and lusting after rebellion. More often than not, her mother's words forced Sophia from the house to the quarry reservoir, where she swam with fierce, cutting strokes. How could she make her mother understand that she might not want to "settle down" or that she felt a keen pleasure in the pure and unadorned sense of being alone? Then there were days, trapped in the house with her mother's loneliness, that made Sophia wild to be married, to belong to someone. To love and be loved. And so afraid that it might never happen to her at all. (58)

We see here that Sophia is caught between her craving to escape and her desire to belong. But before the road she travels is revealed, the causal chain is pushed further back into the past so that the last part of the total reason for the future shape of Sophia's life is understood. That last part is her father's legacy of absence, which has as much to do with her mother's words and her own behavior as those two things have to do with each other.

Sophia's father deserted her and her mother years ago, leaving, according to Mrs. Darling, because she did not heed her own advice, the advice she tells Sophia, "I give to you." The fact of her father's defection, however, is not enough to convince Sophia that the behavior her mother suggests is "the path to being a successful woman —a *wife*." She sees in what she remembers of her father the same wandering self alive in her, and she longs for freedom. Thus, even as she questions how a man could not want someone so compliant, she decides she does not want her mother's life. This she cannot tell her mother, nor can she make possible a life for herself that is different from her mother's. "Conditioned by a life without her father coupled with the longing she felt for him," Sophia becomes too afraid to make her own choices. Thus, life begins making choices for her. So much so that she ends up repeating the pattern her parents marked off; the pattern of "the woman who stayed and the man who walked away" (58–59).

The first piece of her life's design is laid out during what is also Sophia's first date with Preston Richards. Afraid Preston will confuse the dress and makeup she put on for her mother's benefit with the person she is, she takes him to a place she feels "belongs to her," defines her: the quarry where she spends most of her afternoons swimming in solitude. She believes that she has been right in her decision to do this when, upon their arrival, Preston states "I love it. [. . .] This place looks like you." Delighted to be thus understood, Sophia gets reckless, immediately taking off all but her underwear to execute a dive from one of the quarry's cliffs. Surfacing from the dive, she finds herself in Preston's arms, her mouth covered by his, "knowing what she will say and without hesitation. Yes." But permitting Preston "access to her body without revealing what was in her heart" does not open the world's doors to Sophia as she thought it would. It does not put her in a position to swim the globe, coming and going as she pleases. Rather, the "consequences of her actions" force her "into the life she had been raised to live" (61–74), her future decided. She will remain fixed right where she is, with only the memory of longing to comfort her.

After she marries Preston, after she has two more children, Pres and Edie, following her first child, Duff, she notices how much of her mother's life she is living. While a secret part of her still swims the world over, straying like her wandering father, another part does what is expected from her as her mother's daughter:

> It is expected that Sophia will do as her mother did; this is the legacy of the time into which they are born. Sophia lives with the inheritance of her mother, who lived with the inheritance of her mother. She is not expected to attend to her own intrepid journeys or follow her own desires. Her time does not encourage it. (73)

Still, each day at home with her children reminds her of what prevented her from joining the ranks of "women who saw things and did things" (74). Thus, she begins resenting Preston for the traveling his profession requires. In answer to her resentment, Preston takes an unsatisfying job collecting soil samples in Grasse. But even this does not satisfy Sophia, for now she imagines "[. . .] him pushing down the desire inside himself to leave and see all those places they talked about so many years ago." Squelching the part that was her father in herself, she sees, instead, her father in Preston. To prevent history from repeating itself, she heeds the only advice she has ever been given about how to make a marriage work—her mother's—almost completely believing now that "[. . .] if she makes herself so perfect, so unimpeachable in her behavior, he will be forced to stay, will have no legitimate reason to leave" (75).

Such behavior is unnatural to Sophia; it leaves her feeling "duplicitous," fragmentary. But she still can not be truthful with her husband about her wish "to throw it all over, pack the kids in the car, and take off with Preston to all those places. See all those things she longs to see and fall in love all over again [. . .] to tell Preston that she loves him, wants to be less rule bound with her children." Thus, she finds another way to work with the emotional scraps of her existence: "[. . .] she spends one night a week piecing together bits of fabric with a group of women. As if she could piece together all the things she feels inside, stitch them together and make everything seem whole and right" (76).

Although the Grasse Circle would like to move away from traditional patterns to work on a crazy quilt, the type that allows "freedom of color and pattern," the work the group does with traditional patterns is what excites Sophia. It is so much like working with her own life—the "traditional, established pattern [. . .] the true challenge [. . .] to work within a narrow confine. To accept what you cannot have; that from which you cannot deviate" (79). So much has Sophia come to accept the design handed down to women in her time, that when she finds her seventeen-year-old daughter, Edie, pregnant, she urges Edie to marry the father and settle into a life much like her own. With Edie's refusal to do so, Sophia decides Edie must go off to have the baby, give it up for adoption, and then return home to finish school. In words reminiscent of her mother, in a role "she essentially mistrusts; the role she cannot quite abandon," she tells Preston, who disagrees with her decision, "If she would marry the boy, I would feel differently, but she refuses. I won't have a child in my house raising her child without the *sanctity* of marriage. Yes, marriage. Grown-up responsibilities. Wouldn't it be nice if we could all just follow our heart's desire" (83).

Sophia's words and actions here are a displacement of her own anger at having done as her mother did. And such displacement sets in motion a series of occurrences that forever seal Sophia to her mother's fate. In the ninth month of her pregnancy, Edie runs away from the home to which she was sent to have and hand over the baby. Sophia, "not overly worried about her child's escape," agrees that Preston should go in search of her (84). Neither child nor husband returns. And with Duff already grown and gone, Sophia is left at home with her son, holding onto him as her mother held onto her, but nonetheless alone.

Sophia could not repeat a pattern while also altering its design. But that all repeating patterns bear a mark of the changes wrought by time is what

Finn must take from her story. She must understand that what is handed down to us is not all we have to work with. To create your own quilt, to shape your own life, you must find a way to reconcile the design you inherit with the design you have in mind without endangering the integrity of either. Relative to this quilting life lesson is the one contained in the next instructions and story. For as this match—Instructions No. 3 and Constance's story, *String of Pearls*—exhibits, sometimes it is not a prior pattern we have trouble with, but the current conditions shaping that design with which we must come to terms.

In anticipation of the story that follows, Instructions No. 3 parallels a discussion of the fashioning of a quilt to the making of marriages and the founding of friendships. As both have to do with attachments, Finn's training here begins with a general warning about setting boundaries that enforce a whole while also maintaining the individuality of the parts involved: "Do not underestimate the importance of the carefully constructed border in the quilt. Its function is to keep the blocks apart while binding the entire work together both literally and thematically" (86). Then, narrowing the lens so as to deal with one type of fastening at a time, in this case marriage, Finn is told:

> As you prepare to join your blocks, affix them to the dining-room wall or pin them to a set of drapes or arrange them upon the bed you share with your husband. You want to imagine how they will look once bound together. Think about what binds you to your husband and he to you. Marvel at the strength of that bond, which is both abstract and concrete, spiritual and legal. Consider [. . .] the way in which you imagined how the marriage would look before it took place. But perhaps you had other things on your mind before you tied the knot. (87)

Making a direct correlation between the way one plans the final look of her quilt and the way one imagines the future shape of her marriage, this part of Finn's lesson urges her to understand that the circumstances surrounding the conception of even the most carefully sketched blueprint often differ from the particulars accompanying its completion. If this happens, changes may need to be made. Therefore, Finn is instructed, treat the marriage as you would the quilt project: "do not be hesitant in devising new, different ways to link the patches to each other." Perhaps you should look to other quilts—to other marriages—when adaptations are necessary. See what others are doing.

But do not disregard your own ideas, for "what works for one quilt may not be successful for another" (87). Moreover, test your unique ideas; once bound "it is difficult to undo without reducing," without the possibility of "breakage" (88).

Marriage bonds today, Finn interrupts her lesson to comment, are often determined according to the couple involved. She argues, there is more freedom of choice for the woman; "she is encouraged to marry for love, not for family name or political alliance or wealth." But, her instructor tells her, the marriage bond is, nonetheless, like the quilt border—meant to encompass "the entire work [. . .] your life together." Thus, as you should "not be hasty when deciding on a border," because all quilt sashes and borders have the power either to complement or spoil the individual blocks, so you should be careful when deciding the terms of your marriage, understand that where women are concerned especially, "Marriage, too, can heighten the wife's colors or consign her to listless hues and shades." There are no guarantees until the work is done; thus, all these things should be contemplated before final decisions are made. For once the borders are attached, once the bonds are set, they should not be replaced. To do so is to risk "reducing your finished quilt to separate and myriad pieces" (88). Also, in general, remember that once undertaken, a marriage, like a quilt—or like a garden—requires a bit of effort: "it must be carefully tended. Which adds up to a good deal of attention paid; attention you are sometimes not prepared to give." This applies as well, Finn learns, to that other bond we are both drawn to and repelled by—the bond of friendship (91).

The friendship bond, however, is less like a quilt's border than it is like a quilt's binding. The binding, because it holds the layers of the quilt together instead of joining individual pieces, does not carry the dangerous permanency intrinsic to borders; it can be replaced if the quilt suffers from tension, stretching, age, or accident. Friendship bonds work in much the same way, for while they tie us to other people as marriage bonds do, they do so without the required-by-law statements declaring our intent to be together for all time. We are free to refurbish or leave behind old friendships and to create new ones as we grow and change throughout the course of a lifetime. Unlike the quilt border/marriage bond, which swears affection and connection while two things remain together, the quilt binding/friendship bond, the essence of which is found in the friendship quilt, declares "love and faithfulness in the face of parting, perhaps forever" (92).

Still, though they may be different, both the way of a marriage and the way of a friendship are understood in general terms by most of us. These customs come to us from years back. Thus, we, for the most part, willingly embrace them as our own. But some of us, though we accept the customs' fundamental shapes, find that both our natures and the circumstances of our lives do not permit us to engage in them in their original fashion. This is Constance's story.

A loner at heart, happy with her solitude, Constance marries late in life—when she is thirty-three. And she decides to marry Howell, a salesman whose region traverses the Western states, not only because she loves him, but also because what he has to offer is exactly what she needs: a chance to satisfy her curiosity about the West and an opportunity to indulge her solitary spirit—a way to live outside the mainstream without being a rebel (99).

For Constance living outside the mainstream means, to begin, marrying but not being the conventional husband and wife, together day in and day out, locked to each other by permanent living arrangements. In the traditional household, the man is tied to his work, the woman to home and hearth, quietly "shrugging acceptance of all manner of things" (100). Such monotony, Constance observes, results in not only the loss of each other, but the loss of self. This is what she ultimately wants to avoid, and in her life with Howell she does so. From the very beginning, he appreciated her as an individual and accepted her as separate from himself. Thus, "If she had to answer her parents' questions about why she loved Howell Saunders she would have to say: Because he lets me be me." In addition, he respected her enough to be honest with her about the transitory and solitary nature of their life together. Finn writes, "[. . .] he respected her too much to con her. He offered no guarantees except what he could guarantee—none of those silly promises about a future no one can foresee. He would do the best he could."

> When she asks him questions about anything, he considers the answer and delivers it truthfully, not simply telling her what he thinks she wants to hear. Of all the things a man can do, she hates that falseness most of all: someone who tries to edit or predict her response before she makes it. To be second-guessed or "protected" from the truth is to be treated like a child. [. . .] When someone tells you the truth, lets you think for yourself, experience your own emotions, he is treating you as a true equal. As a friend. (100–102)

This consistent honesty, an honesty that maintains the selfhood of both parties, is what Constance likes most of all. It shapes their life together, a life that fills another need in Constance: the need to avoid deep friendships with other women.

A private person, who generally enjoys her own company over the company of others, Constance has never been "wild over the idea of women friends." To her such relationships require too many confidences, too much time with other people. Thus, her "nomadic" life with Howell comes as a "blessing." Finn explains, "After all, if she is constantly being uprooted and moved, then she cannot truly make friends of any sort of depth, now can she?" (93). Nor does she have to, for Howell suits her friend requirements perfectly: he respects her privacy and he is frequently absent, leaving her with plenty of time alone with her own thoughts.

Constance's marriage, then, though it may be different from others, fulfills her in a way she never imagined.

> Since they did not live anyplace long enough to form deep friendships or attach themselves to any house or location, Constance felt no regret at moving on. Nor did she experience a profound searching inside herself, as if the next place would yield something better than the last; she simply packed up and moved, and was often glad to do so.
>
> During these years Constance forgot how to say good-bye or farewell since she rarely left anyone or anything of any significance. This suited her: all that temporary living combined with periods of solitude. [. . .] And Howell and Constance grew closer during his time spent home between trips, being each other's only friend. *Funny,* thinks Constance, *that I should so like being married. I never expected to like it this much.* (102–3)

But the circumstances of her life change over time, and so, she discovers, do her feelings in regard to a typical marriage, a lasting female friendship, a permanent place of residence. When Howell retires, they take up a fixed residence in Grasse, California. For a short time in this situation, Howell gets on Constance's nerves. She "yearns for the vast empty hours that had stretched before her when he was away on business, the sheer pleasure of anticipating his return [. . .] this constant state of togetherness was wearing her out"

(106–7). The feeling, however, leaves her quickly. Soon she finds herself happier with her new stationary life than she was with their old transient one. So much does she begin to enjoy being with Howell on a daily basis, from morning to night, that she misses him even when he runs errands. In her new state of being, she begins to forge, for the first time, a "comfortable kinship" with another woman, Marianna Neale. Moreover, she starts taking part in the community around her, and her first step in this direction is to become a member of the Grasse Quilting Circle. Although she does not really like quilting, the repetition helps her sort through the turn in her emotions, the alteration in her lifestyle; it "functioned as therapy, giving focus to her disjointed and unpeopled life" (108).

When Howell dies she realizes she cannot leave Grasse, not only because Howell is buried there, but also because she has made attachments that have changed her view about picking up and moving on.

> [. . .] she realized that this place, with its quilters and hot
> summers [. . .] and her friendship with Marianna (the first
> real woman friend she ever had, who gardened by her side or
> she by Marianna's side), had now changed for her [. . .] it had
> become someplace else, someplace she could not leave. (110)

So much has Grasse altered for her, so much has she transformed, that she tells her new friend since Howell's death, Dean, the husband of Em, another quilting circle member, that

> [. . .] only someone very young can do that—move without
> hesitation—because the older you are, whether you intend it
> or not, you get attached. You lay down roots, feel an uncom-
> fortable kinship with the soil beneath your feet. Certain things
> become meaningful and irreplaceable and no matter how
> much you like to travel or adore your destinations, you will
> always return to that thing that only exists for you here. (114)

Still, all her feelings of finally coming home, so to speak, do not completely assuage her loneliness. For relief, she turns increasingly to Marianna, who is safe territory, and to Dean, who is not. And as her relationship with Dean causes strife within the quilting circle and confusion within Constance herself, Constance drops out of the circle for a while to spend some time alone—to look again on marriage, to figure once more what friendship means.

The importance of thinking over these relationships is one of the things Constance's story illustrates to Finn. For it shows her how necessary it is that she determine for herself what she needs in relationships before deciding how to fit them into her life. But Constance's story also suggests that Finn must be prepared to rethink her conclusions, given life's many unexpected deviations from even the most carefully laid plans, given the many different people she will meet along the way, people with their own and often very different ideas about these very same issues. Take the idea of marital love, for instance. What happens when two people marry having no knowledge of each other's feelings in regard to this? Instructions No. 4 and Em's story—"Umbrellas Will Not Help at All"—provides Finn with at least one answer to this question.

In Instructions No. 4 Finn is shown how closely related is the preservation of a quilt to the treatment of love in a marriage. Preserving a quilt is done with the utmost care, and for one of two reasons: to display it or to store it. Still, either reason for preserving a quilt has its problems. To display a quilt is to risk finding "another use for the quilt other than display," is to risk growing tired of having it on show, is to risk exasperation at always having to look at your own work. And storing a quilt, though it "may protect it from the elements of heat and dampness and light," does not "afford anyone, including yourself, any pleasure in its beauty." It is "to own but not to enjoy" (120).

In addition, Finn is told, particular modes of display present their own drawbacks. For instance, the most popular display method, the Plexiglas box, includes

> [. . .] losing a sense of intimacy with the work. The desire to touch the quilt will be harbored within yourself as well as within your guests [. . .] but they will simply have to imagine the feel of the small stitches, softness of the material, unevenness of the texture (all of which gives your quilt its look of life), the extra puff of stuffing in selected areas of the top cloth, not to be confused with the layer of cotton batting that lies between the backing and the top work. Do not neglect to note that this sort of display treatment renders the quilt more formidable as a work of art. An ordinary, useful household item transformed. Shake your head at such transformation. [. . .] You could find yourself overwhelmed by all

the precautions necessary to protect your quilt, all the machi-
nations to keep it in good condition. (122)

That is, at the same time this preservation method makes the quilt a part of
your everyday, it makes it no longer a part of your life, something outside your
realm even as it holds a prominent place in your home. It begs your attention,
but it prevents your touch, your involvement with it. It is a temptation you cannot indulge.

The problems surrounding the purposes and methods of quilt preservation are not unlike the ones you may encounter in a marriage, Finn's instructor points out, depending on the way you and your partner handle your love.
For as the preservation process can damage a quilt, both in the abstract and in
the concrete, if one is not cautious, so "a careless couple can murder love if left
unchecked" (121). Say, for instance, you treat your love like a quilt on display,
something you no longer give day-to-day attention. Or maybe you take a look
at it from time to time, only to find that what you created no longer interests
you, or that your careful treatment of it has distanced it from you. Then again,
perhaps you treat your love like a quilt to be stored, a possession, something
you are proud to have but too afraid to show for fear of losing a thing so dear
to you. You stash it away, thinking if you keep it hidden it cannot be lost or
harmed. And, finally, maybe you deal with your love as you would deal with a
quilt placed in direct sunlight. You know the light will "ultimately damage the
quilt," but you leave it there because "[. . .] you like the way it looks when the
early-morning sun lies across it, lazylike, taking its sweet morning time [. . .]
brings out the colors." That is, you inflict your way of loving upon your partner,
knowing that it causes him or her pain, but remaining addicted to the pleasure
of fulfilling your own desires nonetheless. You fail to understand that love
"does not mean the same thing to everyone" (123). But this is what you must
accept in order for your marriage to survive, as Em's story, "Umbrellas Will
Not Help at All," shows Finn.

Finn's visit to Grasse finds Em not looking forward to the circle's pro-
posed summer projects. For one thing, Em fears she will not be able to lie
about the personal meanings behind her supposedly random contributions to
the crazy quilt. And, for another, she "does not know if she has the patience to
put herself into a work that holds marriage as its center"—the bridal quilt.
Both these reactions, Finn learns, have to do with the state of Em's marriage
to Dean.

Em and Dean's marriage is based on a pattern of betrayal, refusal, and acceptance set early in their marriage. In the initial days of their love, Dean had hoped to be an artist and Em had hoped to reap the benefits his artistic unconventionality seemed to promise. But when Dean is forced to teach art rather than create it, he exhibits his unconventionality in an illicit affair. And Em, refusing to "believe Dean's betrayal at first," finds herself wishing for a "'normal husband.'" Yet she knows that what she now wants in Dean is something she will never have; Dean is simply incapable of being a "decent man." Therefore, Em decides to accept Dean's unfaithfulness this time, blaming it, as he does, on his thwarted talent and subsequent restlessness and seeing her ability to forgive as something that "would make her so powerful nothing could touch her" (126–28).

However, when Dean engages in another affair she realizes she is all too corporeal still. During this relationship, Em comes to the conclusion that she and Dean view love differently. To Em, love is sacred and requires self-sacrifice, forgiveness, and understanding. To Dean, love is simply a need to be satisfied, a chance to be taken. He tells her, "the only thing I can change or control—the only adventure I can find is love." And with this realization, Em walks out on Dean. But she soon returns, not because she is pregnant and soon to give birth, but because she comes to terms with the fact that Dean's "romantic nature canceled out long-term happiness," and because she decides she would rather live with their differences than without Dean altogether (131–34).

This decision takes its toll on Em, becoming especially hard to live by when, much later in their marriage, Dean forges a friendship with Constance Saunders. One night while Dean is with Constance, Em once again considers leaving him. Thinking back on the long trial that has been her marriage—Dean's selfish love that requires her selfless love in return—she goes into his painting studio in search of a trinket she wants to take with her, a silver heart Dean bought for her years ago. There, in a place she is normally forbidden to go, she finds a series of paintings of herself done by Dean, beginning right before they married. Unable to "fathom that all these poses and pieces" of her are her, she "marvels at how well Dean seems to know the many sides of her."

> What strikes her as well is what these perceptions of her reveal about Dean: eroticism, contentment, adoration, anger, possible danger, resentment, coolness. She finds herself

saying to no one, *I swear he loves this woman,* as if it is not
her, but another of Dean's Women. (138)

These paintings, like quilt patches, tell a story that reveals as much about Em
as it is does about Dean, and as much about the two as individuals as it does
about them as a couple.

Thus, Em suddenly comes to the conclusion that she cannot leave
Dean, "cannot leave a man who knows her in this way. Cannot walk the world
without him, seeing that she has to leave so much of herself behind." Her marriage may not be what she would ideally have it be, but seeing now "how married they really are," she cannot abandon it (138). Instead, in her contributions
to the crazy quilt she will pay tribute to it. She will donate yellow roses to signify the deep knowledge she and her husband have of each other and silver
hearts in commemoration of the unique ways of loving they share. And her contributions will suggest to Finn that sometimes what we are given, though different from what we wanted, is precious in its own right. Sometimes we must
learn to accept if not embrace that which we cannot change, an idea elaborated
on in the next instruction and story pairing.

Instructions No. 5 continues the discussion of storage methods begun in
No. 4, while also touching on quilt cleaning. Here Finn learns that when not in
use or on display, "a quilt should be kept clean and properly stored." The problem
is that while both treatments require a number of tedious steps, neither cleaning
nor storage guarantees the quilt against damage. Cleaning, though it prevents the
quilt from becoming dirty, takes its toll on the delicate fibers; eventually they
begin to show the signs of age and care. Even if stored away, it could still incur
harm from the elements or from unseen pests inhabiting the storage area.

> And remember, no matter how careful you are, you might not
> be able to prevent some damage to your quilt —no matter how
> attached you are to it, or how much of your skill and time you
> have invested in it or how carefully you followed all the rules
> for care, something unforeseen may ruin it beyond repair; leav-
> ing only the memory of the quilt behind. Do not castigate your-
> self; you may not be to blame. You did your best. These are
> fragile textiles. These things happen. (142–43)

In other words, Finn must recognize that no matter what we do, no matter how
much we care, we can no more prevent than we can predict the outcome of
our labors of love.

Finn sees this quilt care as similar to women's vigilance for their families. She ponders over the fact that like the quilt, a loved one may come to injury regardless of your efforts to make him safe, to keep her out of harm's way. The helplessness women have experienced as a result, Finn tells us, they have documented in their quilts, especially during times of war. Quilts made on these occasions, like the Names Quilt of today, were women's monuments of the lives they could not protect from damage; they were testaments to battles afar and battles within, not an end to injury and loss, but evidence of it.

> These things are not glorified, just recorded. Tattooed on the
> heart; burned into the family's history. This piecing together
> of the life of your child; this homage; this attempt to put it all
> in order [. . .] (146)

It is a cry against a ruin both inevitable and irreparable, a ruin causing a pain that will remain with you no matter how much you wish it gone (146). Quilting circle member Corrina Amurri and her husband, Jack, know this. Their story, "Outdoors," is about the attempt to shield the self from damage when damage is always already a given. It is about learning to live with loss.

When Laury Amurri goes off to serve in the Vietnam War, his parents, Corrina and Jack, handle his absence in different ways, their unique reactions a result of their own roles during the war of their youth: World War II. Jack fought in the war, witnessed the horror of it, and wished to retreat from it. Thus, while his son is away, he seeks open space, escape from the house in which his fears "gain in density and strength" (150). Corrina, on the other hand, like so many other women of World War II, was forced into the position of patient waiter, staying at home hoping and praying her man would be returned to her alive. During this waiting period she worked as a switchman for the railroad nearby. Refusing a better job farther away, she allayed her fear of loss by keeping her life unchanged while Jack was gone, "so that when the war ended he could simply slip back into it, as if he had never left her at all." She behaves in a like manner while her son is away, remaining homebound, "as if she can only keep her worrying about Laury under control if she can keep her home in tact" (152–55).

Corrina's attempts to hold the pain of loss at arm's length fail, however, when Laury is listed as missing in action. Then the sense of inevitable loss surfaces and she realizes, as Finn explains, that

[h]er reserve of patience had been used up when Jack was in
Europe; none was left for Laury who remained unheard from.
She could not pray because she wanted to shake her fist at
God, at the unfairness of being forced through the ordeal of
waiting for a soldier, not once in her life, but twice. She
wanted to scream, How much am I supposed to endure? (157)

Now she must recognize what she could not permit herself to contemplate
before. That she cannot help feeling angry that her friend's son remains safe at
home while her son is somewhere far away and in danger. That no matter what
she does, no matter how much she tears apart and restores her house, "with
fury and with hope," she cannot control the outcome of war, she cannot keep
her loved one protected. And, finally, that she cannot keep herself out of the
way of her own sorrow. For when her son's imagined death becomes a reality,
she sees that loss is a thing that must be reckoned with, a constant in life one
must find a way to endure. Paired as it is with a lesson on quilt storage and
cleaning, Corrina's story is meant to teach Finn that there are times in life
when one must relinquish control. But as Instructions No. 6 and Anna Neale's
story show her, there are also times when one must take it back. The trick is
knowing the difference.

As Anna Neale is the descendant of slaves, the instructions that pre-
cede her story begin with a lesson in the history of slavery, especially as it
relates to sewing and quilting. Finn is told that the sewing slave was worth a
great deal in slavery's day, for she could be put to work in the fields during the
day and set down to sewing at night. This slave was to consider herself "[. . .]
fortunate to be in a household that allowed her specialized work like sewing
exclusively." And yet, Finn is questioned, how can one feel fortunate to have
no control over the work one does, no choice in the matter? What makes the
work worthwhile is having both the freedom to choose to do it, and the freedom to choose what to do, "the designing and creating [. . .] as if you are talking beauty with your hands. Make yourself heard in a wild profusion of colors,
shapes, themes, and dreams with your fingertips." Without this freedom, "the
tedium of quilt construction some days can make you cry; you long to express
yourself. To shout out loud in silk and bits of old scarves" (168).

Through this history, Finn is urged to see quilting as more than a task,
the quilt as more than a product of the hands. Quilting, Anna Neale asserts, is
a mode of self-expression, the quilt an extension of the quilter, a way to tell

her own story, sometimes the only way she can—"with fabric and thread." To illustrate this, she presents a list of the quilts she has designed and created, outlining each in terms of some element of her life, some aspect of her person, some lesson she has learned. For instance, *The Life Before* quilt is described as a "reminder of ancestors. What cannot be told to someone who does not want to listen or does not express curiosity." The *Broken Star* quilt as a reflection of her long-ago wish to "study the stars." And the *Friendship across Time and Distance* quilt underscores the fact that "friendship arrives from the least likely sources and flourishes in the least likely locations [. . .] that someone can know you very well though you have not told her about yourself" (170–72).

These uniquely personal works reflect Anna Neale's quilt tastes. Anyone, she explains to Finn, can appropriate a design or buy a pattern to work with, but such work is not nearly as valuable as the work that contains your own ideas, "your own heart involvement" (169). She refers Finn to the Hawaiian quilter's philosophy, for "[. . .] they believe it is bad luck to appropriate another's design, to tell another's story." They feel as Anna Neale does, "that to share your personal pattern is to share your soul. To compromise your power" (173). Inserting the story of a mainland woman's appropriation of a Hawaiian woman's quilt to emphasize her points, she urges Finn to see that appropriation is a loss of power, a loss of history, on the one hand, and a false power, a false history on the other. In other words, it is dangerous to steal someone else's design and pass it off as your own. To be worthwhile, the pattern you follow must be your own. Anna Neale's own story proves that she knows what of she speaks. For *Tears Like Diamond Stars* is about her firsthand experience with forging her own path in life.

Tears Like Diamond Stars begins with words spoken by Anna Neale to herself:

> I refused at an early age, to be a specter in my own world. I decided that I would not be whisked away, so I sought to anchor myself to society, to make them see *me*, Anna Neale, child of a black mother (deceased) and a white father (whereabouts unknown and unacknowledged); gave birth to one child, my daughter, Marianna Neale; became undisputed leader and founder of the Grasse Quilting Circle (recognized nationally for superior and original work). Of course

> I know that outside of the quilting world the Grasse women
> remain unknown. But I am not invisible because of this
> closed circle; I am not unknown. I learned to speak with
> needle and thread long before society finally "gave" me a
> voice—as if society can give anyone a voice; it can only take
> it away. (174–75)

Reaffirming the essence of the lesson brought out in the instructions section,
here Anna Neale insists that through her own resolve she created herself,
through her own work she found her voice, a way to tell her own story—the
story she permits Finn to share with us.

Anna Neale was raised by her great-aunt, Pauline, in a house owned
by the couple for whom Pauline worked. As a young girl, there were two things
Anna Neale loved. The first thing was

> [. . .] a quilt that had been made by her great-great-grand-
> mother, called *The Life Before*. [. . .] It was divided into
> fifteen large squares filled with appliquéd animals, birds,
> men of dark brown, hovering angels blowing trumpets, ser-
> pents as large as life, stars, the outsized sun, flaming candles
> of dripping wax. These were African scenes: animals with
> tusks, warriors clashing with spirits and themselves and
> beasts. Candles that burned upside down. Giant fish devour-
> ing unfortunate men, who tumbled from enormous balanc-
> ing scales. The colors of dense earthy tones; yellow stars
> blaze a midnight field; the unforgiving sun. [. . .] The quilt as
> dream-desire placed against the reality of the world.
> (175–76)

This first love Pauline promises will be Anna Neale's one day. But so she
promises will her second love, the sky, with its "heavenly bodies, stars, and
comets," for Pauline will find a way to buy her a telescope, one that will be her
own so she no longer has to use the one owned by the man of the house. However, the only way Pauline finds to make the second promise possible is by
breaking the first one. In order to get the money she needs to buy Anna the
telescope, she sells *The Life Before* quilt to the Mrs.[21] This so upsets Anna that
she refuses even to think about a telescope. Pauline, therefore, tries to buy
back the quilt. But the Mrs. refuses, hanging it, instead, in the sitting room

where it is a constant reminder to Pauline of her mistake, where it is admired by friends of the family who beg the Mrs. to have Pauline make them one. Imagining her refusal, Pauline hears herself telling them, "Don't you know that only you can tell your story? You can't buy someone else's life." The problem, she realizes in listening to her own thoughts, is that the quilt contained her family's history, her family's stories. Hence, the sale of the quilt *is* the sale of a life, of many lives.

As time goes by, Pauline grows increasingly distraught "by the theft of her history, appropriated by someone for whom the quilt is an ornamental object and nothing more." And Anna, disturbed by her aunt's pain, becomes unable to be in the same house with the person she sees as the cause of it, the Mrs. Thus, at sixteen, she takes control of both her future and her history— she goes off to find work in San Francisco—and, fulfilling her aunt's promise to her herself, she takes the quilt with her.[22]

During her employment as a maid on a ranch in Bakersfield, California, Anna becomes pregnant by the white son of her wealthy employers. Determining her own fate, she decides not to tell the father, but simply to quit her job and walk away. She then takes a job as a housekeeper in Grasse, in the home of the Rubens, people who take in wayward girls expected to give their babies up for adoption. In this new home, Anna feels the slightest bit of chill from Mrs. Ruben, the tiniest bit of resentment in her careful treatment of her, her use of Anna to show the world "how charitable she could be to the 'less fortunate.'" And as she suspects that the Rubens's daughters, Hy and, especially, Glady Joe, share their mother's attitudes, she feels bitter at what she believes are their less than genuine offers of friendship (189).

Anna does not feel a part of the life going on around her, nor is she sure she wants to be a part of it. It both repels and attracts her. In order to deal with her ambivalent feelings, she decides to limit her contact with this world. Confining herself to solitude when she has time off, Anna begins quilting with the scraps sent to her by her aunt. This time alone with her work is therapeutic; it helps her "forget about being seventeen, unwed, unloved, pregnant, outside the mainstream." But her solitude is short-lived, for it only draws Glady Joe more to her. She comes to Anna's closed door with offerings of friendship nearly every night—a book, tea. Finally, the girls begin spending time together. Anna quilting while Glady Joe reads to her from one book after another—*Wuthering Heights, Jane Eyre, Pride and Prejudice*. Then, as Glady Joe tries her hand at quilting, Anna reads to her from books sent to her by her now retired Aunt

Pauline—books of her mother's culture, like *Spunk* by Zora Neale Hurston.
These steps toward companionship entail a conscious relinquishing of control
on Anna's part. But it feels good loosening her hold, it feels like the right thing
to do in this instance. However, just as a tentative bond is formed between the
two, Anna gives birth and must take charge of her life again. For she does not
want to do what Mrs. Ruben expects her to do: give her daughter up for adoption. Therefore, adept as she is at making her own way in life, she opts instead
to move into her own place and take a job as a bookkeeper to support her new
family.

Were it not for Glady Joe, Anna, in her new life, would be friendless.
But Glady Joe is a constant visitor to Anna's office and home, reminding Anna
through her steady devotion that letting someone in does not necessarily mean
letting something go. Thus, when Glady Joe is expecting her twins, and she and
her husband, Arthur, ask Anna to move in to help out, Anna agrees, affirming
her ties to this other person.

Living together, day in and day out, the two women begin quilting
again on a regular basis. In this work they truly strike a balance. For Glady Joe
enjoys the "tedious grunt work," and Anna would rather "devote her energy to
design and detail." Because of this, Finn explains,

> [t]wo things happen: Glady Joe begins her circle with Anna
> as the unspoken leader and teacher; black Anna and white
> Glady Joe find equal footing. They become true friends
> because they share, complement each other; one does not
> solely take on the role of comforter or comforted; one does
> not exclusively receive while the other takes. Theirs is an
> exchange. (205)

Over time, these aspects of Anna's life make her feel, unlike other black
Americans still fighting for civil rights on the larger stages across the country,
as though she has achieved her own kind of equality right there in the "little
town of Grasse." She thinks, "Let anyone try to tell her otherwise or wrest it
from her. Just let them" (206). Thus, years later, looking at old slides and
snapshots of her combined family, Anna will see her life as bound to the others',
will understand that there is no "simple way" to show her personal history
without including theirs and vice versa. And, having learned that there is a
holding on and a letting go to everything, Anna will embrace this fusion. But
her daughter, Marianna, will spend much of her life struggling with blendings

of this sort, joinings that seek to create a thriving whole out of two diverse things.

Setting us up for Marianna's story, Instructions No.7 works its own combination; it joins quilt stitching pointers with plant grafting directives, and these two things with a history lesson about past laws pertaining to the intermingling of blacks and whites. The layers of a quilt, Finn is told, are stitched together "with silk thread, embroidery thread, nylon thread." And, "the stitches must be small, consistent, and reflect a design of their own." This singular design, the stitches *mapping* the quilt's arrangement, will go virtually unnoticed by the nonquilter, but it will be what holds the quilter's interest when she observes her finished work. She will consistently worry over her delicate outlining, Finn learns, much as the grafter will attend to the tedious seaming required to create a plant that will "not only withstand the hostile environment, but thrive within it." Both quilter and grafter will be so concerned, for it is a difficult thing this "[. . .] combination of disparate elements." So difficult, Finn's instructor points out, that in the past certain alliances of unlike elements were forbidden altogether—specifically, the union of blacks and whites (212–15).

Here Finn's instructor lists the many attempts made by American policymakers to keep these seemingly dissimilar people apart, the many laws created to assure blacks and whites did not join themselves to each other or make the mistake of assuming they were one and the same. The examples she provides span a time period of almost two hundred years, ending with the situation existing during Marianna's growing up, 1935 to 1953. It is a situation not much changed, an America that still wants to forget Marianna exists—her white and black blood a continuous paradox articulated in a custom of exclusion Marianna cannot accept. Her quilting, Finn is told, reflects this disavowal; her abstract style a rejection of tradition in favor of her own form, which, in turn, is much like her life. For her life is a break with what is expected of her in favor of what she wants for herself—an acceptance of the fusion she is. The problem is that just as she accepts her quilting style regardless of what others think, she must learn to embrace the graft that is herself, whether others affirm her combination or not. Marianna's story, "Grafting Roses," shows us this is a difficult task, yet it is perhaps the most valuable lesson Finn has yet to learn from the Grasse quilters.

Like her mother, Marianna is a woman weary of closeness, a self-contained woman of her own mind. As an adult, she will swear off what others expect her to do—keep house for others, for instance, as her mother did, because she is a woman and she is considered black—choosing instead to study and then work in agriculture. However, the Grasse community finds this choice strange; the farmers of the town exhibit their disapproval by refusing to hire "a woman, a negro woman" when Marianna goes in search of a job following her college graduation. So, Finn tells us, "Marianna ended up tending roses in the south of France, fairly close to a town called Grasse [. . .] for a company that supplied flowers to much of Europe" (221). There, as she waits for her graftings to germinate in outdoor soil, she anticipates the growth of her own union in perfect love. She fancies herself loving but one other person, experiencing an exclusive love, making two people, one. However, she ends up developing a love life that is not the offshoot she had foreseen when she imagined love in her life, but a reflection of her own inner struggles. She falls in love with two men, Alec, who is white, and Noel, who is black, unable to choose between the two, just as she cannot choose between the black and white parts of herself, the American and French, and so on.

> It was becoming more difficult for people to determine her background. She knew she could "pass" if she so desired, that she could be taken for white and not black; she resembled her father as well as her mother [. . .] But she refused to deny her African-American heritage, for to do so would deny Anna, and that she would not do; act as if her mother had never existed! She considered Anna's blood the proudest part of herself, not something to be falsified.

Yet,

> [. . .] her white history would not be ignored, either. [. . .] her body was some sort of quiet battleground, with her father's side slowly but surely assuming more and more territory. It was frightening to see in herself the man she never knew; become someone she did not know. [. . .] Everything in her life is at war with everything else: her mixed blood; her Americanism transplanted into French soil; her attraction to catastrophic love (she can love more than one person at a time); being a woman working a man's job. She cannot be made whole, cannot be joined together with herself—or with someone else. (224–26)

Thus, she breaks off with both men and has one affair after another, never committing herself to a relationship long enough for it to move into marriage. She tells herself that it is not for a lack of love that she refuses her lovers' offers, but for a lack of interest in that lifelong juncture that makes her eventually move on to another man and then away from love altogether. Her decision not to join herself to someone else buttresses her decision to withdraw from grafting, her reason for leaving her career calling to mind her real reason for banishing love from her life. Finn tells us:

> No matter how well she did it, it would always have to be done again to new plants. The roses simply could not be bred to stand alone; they would always require a hardier base. The fusion of the bushes can only give the illusion of oneness but can never truly be one. Finally, she recalled her many love affairs, she became convinced that they indicated a cold heart, one that will not allow closeness or for anyone to be close. This astonishes her, because she used to think that her many lovers were the sign of a great capacity to love, a capacity greater than any one of her lovers could match. Now she knows that it was an inability to love. (228–29)

What she does not know, however, is that she is unable to love others because she has yet to learn to love herself. This is what causes her emptiness, makes her hungry for her mother, and prompts her return to Grasse.

There, Marianna takes over the maintenance of Glady Joe's garden, gaining, through her return to her mother, enough "pride and self-worth" to ignore the suggestion, mostly made by whites, that to do so was to compromise herself as an educated black woman.[23] Like her mother's quilting, which Anna now makes a living by, Marianna learns to see her work as a "small miracle, her contribution to beauty," in a place resistant to it. In addition, Marianna forms a friendship with Constance based on their mutual love of roses and their shared respect for private space. The two spend many days working side by side in Constance's garden, sharing a "comfortable silence." Moreover, their relationship brings Marianna to the Grasse Quilting Circle. And it is because of this circle that she learns to accept the differences that are herself, finding in the circle a place where the expression of differences—something she and her mother personify—is not only accepted but necessary to survival. In concluding Marianna's story, Finn tells us:

> The quilters accepted Anna and Marianna, and no one ever
> made the mistake of saying, "We don't even notice color; they
> are just like us." It was this recognition of their differences
> that allowed the group to survive, not pretending to tran-
> scend them. The impulse to unify and separate, rend and
> join, is powerful and constant. (232)

It is at the heart of the group these women form, of the work these women do. Coming together in this fashion, doing this work, benefits each circle member in some way—creatively, emotionally, or spiritually—depending on her need, the shape of her life. And so it should not surprise us to find—as we do in the book's final section, "The Crazy Quilt"—that observing the group, learning their craft, has benefited Finn in her summer search for a sense of herself.

This last set of instructions is less a lesson than it is a summing up of what Finn has come to know through Anna's tutoring and storytelling. Thus, she returns to the crazy quilt here because it is, quite simply and appropriately, her emblem of those things. For like the crazy quilt, the instructions and stories passed to her are a collection of "odds and ends [. . .] with nothing, no tiny scrap, wasted" (233). Although her attention may have been directed to one piece at a time, as a quilt observer's eye may be drawn to one patch at a time, she knows now that no one piece is to be viewed as more important than another. Rather, like fragments making up a crazy quilt, each quilting lesson, each woman's story, must be viewed in its uniqueness as equally necessary to the whole project that is her journey to know. She provides further evidence of this in a description of the circle's dynamics. As the women come together each week, Finn tells us, the circle's seating arrangement changes, like "some sort of complicated, intricate dance of many partners, facing many different directions." In other words, just as there is no ranking to what each woman contributes to the making of the quilt, what each woman brings of herself to the circle, what each instruction and story set is meant to teach Finn, there is no boardroom hierarchy here. And this egalitarian presentation of women, work, and story moves Finn to understand that the life she feels she is now ready to make with Sam has "as good a chance of being wonderful as it does of missing the mark." Or, better yet, "there is a strong possibility it will be both." As she determines in watching the circle members that there is but one constant in their behavior—they wait for the circle's founder, Anna, to choose her seat before taking their own—so she learns "from talking with Anna about the various quilters" that there is but one constant in life: the probability of its being both happy and sad, both good and bad. Discovering that this has always been the case, Finn is filled with "tremendous relief." She knows now that no one chooses a pattern sure to determine the shape of her life thereafter. The design will continually shift, depending on what your experiences in life bring to it, experiences that will more than likely "hold meaning for you alone." Finn concludes, with all the authority of a virtuoso quilter, "Do not explain. This is your right."

Through the instructions and stories shared with her, Finn comes to understand the very thing Virginie learned in *The Minister's Wooing:* folk culture is a means to wholeness. Just as Virginie's experiences with Mary taught her that needlework could center and sustain a soul, so Finn's experiences with the members of the Grasse Quilting Circle convey to her that she should put together a life as one would assemble and stitch a quilt.[24] Both Stowe and Otto present the actual *doing* of folklore as a way of traversing the rocks and brambles thrown in the path of progress. Together their works show us that what we create—our quilts, our lives, ourselves—is as much a part of the present as it is a thing of the past, a whole out of fragments, a tenuous connection. Take care.

CHAPTER 2

Everybody Loves a Good Story

Charles Chesnutt's *The Conjure Woman* and David Bradley's *The Chaneysville Incident*

Living to Tell, Telling to Live: The Oral Tradition and the
Storyteller in Charles Chesnutt's The Conjure Woman

I own my life. And only mine. And so I shall appreciate my
person. And so I shall make proper use of myself.
RUTH BEEBE HILL

In the introduction to this study, I spoke of my grandfather, who, like the
women of *The Minister's Wooing* and the members of the Grasse Quilting
Circle, has long known how to live through folklore—in this case the folk tradition of storytelling. I pointed out how my experience with my grandfather, similar to Virginie's experience with Mary and Finn's experience with the quilting
circle members, is a journey to myself via a journey to this knowledge; my family's oral lore my vehicle.

The stories my grandfather shares with me fall into two closely
related folklore categories: personal experience stories and family stories.
Personal experience stories, Sandra Dolby Stahl explains in her essay of the
same name,

> [. . .] are first-person narratives usually composed orally by
> the tellers and based on real incidents in their lives; the sto-
> ries "belong" to the tellers because they are the ones respon-
> sible for recognizing in their own experiences something
> that is "story worthy" and for bringing their perception of
> those experiences together with the conventions of "story"
> in appropriate contexts and thus creating identifiable, self-
> contained narratives. (268–69)

Family stories, on the other hand, and yet by the same token, include

> [. . .] any incident retold by one family member about
> another over a period of years [. . .] usually based on real inci-
> dents which become embellished over the years. They are

> relevant to American history not only because they convey
> some factual information, but because they often capture the
> ethos of an era [. . .] They also tell us much about the story-
> tellers and how certain episodes in our national history bear
> upon their lives today. (Zeitlin, Kotkin, Baker 10)

Although it took some time, I now realize that it is this "thick web of shared traditions" embedded in my grandfather's stories that connects his life to mine—his "personal reality and personal sense of history" to my own—and makes me feel grounded in the present (Stahl, *Literary Folkloristics* 119). In other words, it is not simply the stories themselves helping me achieve a sense of who I am in this world; it is also the storyteller legacy my grandfather is passing on to me through a series of storytelling sessions meant to teach me how important the very act of telling a story is to the teller, how much it serves to shape and define that person.

We all love a good story, yet few of us pay attention to the significance of the telling to the storyteller. One of the things I learned from my grandfather is that as much as my family's stories provide me with a sense of history, becoming the teller of those stories is what truly links me to that past, centers me in the present, and prepares me for the future.

In her essay "Personal Experience Stories," Stahl discusses the value of personal experience stories, such as those my grandfather shares with me. Her comments in regard to how personal experience stories serve the tellers of those stories fall in line with my own thoughts as to the role personal experience storytelling plays in my grandfather's life. She asserts, "Obviously there are many reasons why we tell such stories. One outstanding reason is that through personal experience stories we articulate and then test the values that identify ourselves" (275). My grandfather's actions signify to me that he recognizes folklore to be "[. . .] one of the important ways we give life meaning beyond the immediate present." Hence, I believe he tells his own stories, as well as our family stories, because he knows it is through them that "we order our lives . . . we become able to both understand and communicate our experiences [. . .]" (Zeitlin, Kotkin, Baker 8). Learning for myself the significance of storytelling to the life of the teller gave new meaning to the oral tradition. And as my personal life is hardly separate from my studies, I soon found myself searching American literature for a work that focused on this newly important figure in my life, the person I am becoming: the oral storyteller. What I found is that as ubiquitous

as characters who figure as storytellers are, we are rarely asked to pay attention
to what that role means to the character, so focused are we on the story being
told. But there are two works that seem to beg us to give the storytellers their
due—one written almost a century ago, the other, fairly recently. Those two
works are Charles Chesnutt's *The Conjure Woman* and David Bradley's *The
Chaneysville Incident.*

Admittedly, *The Conjure Woman* is a series of "plantation tales" told to
eradicate northerners' romantic notions about the system of slavery, particularly
their rose-colored view of master/slave relationships. Working against a post-
Reconstruction eve steeped in fantasy about plantation life before the Civil War,
the stories presented in *The Conjure Woman* call into question the values that
give rise to the notions of benevolent master and loyal slave. Take, for instance,
the first tale Uncle Julius tells—"The Goophered Grapevine." In this tale,
Henry, a slave on Mars Dugal's vineyard plantation, is goophered into an alter-
nating state of health that follows in line with the seasonal changes experienced
by the grape crop. In the spring, Henry gains a Sampsonian virility, growing hair
on his bald head and exhibiting inexhaustible energy. But in the fall, he begins
withering like the grapevine and spends the subsequent winter battling for his
life. Noting Henry's seasonal health fluctuations, Mars Dugal begins selling
Henry each spring, when his obvious strength will bring a good price, and buying him back at a profit in the winter when Henry's health declines. Making
money off Henry and his thriving vineyard are not enough for Mars Dugal,
however. He falls prey to a Yankee con artist who promises him a method that
will double his crop the following year. Come spring, the crop begins thriving as
never before, and so, as the goophering would have it, does Henry. Like the
doubly abundant vineyard, Henry is stronger than ever before. In fact, he is so
indefatigable that he is indispensable this year; with the anticipated added crop
to harvest, Mars Dugal cannot feasibly afford to sell Henry away. The crop,
however, takes a turn for the worse, eventually failing completely under the
Yankee's suggested ministrations. And, as Henry's health has been conjured to
follow in line with the grape crop's, he, too, enters a state of physical decline,
which results, finally, in his death.

This tale illustrates, as Robert M. Farnsworth writes in the introduction to *The Conjure Woman,* how "black man and nature alike suffer from the
greed and power of the white master" (xv). For, in essence, Mars Dugal's insa-
tiable appetite for money and unwavering lack of compassion cause irreversible
harm to both his precious grapes and his coveted slave. Certainly tales such as

this do much to refigure master/slave relationships. But the interrelated tales of
The Conjure Woman do more than criticize a system, they celebrate a culture
as well. As Eric Sundquist puts it in his discussion of Chesnutt found in his work
To Wake the Nations, these stories are a tribute paid to "a world that was at once
hindered by degradation and ignorance according to the standards of white
middle-class society, but at the same time alive with powerful knowledge and
cultural meaning generated on hidden but distinguishable African American
planes of discourse" (301). Through the collection of tales shared with us in *The
Conjure Woman,* we come to know the personal life of the slave—the importance of family, of community; the bonds of love between men and women,
between parent and child—and a number of black folk traditions—conjuring,
folk medicine, and, above all, the folktale.

The roots of the slave folktale can be traced to traditional African culture. Although in his work *Slave Culture* John Blassingame tells us that "in many
ways traditional African folk tales were similar to those found in early European
societies in their attempts to explain natural phenomena and various animal
traits, giving animals the power of speech and containing gods and heroes, creation legends, magic, witches, and morals," he also maintains the following:

> One of the African forms most resistant to European culture
> was the folk tale. An overwhelming majority of the tales of
> Southern slaves retained the structure and motif of their
> African prototypes. Anthropologists, Africanists, and folk-
> lorists have found so many parallels and identical tales among
> Africans and Southern slaves that there can be no doubt that
> many Southern black folk tales were African in origin. In fact,
> African scholars have traced many of the slave's folk tales
> directly to Ghana, Senegal, and Mauritius, and the lore of
> such African tribes as the Ewe, Woloff, Hausa, Temne,
> Ashanti, and Ibo. (25–26)

In both African and slave communities, the tales were a means of tradition
preservation, entertainment, and instruction; they had unlimited communal
value. But so, too, did the teller of those tales. In slave communities, as in
African societies,

> [i]ndividual members of the Black community became
> known as "good talkers" and were often identified with par-
> ticular repertoires of stories. As the occasion required, these

stories were repeated again and again in flawless and metic-
ulous detail. The audience, acting as an unconscious preserving force, helped to maintain some stability of texts by
calling attention to such story changes as substitutions of
detail and omitted passages. (Blassingame 214)

The folktale teller's importance to the community should not be underrated,
nor should we overlook what the tradition provided—and still provides—the
individual engaged in it. This, I believe, is what *The Conjure Woman* moves
readers to consider. The work's narrative structure alone pushes this figure to
the forefront, begging readers to pay attention not only to the tales he tells, but
also to his relationship with the tradition.

The Conjure Woman tales, although originally told by Uncle Julius, are
relayed to us by John, "a white Northerner who has gone South after the War
in search of a suitable place of business for himself and a hospitable climate for
his ailing wife" (viii). John, as he readily admits throughout the text, is too busy
making his grape-growing plantation work to dedicate much thought to either
Uncle Julius or the tales he relates. When he does, his logical business mind,
focused as it is on plausibilities, forces him to maintain a degree of healthy skepticism in regard to those tales. In his editorial comments, John openly admits his
indifference and the difficulty he has believing Uncle Julius's tales. He makes it
clear that beyond their entertainment value, the tales hold little interest for him;
his interest is in working the plantation.[1] Robert M. Farnsworth, in the introduction to *The Conjure Woman,* writes, "The narrator's preoccupation with the
practical and the immediate is a limitation. It causes him to see only a farfetched
amusing story [. . .]" (xiii). And Houston Baker, in *Modernism and the Harlem
Renaissance,* tells us that John "views Julius as, at best, a useful entertainment,
one who can do odd jobs *and* tell stories. He considers him, at worst, an agent
of annoyance and craftiness" (45). Neither John's skepticism nor his impatience,
however, are born of malice or prejudice in regard to race, but born of the
pragmatism and logic required of a man raised on business matters rather
than storytelling. But it is just these things—John's disinterest and skepticism—
that allow him to portray Uncle Julius so clearly. Because of them, John maintains a distance between himself and Uncle Julius, a distance that warrants a
more objective "showing" of Uncle Julius, a distance that permits us to determine for ourselves the role the tradition plays in Uncle Julius's life.[2]

The most important thing the storytelling tradition provides Uncle
Julius with is an immediate way of identifying himself. He knows who he is and

what gives him such a clear sense of self. This we see the first time John and
Annie encounter Uncle Julius. To begin, in response to John's questions about
the vineyard he is considering buying, Uncle Julius establishes himself as the
keeper and rightful conveyer of such knowledge when he replies, "Lawd bless
you, suh, I knows all about it. Dey ain' na'er a man in dis settlement w'at won'
tell you old Julius McAdoo 'uz bawn en raise' on dis yer same plantation" (10).
And then, instead of supplying simple answers to John's further inquiries, he
launches into the story of "The Goophered Grapevine." The combination of
words and action here is important. For through these things Uncle Julius
defines himself—Julius McAdoo, storyteller—and points to what is the single
most important element in his self-definition—his role as storyteller for the
community.

Identifying himself as storyteller serves to answer a number of questions John and Annie may have about Uncle Julius. First of all, it indicates his
status within his community—there his role affords him a good deal of respect
and privilege—and, therefore, suggests the manner in which he expects John
and Annie to treat him. In addition, it implies what his community responsibilities are—entertainment and relaxation, asserting interests and outlooks,
teaching ideals and conduct, and recording life.[3] The shape and content of the
first story Uncle Julius tells, as well as the fact that he embarks on this story
almost immediately upon meeting John and Annie, make it clear those responsibilities are first and foremost in his mind. The way Uncle Julius introduces
this story alone shows he is not only able, but also, above all, committed to
fulfilling his communal responsibilities as storyteller.

Like all good storytellers, Uncle Julius knows he must begin by gaining his audience's attention. This he does by suggesting the vineyard's history
is rather macabre. To build John and Annie's curiosity, he tells them it is "goophered,—cunju'd, bewitch' [. . .]"—a black folk concept with which neither
John nor Annie is familiar. It is not only the information shared that captures
John and Annie's interest, however, but also the way Uncle Julius conveys what
he knows that makes John and Annie hunger for more. As John writes, "He
imparted this information with such solemn earnestness, and with such an air
of confidential mystery, that I felt somewhat interested, while Annie was evi-
dently much impressed, and drew closer to me" (11–12). John's words attest to
Uncle Julius's talents, for here John admits that Uncle Julius has his audience
where he wants them—in a state of relaxation. And yet, further to set them up
to believe the story to come, he requests that while they relax, they allow him

to fill them in on all the details of the bewitched vineyard. He says to them, "I would n' spec' fer you ter b'lieve me 'less you know all 'bout de fac's. But ef you en young miss dere doan' min' lis'nin' ter a ole nigger run on a minute er two w'ile you er restin', I kind 'splain to you how it all happen'" (12).

Through his request that John and Annie sit still and listen to him explain "how it all happen," Uncle Julius positions himself and John and Annie in accordance with the storytelling event teller/listener schemata found in Robert A. Georges work "Toward an Understanding of Storytelling Events." That is, Uncle Julius makes it clear that he will be the storyteller, they will be the story listeners—roles they assume for all subsequent storytelling sessions. These roles have attending duties and rights, and accepting them indicates an agreement on the part of all parties to "operate in accordance with a specific set of status relationships." The storyteller's responsibilities—"to formulate, encode, and transmit a message in accordance with socially prescribed rules with which he and the other participants in the storytelling event are familiar"—are the story listener's rights. By the same token, the story listener's duties—"to receive, decode, and respond to the message in accordance with socially prescribed rules with which he and the other participants in the storytelling event are familiar"—are the storyteller's entitlements (317–18). It is obvious that Uncle Julius takes for granted that John and Annie are familiar with the responsibilities of story listeners, for he launches into story without a preamble as to what he expects of them. Nevertheless, as we shall see, John and Annie's behavior during this first session proves him right in doing so—they listen intently, attempt to interpret the story (or at least Annie does), and respond to the story in kind.

Once John and Annie assure Uncle Julius that they would "[. . .] be glad to hear how it all happened," Uncle Julius begins a story that not only entertains the two but also educates and manipulates them. In taking advantage of this specific moment, Uncle Julius indicates his knowledge of one of the things storytelling supplies people with:

> [. . .] the much-needed opportunity of relaxing not only their bodies after a hard day of work but even more important their minds. Psychological relief is not the least of the functions performed by oral literature for members of the society. The minds of both performer and audience are relieved of various problems that have been pressing on them throughout the day [. . .] the entertainment at least provides a temporary respite. (Okpewho 108–9)

In terms of entertaining John and Annie, Uncle Julius is quite successful. The story of the Goophered Grapevine is told without interruption and we can only imagine John and Annie sitting quietly spellbound throughout Uncle Julius's narrative. Where educating John and Annie is concerned, Uncle Julius conveys a lesson, as I mentioned earlier, about the system of slavery, especially as it relates to the master/slave relationship. He also divulges tidbits of black folk culture, namely conjuring beliefs and practices.[4] And yet, the most important thing storytelling allows Uncle Julius to do in this instance is manipulate his way into the lives of these people.[5] Although John suspects the story was told to prevent the sale of the vineyard, in the end it appears as though Uncle Julius told his story in order to secure himself a place in John and Annie's new life, which he does. But as John's narrative moves on, from one Uncle Julius storytelling session to another, it becomes apparent that it was not the job that interested Uncle Julius so much as it was expanding his storytelling audience to include these two people who know so little about the world he knows so much of.[6] The job, via the first storytelling session, becomes his means of doing this. Working a "form of conjure" of its own (Pryse 11), the storytelling session secures Uncle Julius a position that enables him to increase the power of his craft and augment his opportunity for creative self-expression.

As I showed in the previous chapters, creative self-expression has a great deal to do with our ability to determine who we are. Without a means of expressing ourselves, we lack a way of figuring how we fit in the larger scheme of things. And not only that, we lack a way of conveying how we view the world. Alice Walker speaks eloquently of the relationship between creative self-expression and self-definition in her essay "In Search of Our Mother's Gardens." Creative self-expression, as Walker views it, be it gardening, painting, quilting, or storytelling, is the artist's way of "ordering the universe." It is work, she writes, that the "soul must have" (241). Although her essay centers on the legacy of black female artistry, what Walker has to say also applies in the case of Uncle Julius. Uncle Julius does not miss the opportunity to engage in his craft. Why? Because in doing so he is able to figure his vision and convey it to others; he is able to make himself known. We see Uncle Julius using the tradition of storytelling for such purposes throughout *The Conjure Woman*. He does so in "The Goophered Grapevine," for instance, but our most explicit examples come in the stories that follow.

"Po' Sandy" is perhaps our best illustration of Uncle Julius's ability to recognize and seize a storytelling moment. For as we see here, he does not narrate this tale while he and John and Annie traverse the rocky ground leading to the sawmill, but begins it when he realizes he has his passengers captive, lulled into passivity by the droning of the sawmill's "rhythmic cadence" (39). Exhibiting again his remarkable ability to draw his audience into his storytelling web, he takes this instant to turn their attention surreptitiously to the treacherous history this trip has brought to his mind. John relates the following:

> When the saw started on its second journey through the log, Julius observed, in a lugubrious tone, and with a perceptible shudder:—
>
> "Ugh! but dat des do cuddle my blood!"
>
> "What's the matter, Uncle Julius?" inquired my wife, who is of a very sympathetic turn of mind. "Does the noise affect your nerves?"
>
> "No, Mis' Annie," replied the old man, with emotion, "I ain' narvous; but dat saw, a-cuttin' en grindin' thoo dat stick er timber, en moanin', en groanin,' en sweekin', kyars my 'memb'ance back ter ole times, en 'min's me er po' Sandy."
>
> The pathetic intonation with which he lengthened out the "po' Sandy" touched a responsive chord in our own hearts.
>
> "And who was poor Sandy?" asked my wife [. . .] (39–40)

Just as he wished, Uncle Julius has been asked to relate his story, a story through which he posits the slave's capacity for love and portrays the very real power their white masters had over that affection. Although to John and Annie the sawmill is no more than a stepping stone to getting a new kitchen built, to Uncle Julius the sawmill is a repository of past events. He cannot visit the place without being reminded of the cruelties inflicted upon his people, and he cannot leave it without conveying to his charges his view of those injustices. Storytelling allows him to meet this abstract and very personal imperative. It provides him with a way of making known his account of history while simultaneously moving his listeners to accept what it means as well.

That storytelling furnishes Uncle Julius with this power is evidenced in Annie's response to Po' Sandy's story. At the story's conclusion she exclaims, "What a system it was [. . .] under which such things were possible." And then, when her husband announces his amazement that she could be "seriously considering the possibility of a man's being turned into a tree," she underscores her empathetic response by replying, "Oh, no [. . .] not that [. . .] Poor Tenie!"

As Annie's words here indicate, although she may have been fully enchanted by the tall tale elements of Uncle Julius's narrative, it is the story's underlying message that resonates for her in the end—so much so that it affects her behavior, just as Uncle Julius intended.

According to Uncle Julius's story, because the schoolhouse lumber was "[. . .] sawed out'n de tree w'at Sandy wuz turnt inter," any building erected with that lumber "is gwine ter be ha'nted tel de las' piece er plank is rotted en crumble' inter dus'" (60). Annie, moved not by the possibility of ghosts, but by her understanding of the injustice the lumber symbolizes, decides that she cannot, in good conscience, allow her new kitchen to be "built out of the lumber in that old schoolhouse" (61). She tells John, after he again expresses his incredulousness at her being influenced by Uncle Julius's "[. . .] absurdly impossible yarn [. . .],"

> I know the story is absurd, [. . .] and I am not so silly as to
> believe it. But I don't think I should ever be able to take any
> pleasure in that kitchen if it were built out of that lumber.
> Besides, I think the kitchen would look better and last longer
> if the lumber were all new. (61–62)

And, as John relates, Annie has her way. The kitchen is built out of new lumber and the old schoolhouse is left standing, untouched—but not long without occupants. For, as we soon learn, Uncle Julius's reasons for telling Po' Sandy's story went beyond his desire to share the "real" story of the southern slave experience; his motives included the more immediate needs of his community.

At the time of the story's telling, the temperance issue was causing dissension among the members of Uncle Julius's church. And Uncle Julius, anticipating the secession of a number of followers from the main congregation, had his eye trained on the old schoolhouse as a place for the expected seceders to hold their own meetings. However, when plans were made to raze the schoolhouse for new kitchen lumber, this option was put in danger. Hence, Uncle Julius tells his story not only to re-piece history but also to secure the schoolhouse's safety; and, more than that, to ensure the schoolhouse, once preserved, would not be put to some other use than what he intended. As Uncle Julius tells Annie when asking her permission to use the building, haunted as it is, the schoolhouse is not fit for anything other than worship services. For only during such religious ceremonies, he explains, are ghosts kept at bay.[7] With this assertion, his final utilization of the tale of Po' Sandy, Uncle Julius exhibits his ability to take full advantage of what the storytelling tradition has to offer the individual and the community. But, as I mentioned earlier, this ability is demonstrated in other stories as well—the story of "Mars Jeems's Nightmare," for example.

By the time this tale is told, John and Annie have become quite accustomed to Uncle Julius's taletelling. As a matter of fact, John tells us, when left with time on their hands, they felt they "might as well put in time listening to Julius as in any other way [. . .]," for they "[. . .] had found some of his plantation tales quite interesting" (70). What John suggests here is that the tales are simply a way of filling moments spent in wait or repose, a form of entertainment. Uncle Julius, of course, knows better. The tales are—at one and the same time—a personal introduction, a preliminary course in southern history and slave life and culture, a way to address his own needs or those of his community. And, as we see, in this instance especially, the tales are a means to change.

"Mars Jeems's Nightmare" delineates the hardships slaves were forced to endure under the watch of despotic plantation owners and their equally tyrannical overseers. It asserts not only the ineffectiveness of such bad business practices but also their wrongfulness. Through these elements of this tale, Uncle Julius reestablishes himself as a man who knows much about the practical workings of this world. But the tale likewise chronicles the personal life of slaves—their ability to love; their belief in conjuring, in the fantastic, in the mystical; their need for self-expression; their resistance to a system that denies these things altogether. It also helps him verify his knowledge of that other side of life, the side that resides in the heart. And this is where his tales help him do his most important work—moving his listeners to alter their conceptions and thus their behavior.

Getting people to change—be it in thought or in deed—is tough work. In fact, according to the Mars Jeems tale, it may take a powerful conjure—one capable of turning a slave owner into a slave—to make a man empathize with those he has power over, to make a man see the error of his ways and begin modifying his behavior. And, yet, what change truly boils down to is emotional incentive. Or at least, we see, this is how the worldly wise Uncle Julius understands it. For in summing up the meaning of this tale, he focuses on the *reasons* the Mars Jeemses of the world should change, rather than on the *way* lore has the real Mars Jeems's transformation come about. He tells John and Annie: if you don't want to find yourself on the other side of the track—conjured from master into slave—and if you don't want to suffer a guilt that spawns debilitating bad dreams, "ter say de leas'," then, for just a moment, put yourself in the position of those less fortunate than you. Try to comprehend their experience and then treat "'po' ign'ant niggers w'at ain' had no chanst to l'arn'" accordingly, with compassion and understanding. Do this, Uncle Julius asserts, because "dem dat is kin' en good ter po' people is sho' ter prosper en git 'long in de worl'" (100).

Unfortunately, even with the added emphasis on change via incentive that Uncle Julius's moral to the story provides, both John and Annie are stymied, once again, by the fantastic aspects of the story. Skeptical of the otherworldly beliefs recorded therein, John even goes so far as to patronize Uncle Julius when he asks him, "By the way, did you make that up all by yourself?" Uncle Julius's first response to this question is simply a sorrowful look meant to indicate his disappointment at John and Annie's inability to see past the conjuring in the story and to recognize the point of the story. But he follows this look with a response that adds significance both to the tale itself and to his telling of it. He declares: "'No, suh, I heared dat tale befo' you er Mis' Annie dere wuz bawn, suh. My mammy tol' me dat tale w'en I wa'n't mo' d'n knee-high ter a hopper-grass.'"

In other words, because this tale is both ancient—older than both John and Annie—and precious—handed down to him by his grandmother—it is not to be taken lightly. The shape of the tale's transmission, from grandmother to grandson, suggests its telling is of an instructional nature; the purpose to which it has been put in this instance as well. What Uncle Julius takes for granted here is what he has assumed on all other occasions when he has engaged John and Annie in the storytelling tradition: a "commonality of meaning" shared between him and his listeners. His use of the tradition always and again represents, as Sandra Dolby Stahl writes in her work *Literary Folkloristics and the Personal Narrative*, "a leap of faith" based on the belief that a personal reality will be shared and understood (119). Although at first it appears as though Uncle Julius's telling of the tale has been for naught, in a moment we will see that Uncle Julius's leap has, once more, landed him safe on his storytelling feet. The next day we learn his tale has spoken to at least one person's heart, just as Uncle Julius intended.

We know from the expository section forefronting "Mars Jeems's Nightmare" that Uncle Julius begins on this tale after John and Annie have witnessed young Mister McLean (Mars Jeems's grandson) beating his mount into submission. However, he does not use the tale to explain further the comments he makes in regard to Mister McLean's misuse of his animal. Rather, he tells the tale to address John's recent firing of Uncle Julius's grandson, Tom, for "[. . .] his laziness, his carelessness, and his apparent lack of any sense of responsibility"

(66). It becomes clear that this is the case when we take into account the fact that while discussing Tom's dismissal with John—prior to telling the tale—Uncle Julius uses words he later echoes while explaining the story's moral: That is, he begs John to "[. . .] make some 'lowance fuh a' ign'ant young nigger, suh, en gib 'im one mo' chance" (67).

John doesn't make the connection between his treatment of Tom and Uncle Julius's narration of the Mars Jeems's tale. But it is apparent, in the end, that Annie does. For the day after the story is told, she hires Tom back. In words verifying that Uncle Julius's tale hit the mark he intended—the human heart, the area, as I mentioned earlier, he knows, once reached, is most likely to produce results—she explains her actions to her husband:

> Oh, Yes, [. . .] I forgot to tell you. He was hanging around the place all the morning, and looking so down in the mouth, that I told him that if he would try to do better, we would give him one more chance. He seems so grateful, and so really in earnest in his promises of amendment, that I'm sure you'll not regret taking him back. (102)

That is to say, she doesn't give Tom back his job because doing so will be good for business, but because doing so will be good for the hearts and souls of both parties. Her "rose-colored hopes," as John calls them, are not pinned on profits but on people, which is exactly where Uncle Julius directs his own, as we see in his treatment of Miss Annie.

The tales discussed thus far show us that Uncle Julius has a sympathetic listener in Miss Annie. She is the one most often moved to action by his words, and, therefore, over time she becomes Uncle Julius's primary focus when telling his stories. Uncle Julius knows that Miss Annie's response has the power to create a ripple effect; like a stone thrown in a pond, it can reach out to affect others as well. Although Uncle Julius will continually work to make John see the master/slave relationship for what it was, as Robert M. Farnsworth tells us in his introduction to *The Conjure Woman*, "[. . .] he clearly appeals to Miss Annie for a stronger response of repugnance to a system in which human beings are reduced to objects or mere capital" (xiv). And because Miss Annie's response is more often than not as Uncle Julius desires, he repays her in kind—with affection and attention; with hope for her well-being; with a tale, the thing through which, as I mentioned earlier, Uncle Julius conveys *himself*, the person he is.[8]

At the start of *The Conjure Woman* we learned that John and Annie moved from North to South on the advice of Annie's physician. "Sis Becky's Pickaninny" begins with John's comments as to the state of his wife's health now that they are settled in this warmer region:

> We had not lived in North Carolina very long before I was able to note a marked improvement in my wife's health. The ozone-laden air of the surrounding piney woods, the mild and equable climate, the peaceful leisure of country life, had brought about in hopeful measure the cure we had anticipated. Toward the end of our second year, however, her ailment took an unexpected turn for the worse. She became the victim of a settled melancholy, attended with vague forebodings of impending misfortune. (132)

John is advised to keep Annie's spirits up or face "grave consequences," and he begins devising ways to lift her mood. His attempts to "cheer her up," however, are to no avail; "[. . .] nothing seemed to rouse her from the depression into which she had fallen" (133). Nothing, that is, until Uncle Julius surreptitiously donates his services, services that come in forms unlike any offered Annie thus far: a tale and, well, yes, to John's incredulity, a rabbit's foot.

The tale of Sis Becky's pickaninny begins when Uncle Julius, aware of Annie's decline, comes around one day to see how she is faring, bringing with him this day his good luck charm, a rabbit's foot. After Uncle Julius exhibits the charm, John, typically skeptical of Uncle Julius's superstition-based faith, is overwrought and exclaims:

> Julius [. . .] your people will never rise in the world until they throw off these childish superstitions and learn to live by the light of reason and common sense. How absurd to imagine that the fore-foot of a poor dead rabbit, with which he timorously felt his way along through a life surrounded by snares and pitfalls, beset by enemies on every hand, can promote happiness or success, or ward off failure or misfortune. (135)

John is unaware that his own words highlight the appropriateness of the rabbit's foot as a symbol of good luck, and Uncle Julius is not about to point this out just yet. He is setting John and Annie up for a story, and so he plays with

John a bit, manipulating him from disdain to curiosity. That is, instead of arguing John's point, he asserts that John is right—well, right as far as a rabbit's forefoot being worthless goes. According to Uncle Julius, no one can expect good things from a forefoot, "De fo'-foot ain' got no power." If someone wants good luck, the foot they set store in must be special, something rare indeed. "It has ter be de hin'-foot, suh,—de lef' hin'-foot er a grabe-ya'd rabbit, killt by a cross-eyed nigger on a da'k night in de full er de moon" (135). In addition, a thing so hard to come by is equally hard to part with, so Uncle Julius explains. This is part of the reason he would never sell his. But he would also never part with it because it really does bring good luck; he has forty years worth of proof. The proof he provides, however—he had a good master, he wasn't sold, he was set free—is too general, too lackluster for John. He wants something more, just as Uncle Julius anticipated, just as he is more than willing to provide:

> "Law, suh! you doan hafter prove 'bout de rabbit foot! Eve'y-
> body knows dat; leas'ways eve'ybody roun' heah knows it. But
> ef it has ter be prove' ter folks w'at wa'n't bawn en raise' in
> dis naberhood, dey is a' easy way ter prove it. Is I eber tol'
> you de tale er Sis' Becky en her pickaninny?" (136)

Uncle Julius knows he has not told them this story; what he wants is a request for a story, which he gets when John, on cue, urges, "let us hear it" (137). With the preliminaries completed now, Uncle Julius jumps into the tale with both feet—hind feet, of course.

"Sis Becky's Pickaninny" is the story of a female field hand parted from her son when her master, "Kunnel Pen'leton," sends her off to another plantation in exchange for a coveted racehorse. Although the colonel dislikes parting mother and child, his avarice overrides his good conscience and, thus, sets in motion a series of conjures meant to bring mother and child together again. While the conjuring is doing its job, both mother and child suffer fluctuating emotions brought on by their separation—one moment, deep depression, the next, euphoria at the thought of togetherness. Finally, just as these turbulent feelings begin to threaten their very lives, Aunt Peggy's "goo-phering" succeeds and the initial trade is called off. The horse is returned to his original owner and Becky is returned to her home and child.

The mother/child reunion restores the good health of both parties, and, in sum, we have a happy ending. And yet, this is not a fairy tale, as John refers to it. It is a lesson in hardship, a lesson Annie grasps and is much moved by. She tells her husband, who, once again, focuses only on the fantastical elements of the tale:

> Why, John! [. . .] the story bears the stamp of truth, if ever a
> story did [. . .] those are mere ornamental details and not at
> all essential. The story is true to nature, and might have hap-
> pened half a hundred times, and no doubt did happen, in
> those horrid days before the war. (159)

In this declaration, Annie makes clear she understands the heart of the tale: greed makes people immune to the very real needs of others; mother and child, whether slave or free, are naturally bonded in ways we can hardly imagine; disregard for that bond causes inestimable harm. Still, John points out to Uncle Julius, bypassing Annie's interpretation, the tale makes no mention of a rabbit's foot, the impetus for the tale. He remarks to Uncle Julius, "[. . .] your story doesn't establish what you started out to prove,—that a rabbit's foot brings good luck" (159). In response, Uncle Julius makes one of his most important moves yet during a taletelling session: he relinquishes to Annie, his primary audience member, the explanation for that omission. That is to say, because the story was told for the benefit of Annie's health, much more so than to prove the validity of the rabbit's foot superstition, Annie is the one responsible for its meaning in this instance. To get to that meaning she must fill in the space Uncle Julius left empty—the space where the missing rabbit's foot should be—and fill that space she does. There is no rabbit's foot in the story, she explains, because "Sis' Becky had no rabbit's foot." If she had a rabbit's foot, Uncle Julius chimes in, "she nebber would 'a' went th'oo all dis trouble." For both Uncle Julius and Annie, no further explanation is needed; the question-and-answer period ends, John returns to the house, and, after a private moment with Annie, Uncle Julius takes his leave.

In the days that follow, however, it becomes apparent that Annie has taken responsibility for the full import of the explanation. Although Sis Becky had no power over her situation—circumstances were beyond her control— Annie has that power; it is up to her to get better. Perhaps she realizes that the reasons for her own troubles are nothing in comparison to the causes of Sis Becky's and her child's. Whatever the case may be, Annie brings on her own recovery. Of course, she also has a rabbit's foot to aid her renewal, as John discovers, and Uncle Julius's rabbit's foot at that. How could she not be well with such power in her pocket?

Through this story Uncle Julius reveals yet another aspect of himself —the altruistic part.[9] For other than helping him establish this portion of his nature, telling this story does nothing for him personally. It is all about doing for others. It seeks compassion for the plight of slave families, it seeks insight into a people's faith, and, through these things, it seeks the good health of a friend. But Uncle Julius is not always so selfless in his storytelling; occasionally a tale is told solely for his own benefit. And when this is done, as in the tale "The Conjurer's Revenge," the tradition is Uncle Julius's means of more fully substantiating the kind of man he is—multifaceted.

"The Conjurer's Revenge" is, perhaps, the only tale in his collection that Uncle Julius uses for the exclusive purpose of revealing and attending to a side of himself heretofore only hinted at, the part that focuses inward. This self-interested component of the human character is likely to be denied by many of us. Uncle Julius, however, does not abjure this segment of himself. He simply finds a way to address it without outright announcing it—through the oral tradition. And, amazingly, with this tool in hand he gets what he needs without stepping on *too* many toes in the process.

It would seem the telling of "The Conjurer's Revenge" comes about as a result of John's decision to add watermelons to his crops-for-profit. For the story begins when Uncle Julius expresses his disagreement with John's decision to buy a mule instead of a horse to take care of the additional work the new planting will make necessary. However, in declaring his opposition to John's decision, Uncle Julius is not setting up John for a story regarding the value differential between horse and mule, but laying the foundation for a taletelling session meant to get Uncle Julius something he wants—a new suit.

Still, to make it seem as though the story is for John and Annie's benefit alone, Uncle Julius lures John and Annie into a question-and-answer period about his distaste for mule husbandry that leaves too many particulars to the imagination. In fact, so much mystery and unbelievability surrounds his answers that John and Annie eventually find themselves begging Uncle Julius to account fully for what he has only alluded to thus far. That is, they wind up pleading to him to tell them a tale, just as Uncle Julius would have it. And so he begins the story of the slave Primus, a man conjured into a mule, sold for a shared profit, worked like an animal, and, finally, conjured back into a man again. All except for one foot, Uncle Julius asserts, which remains, to this day, so much a reminder of the conjurer's power and the parallels between slave life and mule labor that he cannot, in good conscience, work a mule for fear of doing what he proclaimed, prior to telling the tale, he most wanted to avoid: "[. . .] imposin' on some human creetur [. . .] some er my own relations, er somebody e'se w'at can't he'p deyse'ves" (106).

At the close of the tale, Annie expresses her tremendous dislike for it. She tells Uncle Julius "The Conjurer's Revenge" is not up to par, "it isn't pathetic, it has no moral that I can discover, and I can't see why you should tell it. In fact, it seems to me like nonsense." Uncle Julius is quite chagrined by this, his favorite listener's response. Yet he makes from Annie's reaction an opportunity to expound on the fine line between reality and fantasy.

> [. . .] I be'n hearin' de tale fer twenty-five yeahs, en I ain' got
> no 'casion fer ter 'spute it. Dey's so many things a body knows
> is lies, dat dey ain' no use gwine roun' findin' fault wid tales
> dat mought des ez well be so ez not [. . .]. dis is a quare worl',
> anyway yer kin fix it. (128–29)

In other words, according to Uncle Julius, one man's truth may be another man's fiction; taletelling has always been used to deal with and express reality's subjectivity. It is a method as good as any other. In fact, it is Uncle Julius's method of choice when it comes to navigating his own reality. And, as we see in this instance, it does not fail him. "The Conjurer's Revenge" precipitates John's buying of a lame horse belonging to a friend of Uncle Julius. Not long after the worthless animal's purchase, Uncle Julius appears decked out in a new suit of clothes. Knowing that Uncle Julius's wages could not compensate for such extravagance, John suspects he has been hoodwinked by Uncle Julius's taletelling. That is, he believes Uncle Julius told his story in order that John would buy his friend's horse, a purchase producing profits Uncle Julius was to share in, profits he all along intended for the acquisition of the expensive suit of clothes. John has no way to confirm his suspicions, of course. But his subsequent actions, which include taking Uncle Julius's advice "[. . .] only in small doses and with great discrimination," prove that through taletelling Uncle Julius has made known another side of himself—the shrewd, self-serving side —rounding out his own image (131).

Through his taletelling, Uncle Julius reiterates and attends to this portion of his person quite often. For instance, when he tells the tale of "The Gray Wolf's Ha'nt," he does so not simply to protect John from the wrath of those buried on the tract of land John wants to clear for planting, but also to prevent John from disturbing something on that land Uncle Julius has long held sacred to himself—a honey-filled bee tree. Crafty and calculating though his actions on such occasions as this may prove him to be, he is, above all, a man devoted to others. Perhaps this is why John finishes his portrayal of Uncle Julius and his record of his tales with the story of "Hot-Foot Hannibal." For this tale, and the view of Uncle Julius its telling supplies us with, is a final guarantee that Uncle Julius's "[. . .] concern for those he cares about transcends gain [. . .]" (Render 24); that his friendship is, without a doubt, an invaluable commodity.

Prior to the telling of "Hot-Foot Hannibal," John informs us that his wife's sister, Mabel, who has been staying with them, has just had a lover's quarrel with her fiancé, Malcolm Murchison. The quarrel, brought on by Mabel's jealousy and exacerbated by Malcolm's pride, results in the couple's calling off their engagement. Ten days after the disagreement, Uncle Julius appears to take John, Annie, and Mabel for a rockaway ride to a neighboring vineyard. Uncle Julius prefers reaching their destination via the long route, or "big road" as he calls it, but Miss Annie insists they set out on the short road so that she can pick some flowers from the trees that border this path. Uncle Julius concedes to her wishes. But when they attempt to restart after stopping for the coveted blossoms, their horse, Lucy, makes it known she shares Uncle Julius's resistance to Annie's chosen route. She goes but a few yards before refusing to go a pace farther, planting her feet regardless of prodding. Uncle Julius can explain her problem, of course. After all, it is also the reason he wished to take another route—their swampy surroundings are frequented by Chloe's haunt. The mare can see her just ahead, he asserts. This tantalizing but partial explanation elicits from John and Annie the required appeal for further clarification—a story—and so comes the tale of "Hot-Foot Hannibal."

Uncle Julius is aware that place has much to do with a story's effect. And, according to John, Uncle Julius sure picked the right spot for this story:

> [. . .] the amber-colored stream flowing silently and sluggishly
> at our feet, like the waters of Lethe; the heavy, aromatic scent
> of the bays, faintly suggestive of funeral wreaths,—all made
> the place an ideal one for a ghost story. (203–4)

But "Hot-Foot Hannibal" is not necessarily a ghost story; it is a tale of jealousy's evil effects, a tale of love lost. The lovers in this story are Chloe and Jeff, two people who use a conjure to rid themselves of the one obstacle to their being together—Hannibal—the fellow house servant to whom Chloe has been

promised against her wishes. Unfortunately, Chloe and Jeff are not only careless in their conjuring, they are reckless in their estimation of Hannibal's reaction to being thrown out of the big house and returned to the fields. They do
not suppose that Hannibal would get so angry over his conjured change in sta-
tion that he would decide to take revenge on Chloe and Jeff, but he does.

Wise enough to know that jealousy makes people behave rashly, Hannibal plants a bug in Chloe's mind regarding Jeff's fidelity. He swears to her
that it was Jeff he saw with another woman "[. . .] down by de crick in de
swamp eve'y Sunday ebenin', ter say nuffin 'bout two er th'ee times a week."
Then, after sowing these seeds of doubt, he stages and stars in a drama sure to
make those seeds take root. He sends a note to Jeff telling him that Chloe
wants to meet him that Sunday down by the creek. Confident that Chloe is
now suspicious enough of Jeff to go spying on him, Hannibal also dresses up as
Chloe/the other woman and goes down to Jeff's waiting place by the creek to
make the meeting with Chloe/the other woman complete. So good is Hannibal's deception and so fully has Chloe's jealousy overridden her good judgment, that after witnessing Jeff rushing into the arms of Hannibal—disguised
as the other woman for Chloe and as Chloe for Jeff—Chloe hurries back to
Mars Dugal to tell him about the conjuring she and Jeff played a part in, the
conjuring that resulted in Jeff's taking Hannibal's position in the big house.
Knowing that conjuring is a slave practice of which Mars Dugal disapproves,
Chloe is sure her report will produce a less than favorable future for Jeff. And
she is right. Mars Dugal sells Jeff the next day to a speculator who puts him on
a steamboat destined for Alabama.

Shortly after these occurrences, Hannibal is brought back into the
good graces of the household and reveals to Chloe what he did to rectify his
situation. When Chloe realizes that it was also her own jealousy that brought
about the sale of Jeff, she falls into a state of depression. Subsequently, Mrs.
Dugal persuades her husband to try to buy Jeff back, only to learn that Jeff
drowned while en route to Wilmington. This news quickly reaches Chloe, who
sinks deeper into despair, finally committing suicide on the very spot where
Jeff's illicit meeting was to have taken place. There she waits still, Uncle Julius
tells his listeners:

> [. . .] [her] ha'nt comes eve'y ebenin' en sets down unner dat
> willer-tree en waits fer Jeff, er e'se walks up en down de road
> yander, lookin' en lookin', en waitin' en waitin', fer her sweet-
> hea't w'at ain' neber, neber come back ter her no mo'. (225)

Now, a variety of lessons can be learned from this story, all directed at John and Annie's young and willful charge, Mabel. To begin, the story is meant to show Mabel that although slaves had little control over their personal relationships and, as a result, often took extreme measures to be with those of their own choosing, measures that sometimes did more harm than good, she can choose her own partner in life. It is up to her. She need not resort to conjuring or the like to be with the man she loves. She must simply learn to trust him. For as the story also illustrates, whether slave or free, distrust and jealousy can ruin a relationship.

That these lessons have struck the cord intended becomes apparent when, after changing course at the story's end—opting for the main road vs. Chloe's ha'nt—the party runs across Malcolm Murchison's servant driving a cart laden with Malcolm's personal effects. The baggage weighing down the cart, asserts the servant, is destined for New York, as is Malcolm, who is following a short distance behind. Shortly after the servant and buggy move on, Annie tells Uncle Julius to stop again; there are some trumpet flowers by the road she would like John to retrieve. Upon returning to his own cart, John finds Mabel missing. Annie tells him Mabel has decided to walk on ahead of them, that they will catch up with her momentarily. However, this meeting is delayed when Annie insists Uncle Julius return to the spot of the trumpet flowers to get the fan she dropped while there. Uncle Julius takes, as John tells us, "an unconscionably long time finding it [. . .]," but obviously just long enough for Mabel to put to work the lessons learned from Uncle Julius's story. For when John, Annie, and Uncle Julius finally overtake Mabel, they find her walking with Malcolm, her arm linked in his, both their faces "[. . .] aglow with the light of love" (228). Apparently the lovers have resolved their differences.

John fails to connect the story to the outcome of the day. Instead, he focuses on the possibility that Uncle Julius and Murchison arranged the lovers' "chance" meeting beforehand. Why else, we can imagine him pondering, would Uncle Julius insist the party take the long route in the first place? And when refused, why else would he tell the story of Chloe's ha'nt but to prevent their continuing on their chosen path? John, in all his pragmatism, will remain skeptical of Uncle Julius's motives even as Uncle Julius refuses anything more from Murchison than friendship in the years to come. Of course, only Uncle Julius can know the truth. But, as we know from other instances, Uncle Julius rarely tells a story solely for his own benefit. In fact, all his stories have the capacity to reach beyond his own personal desires. It depends on the listeners' abilities to interpret the stories in light of their own situations. Annie has already exhibited this ability, and this taletelling session shows us that Mabel has it as well. So affected is Mabel by the story of Hot-Foot Hannibal—it moves her to tears—that when losing Malcolm for good seems a very real possibility, she rises to the occasion, the story's import spurring her to action. Whether Uncle Julius and Malcolm arranged the meeting or not, it was still up to Mabel to take advantage of the encounter. Regardless of what John may think, without Uncle Julius's help—coming as usual in story form—it is doubtful she would have seen the error of her ways and taken it upon herself to rectify the situation. Hence, through his quiet involvement in the lover's reunion, Uncle Julius proves himself the most faithful of friends; the tradition of storytelling is his way of so identifying himself.

When we take the collection of stories and storytelling sessions as a whole, we see that in the hands of Uncle Julius, storytelling is put to multiple purposes. It is used to teach Annie the brutality of slavery; to chronicle the slaves' beliefs in supernatural or mystical forces, in hauntings, conjurings, and the like; to fulfill the tangible needs of his people; to transmit Uncle Julius's vision of the past, understanding of the present, and hopes for the future; and to help others help themselves. Finally, Uncle Julius uses storytelling to define himself for others. In other words, Uncle Julius makes storytelling attend to both the community *and* the individual. As well it should. The oral tradition of storytelling is not meant to serve the community exclusively. Rather, as Isidore Okpewho tells us in his work *African Oral Literature,* this form of art succeeds largely because the personal interests of the artist are involved in one way or another" (35). There is room enough in the tradition to accommodate a group's "cherished heritage" as well as "[. . .] the personal interests and outlook of the individual artist" (39).

Uncle Julius knows John and Annie are unfamiliar with his world, the black world. Moreover, he knows they have little real knowledge of the system of slavery, and he recognizes that without a fuller understanding of his people, of that system, they will never comprehend the "impact of slavery on blacks," they will never accept responsibility for affecting change in the days to come (Farnsworth x). These issues are paramount in Uncle Julius's life, as they are in the lives of all members of his community. Hence, addressing these issues through storytelling helps him fulfill objectives that are both personal and communal and gives him a solid sense of self, an unparalleled degree of power, and a priceless measure of self-worth. Likewise, he uses storytelling to ascertain that self, display that power, and define that worth. The main character in David Bradley's *The Chaneysville Incident,* however, does not recognize that he has at his disposal such a multifarious tool. Thus, he is at a loss in terms of not only getting what he wants from life but also in determining who he is and making himself known to others. At a loss, that is, until, like Uncle Julius, he embraces the oral tradition as his own means to survival.

Returning to the Oral Tradition to Find the Past: Speaking History, Speaking Self in David Bradley's The Chaneysville Incident

The past is myself, my own history, the seed of my present thoughts, the mold of my present disposition.

R. L. Stevenson

When I interviewed David Bradley, the author of *The Chaneysville Incident*, we discussed at length the idea of an oral tradition in literature. We agreed that since all cultures began in some way with an oral tradition, the issue is not whether or not there was an oral tradition, but the role played and the significance held by that tradition. The larger the role, the more significance given to the tradition, the more likely it will be to appear within the literature of the culture being studied. That African American literature should contain an oral motif is perhaps both logical and problematic. The fact that the institution of slavery served to maintain the use and significance of the oral tradition in passing histories and maintaining ties within African American communities longer than in other North American communities makes it perhaps logical that such a tradition should be preserved or in some way resonate in the literature created by African Americans. Typically, it is the writing that is looked to for evidence of the oral tradition's influence; we study whether or not and how authors use the tradition to structure their texts. But proof of the tradition's preservation need not always and only be a matter of stylistics; it can also be a matter of thematics. That is, the significance of the oral tradition can be what the story is all about. This is the case with *The Chaneysville Incident,* for what John, the main character in the novel, learns through his experience with the oral past is the relevance of the tradition to his life in the present.[10]

Nevertheless, when we first meet John he wants no part of the past; his present disposition toward it is one of anger. As a historian, John makes his living digging up objective facts about the past and putting them together in a

logical way in order to create and document indisputable histories. What he
knows of his own past, however, has come to him through the oral tradition of
storytelling, from his friend and mentor, Jack Crawley, "the old man with the
stories," as John's white lover, Judith, refers to him, somebody she thought
John made up, someone "indestructible [. . .] Or a lie" (3). Thus, John doubts
his past's authenticity, attempting to write it off as hearsay. This proves impossible when he is called back to his hometown to tend to Jack during his final
days. For during this visit John's past—a past full of anger, anguish, betrayal,
slavery, racism, and triumph—comes back to claim him and to be claimed.

John has not been home in years, and he resists going this time. To
John home is a place

> [. . .] to which you belong and which belongs to you even if
> you do not particularly like it or want it, a place you cannot
> escape, no matter how far you go or how furiously you run;
> even if you do not like it, even if you hate it, you get a tiny flush
> of excitement when you reach the point where you can look
> out the window and know without thinking, where you are;
> when the bends in the road have meaning, and every hill a
> name. (14)

Still, John's resistance to returning to the place of his youth has less to do with
the typical hometown malaise he defines here than with the notion of encountering Jack. Jack had been John's teacher. Through Jack, John had learned the
survival folkways ingrained in the mountains of his hometown. In addition, Jack
had been for John a man full of stories about John's father, Moses Washington,
full of stories about the past. Hence, encountering Jack means John's meeting up
with a part of himself left by the wayside on his way out of town years ago, a part
he believes he has no need for, a part he has made it his business not to know.

That he will be forced to know it again becomes clear to him as soon
as he steps off the bus from Philadelphia and onto the road leading to his old
stomping ground, "the hill."

> I knew nothing about the hill any longer, I had made it my
> business not to know. But now suddenly, inexplicably, I was
> curious, and so I thought for a moment, pulling half-
> remembered facts from the back of my mind—scraps of
> information—and made extrapolations. (17)

When he finally reaches the top of the hill, the place of his family's home, he moves from conjecturing the present state of the world around him to remembering what he knows of what happened there in the distant past. Most specifically, what happened there to create a legend out of the man who was his father, Moses Washington. His memory of these occurrences, of this man—disjointed and fragmented, splintered by time—exhausts him; his fatigue permitting "the growing of old tensions, a sudden chill at the base" of his belly that he tries to ignore (24). But his attempts are hampered by even more memories as he crosses to the far side of the hill, the side that was *"dif-ferent* [. . .] guarded by ghosts," or so the stories reported. John remembers that although the adults found such tales humorous,

> [c]hildren dared each other to take the first few steps, to go
> and bring back a rock or a bit of brush from beyond the
> point where the path made its first precipitous drop and van-
> ished into undergrowth; those with imagination and bravery
> [. . .] would go far enough not to be seen, wait awhile, then
> come back, claiming to have discovered [. . .] almost any-
> thing. (27)

More importantly the far side of the hill was the place where no one but his father's friends, Josh White and Old Jack, lived, a place John lacked the courage and imagination to enter until the evening following the day of his father's death—the day Old Jack Crawley summoned him to history.

Standing at the crest of the hill now, an adult, John's memory of that experience comes back to him. He remembers how Old Jack came to his house, full as it was of mourners, and told John to come with him, "shouting drunkenly about Moses Washington's last will" (24). However, because no one, not even John at the time, understood what Jack wanted, Jack's demand was met by fear, anger, and refusal; the adults took him from the house kicking and screaming and put John to bed.

When John woke up later that evening, he understood why everyone, including himself, had reacted to Jack as they did—they were afraid of the unknown. His young mind grasped the "pointlessness" of such fear. Thus, he decided to go and "find Old Jack, go and find him and ask him what he wanted" (28). John remembers how that night his sense of purpose filled him with a feeling of invincibility, and so he crossed over the hilltop and descended in darkness to the door of Old Jack Crawley's shack.

His meeting with Old Jack that night was one of revelation. For Jack understood Moses Washington and, therefore, understood the boy's indifference to his father's death. John recalls how Jack articulated his own lack of feeling:

> It ain't nothing to be ashamed of [. . .] Can't nobody make
> you feel somethin' you don't feel, an' there ain't no point in
> tryin' to pretend you feel it. Hell, I bet you didn't even like
> him. [. . .] Me, [. . .] I guess you could say I loved him. He
> saved my life moren one time. But I'll tell you the truth—way
> Moses went about things, he was like to save your butt by
> kickin' you in it to get you movin' in the right direction. You
> mighta loved him for it later on, but right off you wasn't likely
> to be too damn grateful. (31)

John also recalls how Jack's recognition of the underlying cause of John's inability to feel for his father—his lack of knowledge about the man—spurred Jack to use that night to begin introducing son to father, past to present. Hence, while savoring his first taste of whiskey, sitting quietly among the shadows of Jack's ramshackle home, John learned of his father's love for him, his pride in him, his admiration for John's hatred of him, his carefully laid plans in regard to him—plans that included, in the event of Moses' own death, Jack teaching John to "hunt, an' teach him to fish, an' drink whiskey an' cuss." Jack tells John, "Teach him to track.' That's what he said. An' then the damn fool went out huntin' groundhog" (35–36). Yet, to truly bring Moses to life for John, Jack describes him in terms of a legend:[11]

> [. . .] I don't guess it changes nothin' to speak of him. Every-
> body else is. They *been* speaking of him. Most folks they gotta
> be dead an' gone 'fore there's a chance anybody'll talk about
> 'em. Not Mose. They was probly talkin' about Moses Wash-
> ington 'fore he was ever born. Wasn't nobody that knowed
> nothin' about him, though. I knowed some. Josh knowed a bit,
> but he wasn't the kind of man that set too much store by
> where a man come from or where he went when he was outa
> sight. An' he's dead anyways. But not knowin' facts don't stop
> folks talkin'; hell, it just sets 'em goin'. Most folks'd a hell of a
> lot rather listen to rumors than go around the corner to see
> what's what. And Mose helped 'em right along. He let 'em

talk, an' if they was to ast him a question—an' there wasn't many that had the nerve—he'd just smile an' let 'em think what they wanted. Pretty soon you cound't go anywheres in the County without everybody knowed his name, an' who run with him, an' three or four stories about what we done. Wasn't half of it true. Fact is, you found out somethin' about Moses Washington, you knowed for sure either he wanted you to find it out jest 'xactly the way you done it, or it was a lie. An' most times, it was both. (36)

Something about Jack's look following the dissemination of this information about Moses frightens John. He remembers how he looked for a way to leave but instead was manipulated into accepting more whiskey and something even more potent than liquor to cast a spell over the mind—a story. He tells us Jack overfilled his cup, waited to see the toddy's unmistakable effect, sat down across from John and said, "You wanna know how I met your daddy? [. . .] Do you? You want a story? [. . .] Then fetch me the candle [. . .] It's there, by the door" (37). In this instance, Jack calls to mind the actions of Chesnutt's Uncle Julius. If we remember, Uncle Julius was incredibly adept at recognizing and seizing a storytelling moment; he knew that time and place mattered to the telling of a story. Jack's actions here indicate that he knows this as well. He does not begin an actual story until he has John's full and rapt attention. Similar to the way Uncle Julius lures and positions John and Annie for taletelling sessions, Jack spends a good deal of time enticing John with bits of information about his father and lulling him into a state of passivity with a warm fire and a generous taste of whiskey before embarking on the first real Moses story. Only then do the first of many stories told by Jack come, stories that prove to be more than a simple means of entertaining a young boy after the death of his father. They are John's legacy, a legacy he refuses to recognize as such. Until he goes home—that is, until Jack's acrimonious greeting upon his return forces him to face the wrongness of his having stayed away so long and subsequently sends him reeling into the past once again, to the days he spent as Jack's survival folkways and storytelling apprentice.

He remembers Jack's having taught him how to build a fire, how to traverse the woods, how to move in silence, how to accept his "own limitations and compensate" (44). In helping Old Jack as he dies, John must summon these very same survival skills. He is surprised by how much of what he learned still remains with him, ingrained in him. For instance, after managing

to retrieve clean water from the "shallow, leaf-choked spring" behind Jack's
shack, he writes, "I did remember. Something in me did, and I was calm and
patient when I needed to be, and I was strong and steady when I needed to be
[. . .]" (46). But he is also distressed by how these woodcraft tests recall to him
and awaken within him a hunger for stories of his father, a hunger Old Jack was
always also more than willing to satisfy. Recollecting this hunger, John writes:

> I always wanted to hear about Moses Washington, about
> what he had said and what he had done, about the adventures
> that had taken him, and Old Jack Crawley and Uncle Josh
> White, tearing across the mountains pursued by lawmen and
> irate fathers and angry farmers. The stories were endless,
> and I had never tired of them, at least not for years. No; I had
> never tired of them. But somewhere along the line it had
> occurred to me that the stories were not just stories. They
> were something else: clues. The stories had changed then, it
> seemed. [. . .] And I had changed. And none of the changes
> had been for the better. (45)

Jack's stories fascinated John as a boy, but when they return to him now, they
both fascinate and frustrate him. They fascinate him because they are a means
through which he is able to learn again about the legend that was his father,
but they frustrate him because, as a historian, they leave too many questions
about his father's death and his family's history unanswered. The historian in
John battles with two seemingly mutually exclusive issues: that there is little in
the stories he can verify as fact, but that there are clues in them beckoning him
to search for something in which he, at the very least, can believe. In facing the
loss of Jack and in thinking again about his father's legendary life and mysterious death, John comes to terms with why the idea of oral story as history both-
ers him so. He tells us,

> I began to think about what a man's dying really means: his
> story is lost. Bits and pieces of it remain, but they are all
> secondhand tales and hearsay, or cold official records that
> preserve the facts and spoil the truth [. . .] The missing vol-
> umes are often not the most important, but they are the stuff
> of background, the material of understanding, the real power
> of history. The gaps in the stories of the famous are filled even-
> tually; overfilled. But the gaps in the stories of the unknown

are never filled, never can be filled, for they are larger than data, larger than deduction, larger than induction. (48–49)

That one can and must develop one's own truths by becoming the storyteller and filling in the gaps for oneself is the sole fact John's ancestors have left him that he refuses to acknowledge.[12] Urging him to this admission is Jack, a man who knows that

> [i]f you would bend a man, not just influence him or sway him or even convince him but *bend* him, do it with ritual. For even if he claims to have no belief, no religion, no adherence to any formal or informal order of service, there is, somewhere within him, a hidden agenda. And he will respond without hesitation, without thought, almost without knowledge, certainly without will. All you need to do is to guess the beginning of it. With me, Old Jack did not even have to guess—he knew. He had created it. (77)

Jack is cognizant that John not only drifted from his past but also abnegated it. And he is aware that to pull John back to history, to give him back to himself, it will take more than a simple return home, it will take an engagement in a tradition meant to bridge past and present realities. Hence, on the eve of his own death, Jack returns John to the first night they spent together, to the ritual shared and passed on that night—the ritual of storytelling. As John tells us, late that night, "when the meal was finished and the dishes washed, when the fire was stoked and the mugs of warmed and sweetened whiskey were in our hands, he did not hesitate; he did not even ask. He just said: 'You want a story.'" (77). Sure that he returned home only to see to Jack's needs, not to have a soiree with the past, this is not at all what John wants. He wants nothing more than to drink himself into a stupor and fall into a "dreamless sleep." Thus, he refuses to respond as he should, as he did as a child, with an enthusiastic "yes!" Instead, he remains silent, resisting the pull to behave according to the ritual he and Jack established years ago. In fact, when Jack proceeds with the next line of the ritual script—"Then fetch the candle"—John remains sitting, quietly fuming. Jack is only momentarily daunted by John's behavior; he soon goes on with the next lines—"Bring the matches, too. Can't have light without strikin' fire"—and John finds himself, much to his chagrin, giving in to ritual. He honors Jack's request, going through "motions so familiar they were almost painful." Thus, having accepted the old way once again, he is perplexed when, upon returning to the table, he finds the scene from his childhood has disappeared. Jack is not sitting in the chair, waiting to strike the match, light the wick, and sit the candle in a pool of wax, "a prisoner of its own substance." He has moved to lie on his cot. The job of "lighting" must be completed by John himself. This is an important change to the ritual, for it is the first step in positioning John as storyteller. However, as it is not yet time for Jack to relinquish the role himself, he continues on, taking responsibility for the storyteller's last lines of script prior to the story to be told. He tells John, using the same words as before, "Put the matches back." But he stops there, leaving out the final words of advice he had given John as a child. For those words, "Always put things back where you found 'em so you'll know where they are when you need 'em again," are not necessary now. "He did not need to say the rest of it," because this is the storyteller's job, this is what John is there to learn (78).

Nevertheless, John does not yet realize that he is, as he was all along, meant to learn something not only from Jack's stories, but from Jack's storytelling as well. Hence, all John attempts to take from this last storytelling session is the same little thing he took in the past—a bit of information about his father's doings, something to fill out the man who remained an enigma to those who tried to know him. What he finds upon Jack's death, however, is that while he thought the sum of stories would provide him with an image of the man, what he has is only an outline; his father still remains a mystery, his family's past a nagging uncertainty, his own future hanging on this lack of knowledge. As he begins the task of putting the pieces of information together like a puzzle, he runs up against more questions than answers, fragments that don't seem to fit, extras he would like more than ever to discard and forget. The majority of these scraps come from his own memories of his father, of their rare encounters—the most potent memories having to do with Moses' attic hideaway and his erratic behavior after spending time there. John explains:

> Nobody went up into the attic except Moses Washington. Nobody would have been welcome. Nobody *wanted* to be welcome [. . .] all we ever knew was that every day he would climb up there and pull the staircase and the trapdoor up after him. You could hear him rattle around for a while, and then the floor would creak as he would settle down to do whatever it was he did. There was no set time for all this; [. . .] if he did come down, it was well to be out of sight, because his actions were totally unpredictable. [. . .] Once he

had descended and grabbed me by the hand and dragged me down the stairs and out the back door and on a long and exhausting and silent tour of the Hill, hauling me by the hand up one street and down another, again and again, for two solid hours, without saying a single word, and when he was finished with whatever it was he was doing he had picked me up and kissed me wetly, and there had been tears in his eyes. Another time, shortly before he died, he had come down slowly and heavily and had stood above me as I sat reading a book. I had tried to look up at him, but he had put his hand on my head and forced me to look at my book, and we had stayed like that, a tableau in tension, until, for reasons known only to him, he had let me go. I had turned to look at him then, and had found that I could not look away; his eyes met mine and held my gaze more firmly than his hands had held my head. We had stayed that way for a while, and then he had turned and gone back upstairs. (138)

John remembers that Moses' behavior was so strange after time spent in his hideaway that his family avoided the place entirely. Even after his father's death, John waited three years before venturing there, for he surmised the place probably had something to do with Moses' demise. After all, he tells us, before going on the wild run through the woods that resulted in his "killing himself," Moses had been up there (138). Moreover, when John finally went to the attic it was not out of curiosity, it was out of need. Homesick, and having read everything in the house including the Sears catalog, he went to the attic in search of fresh reading material. Once up there, however, he met another need he had long ago learned to squelch—the need to know his father. So began, as John describes it, "a magic time":

I had dedicated myself to the task of unraveling the whys and wherefores of Moses Washington; [. . .] I was thirteen but I was not stupid—I knew that there was a great deal I needed to know before I would be ready to confront so great and absolute a mystery [. . .] And so I had developed a plan, and I had followed it to the letter. (144)

His plan was to work like a historian, to identify this figure from the past logically and methodically.

I had spent a month writing down in a loose-leaf notebook
everything I knew about Moses Washington from my own
observation and recollection. I had spent the next month
writing down in a second notebook anything I could find out
from other people, keeping those facts cataloged according
to source. Then I had collected data from records—or I
had tried to: there was practically nothing about Moses
Washington written down anywhere in the County besides
the recording of the deed to the property and the coroner's
certification of his accidental death.

Then I had composed two lists of questions. One set I
labeled preliminary questions: Where had Moses Washington come from? Why had he come to the County? Why had
he stayed? Why had he been a moonshiner? Where and
when had he learned to read? What had happened in the
war to make him change? The second list was only two questions long; I labeled it final questions: What had he been
researching up in the attic? Why, after a ten-year hiatus, had
he taken up his gun? (144)

Erasing his emotions from the search for answers, John made his father a project to be completed, not a person to know. Therefore, although the work
opened the door to his interest in history, an interest that led to his brilliant
adult career, it slammed the door—for the time being—on his understanding
his father. As a young man, he finally decided that such understanding required
something he did not have: imagination, "and if you cannot imagine, you can
discover only cold facts, and more cold facts; you will never know the truth"
(146–47). Frustrated by what he lacked to see beyond the facts, he abandoned
his father, his history, his heritage. But it did not abandon him, it continued to
visit him in his dreams. And in his dreams he met with the person who had all
along been trying to teach him a way to imagine: Old Jack.

In his dreams, Old Jack was as much a guide, and a mentor, as he was
in John's life. Still, in sleep as in waking, John did not grasp Jack's role, nor did
he understand his own part. And so, the dreams plagued him into adulthood,
eventually becoming nothing more than an "all-encompassing sensation of icy
coldness, and a visual image of total white. No sound. No smell. No feeling
really; just the cold," consuming him to such a point that he has to be awakened
by others in order to escape his own subconscious, in order to escape the past

that haunts him still (149). Jack's death brings this past from the depths of dreams to the light of day. To decipher it, to come to terms with it, to know himself through it, John must develop and learn to heed the imagination he professes not to have. Jack has positioned storytelling as a means to this end, as John's means to himself. It is up to John to make this realization, to engage in the tradition meant to save his life.

Up until now, John has successfully avoided the role of storyteller where his own past is concerned. As John reveals in his recollections of past conversations with Judith, in his years away from home, he has learned to hide behind documented didactic history. He has told her facts about his hometown, but nothing that had to do with his family or himself. When she asked him why he never talked about home, he responded with silence. When she insisted that although he talked all the time, about "the Ottoman Empire or European nationalism," he never discussed anything that had to do with himself. He told her, "That is what has to do with me, I'm a historian." John's words here were quite telling. But Judith's retort was even more revealing, for it predicted and summed up the problem John would encounter in coming face to face with the past via his call home to care for Jack. She declared, "That's what you hide behind. All the Goddamn time. Quotes and anecdotes. Humorous little lectures guaranteed to make you the wittiest fellow at any cocktail party" (69–70). Home once again, the stories returned to him, John finds them imbued with different meanings. And he suddenly realizes that he must close the historical gaps in his family's history before he can continue with his own future. Such an act is essential to John's whole survival. But in order to fill in the past, he must take on the role of storyteller. And in order to take on that role, John must first admit that "truth, that elusive historical goal, can also lie in the intersection of narrator and discourse [. . .] for the act of authoring is a claim to authority" (Tonkin 8). Then he must find a listener who will ask the right questions that will lead him to fill in the gaps, a listener he trusts enough to allow him to construct his own truths and come to terms with them. Judith's arrival at Jack's cabin, after his death and her later threat to leave for good, provide John with both a reason to tell the stories and a listener to help shape them.[13] Just as in *The Conjure Woman* it is Annie who advocates Uncle Julius's storytelling, in *The Chaneysville Incident*, it is Judith who encourages John to speak; her questions inviting him to mold the story himself.[14] Thus, although Judith's role is not central to the novel, she is a crucial element.

When Judith arrives on the scene, she tells John what she has come to realize during the trip to meet him. In words reminiscent of their previous conversations, she proclaims:

> You hide things. Not just some things; everything. You don't even think; you just hide them. You've got a big lead vault in your head and you put things in it. If there's anything you haven't figured down to the last quarter inch, anything you're not absolutely sure about, anything you haven't torn to pieces a hundred times, you keep it there. And if there's something you never understand in there, it will stay; nobody else will ever see it [. . .] you never brought me here because you didn't want to share even that. [. . .] There's something here that terrifies you. But you won't share it [. . .] (260–61)

And with these words, Judith spurs John to action. He begins, finally, on the project of reconstructing his family's history. He runs quickly into problems.

Although he finds written testaments of the man who was his father, a man who spent a good portion of his life searching for rather than denying his history, and the man who was his great grandfather, C.K., a historian of sorts himself, they do not provide enough facts for him to create a detailed family history.[15] The questions John has about his father's mysterious death remain unanswered, for the facts alone do not present a connection between his father's movements and his great-grandfather's life.

Lining himself up with the tools of his trade—color-coded note cards, factual journals, and earmarked books—the things that furnish him with names and dates, he finds himself frustrated, for he is unable to establish emotion, motive, frame of mind.

> I had tried all the combinations; I had merged the white cards with the blue, I had mixed in the red, I had tried red and white alone. I had put in the orange. I had cut out the white cards and mixed in the gold. I had made notes. None of them made any sense. Once or twice I thought I had something going, but it was nothing but smoke. I picked up the pad and tore off the sheets with the notes on them and balled them up. I went and dropped the papers into the fire,

watched them crisp brown and blacken and burst into flame. For a minute I thought about doing that with everything; the cards, the notes, the notebooks, everything. For a minute I wanted to burn it all. (291–92)

At this point, John is, in a sense, like the novel itself—overburdened with factual information—so overburdened the story in front of him is almost subsumed. But this crafty move by the author only serves to illustrate the oppressive weight our reliance on documented facts soon becomes when we are no longer able to see our necessary participation in the stories that surround them, providing the foundation for them. That the facts do not hold water for John is simply because he insists on maintaining the historian's interpretive distance. Thus, he refuses to construct his own story, which is the only way the facts will become relevant to his work and his life. He must learn to place his own oral history alongside the written facts. Moreover, he must learn to speak-weave them together as a story, not a didactic chronicle, in order to place emotion, motive, and frame of mind in their proper place, at the heart of the history.[16]

Part of John's problem, however, is his own emotions, motives, and frame of mind. Moses was a distant and difficult man. For these reasons, John hated him and his return home reignites that hate. But when John learns that he is more like his father than he realized, for Moses, too, was fascinated by history and had been subsumed in his own search for his family's history, the more tender feelings of pride and love surface. Thus, although he begins his search driven by anger, he continues it in order to know his father, in order finally to understand the man and the history Moses spent his life in search of.

This turn from the objective to the subjective is a difficult move for John. The historian in him is adamantly resistant, but when the psychoanalyst that is Judith asks him again and again to talk to her about what he is finding or not finding, things begin to fall into place. She says to him, "Maybe if you talked to me about it." And, then, when he tells her there is nothing to talk about because none of the facts connect, she asks him a question—"How did you get here? It sounds so horrible. It sounds like nobody wanted you here and you didn't want to be here [. . .]"—that gives him what he needs to begin making those connections he longs for: a place to start (293). Pushing his thoughts back to how black people came to "The Hill" in the first place, Judith gets John to give voice to what he has heretofore only recorded in his mind. As he does so, he realizes what he must do to truly bring the facts to life. He must put the cards and notebooks aside and return to the places and folkways Jack had so diligently shown and taught him, but that he had written off as quaint and illogical. He must seek out the legends entrenched in the mountains surrounding his father's home. He must go to the place of his father's mysterious death, retrace the footsteps, listen to the voices of his ancestors, and learn to use his own voice to bridge the gap between the past and the present. And, yet, as he tells us,

> I did not want to go. I did not want to go at all. I would rather have sat in the cabin, sipping toddies, listening to Judith's snoring, even looking at those damned cards. But there was nothing in the cards for me; I knew that now. And I had gone to every other place on the map, visited the caves and the hollows and the hideouts, all of it. There was only one place left. Only one chance left for me to understand. If there was a chance at all. (306)

In order to find his way through the mountains, John must now rely on his own instincts and intuitions. He must combine what he has learned from the maps and books with the knowledge of his father provided by Jack's stories, the things Moses would or would not have done. Moreover, he must come to know that where his history is concerned, what he has learned of it through the oral tradition is equally, if not more important, than what he has gleaned from the books and maps left to him.

While traversing the woods, searching for the spot of his father's death, John, at Judith's continual urging, turns his family's history into a tale. Going against his training as a historian, he substitutes his own ideas and assumptions for facts when they are lacking, attempting, as he explains, "to forget everything, all the clashing facts on the red cards and the gold cards and the orange cards, trying to separate out the ones on the white, and trying to forget I didn't know the why of any of it" (323). He is only partially successful in this endeavor; the historian's need for a factual basis to his findings still gets the best of him when he finally comes to the spot where his father died. Because the spot does not reveal to him the facts surrounding his father's death, he feels as though the answers and connections he had hoped to find there will forever elude him. Hence, John returns with Judith to Jack's cabin wrongfully assuming that he can go no further for he has run out of facts.

Back in the cabin, however, John realizes that like Jack, the mountains hold a story for him, they are full of the voices Jack had once urged him to listen to, forced him to acknowledge. Although as a young man John had heard the voices, his belief in logical conclusions forced him to reject them:

> I had gone away from the mountains, down to the flat land,
> [. . .] I had promised myself I would never hear it again, that
> I would never go up into the mountains again. I had kept that
> promise, until now. Only now I knew where the lie had been:
> I had stopped hearing, but I had not stopped listening. (383)

His return to the mountains and the footsteps of his ancestors makes him eager to hear the voices again. Moreover, it makes him long to become a part of those voices. And, with Judith's persevering help, he does. Still hungry to know those parts of John embedded in his family's history, Judith again insists John forget the facts and simply tell her what he thinks. Much to his own amazement, John hears himself say: "You want a story do you? [. . .] Fetch the candle" (393).

With these words, John takes on the role of storyteller, a role that serves to blur his previously established notions of the known and the unknown, of time and space. And this fogging of the clear lines of demarcation set by the historian, is essential, for it finally and forever eradicates those other lines set by John to distinguish his oral history from his written history. These lines gone, John is able to sift through written facts for actual movement and through the oral stories for those essential elements missing before: emotion, motive, frame of mind. With Judith as listener, providing questions that lead to elaboration on John's part, a filling in of the gaps with his own conclusions and assumptions, he begins to speak-weave the written and the oral, which, when the facts and reliable markers have once again run out, ultimately enables him to move beyond the end of the written history into the oral history that will merge with his own existence. John is forced, by his own actions, finally to give credence to the notion of speaker as author/authority.[17] Furthermore, as he tells his family's story—creating the missing written parts—he learns that "far from dealing only with ourselves when we tell about the past, we incorporate the experience of a multitude of others along with our own; they appear in what we say through our marvelous capacity to express other perspectives" (Schrager 76–98). As John talks, he suddenly no longer exists simply in that day in those mountains, he is now also a part of his father's day and his great grandfather's day, a part of the mountains both C.K. and Moses traversed years before him, a part of their very minds. What happens to John is what Elizabeth Tonkin describes in her work

Narrating Our Pasts, when she tells us that an oral story "told as it must be in a
specific time and in a phase of irreversible time [. . .] creates a special time, 'a
time outside time'" (3).

In creating his own story and telling the story to Judith, John comes to
realize that "to tell history is to act" (Tonkin 11). For if the past you are reconstructing is directly linked with your own, the telling allows you to become a part
of that past, provides you with a means of reconciling the way that life intersects
with your own present state of being. Moreover, he learns that although with
written texts "the setting in which one reads [. . .] is often irrelevant to its interpretation," with oral texts, the setting is vital (Tonkin 51). Where any oral history is concerned, the listener(s), location, and circumstances that occasion the
telling are directly related to what the story becomes in terms of both content
and meaning. As John tells us, his family's story—his story—comes together
because in Jack's cabin "[. . .] it was as it had always been: the wind slipping
through the chinks in the walls, stealing through the cabin, making the candle
flicker, making the shadows dance; the air rattling and roaring in the flue" (393).

By returning to the oral tradition and taking up Jack's position as oral
historian, John stops viewing the past as simply "a resource to deploy, to support
a case or assert a social claim" (Tonkin 8). John has become an essential participant in the past—a role his reserved and haunted father was never able to play,
for he closed himself off from those things necessary to our stories: occasions
and listeners. Having a trustworthy listener and an essential occasion helps John
shape a past that makes the factual truths more meaningful. What he creates
while telling the story to Judith becomes enough for him, for the story he weaves
is a past he has a stake in and has played a part in, a past he can and must believe
in. And his active involvement in the re-creation of his family's past helps him
finally understand the ways in which he has shaped his life in light of the past.[18]

Because Moses could not come to terms with the past himself, he left
John an incomplete trail to follow, but it is a trail that eventually leads John to
the creation of the truth for himself. For John, this truth, a combination of
written fact and oral interpretation, is a truth more meaningful than any written history alone could be, for it is a truth by which "descendants and ancestors achieve living reciprocal relationships" (Pavlic 165). Hence, John knows he
must do for the next family members in search of the Washington history what
Moses did for him. He must give them room to create and tell their own story.
And so, upon leaving the cabin, he tells us the following:

> [. . .] I took the folio down and put the books and pamphlets
> and diaries and maps back where they belonged, ready for
> the next man who would need them. I sealed the folio with
> the candle wax, as my father had done for me. Then I gath-
> ered up the tools of my trade, the pens and inks and pencils,
> the pads and the cards, and carried them out into the clear-
> ing. I kicked a clear space in the snow and set them down,
> and over them I built a small edifice of kindling and then a
> frame of wood. I went back inside the cabin and got the
> kerosene and brought it back and poured it freely over the
> pyre, making sure to soak the cards thoroughly. [. . .] I struck
> the match [. . .] dropped the match to the wood and watched
> the flames go twisting. (431–32)

In the "spirit of understanding" (Cooke 21), John leaves this incomplete written history, for he has learned that if one does not speak, one has no past.
Although John's memories are not all his own, by speaking he has broken into
the silences surrounding him. The previous stories and his telling of them *and*
his own have freed John to value the oral tradition for the bridge only it can
provide.

From *The Conjure Woman* and *The Chaneysville Incident* we learn
that "oral accounts of past events are also guides to the future, as well as being
social activities in which tellers claim authority to speak to particular audiences" (Tonkin). Unfortunately, the differences between written history—
fact—and oral history—interpretations—often serve, in this logic-based
world, to make one less important than the other. However, what Uncle Julius
strove to convey to his listeners and what John learned from his struggle is that
"personal history can amplify—or alter—official history" (Campbell 136).
Moreover, that history as recorded and history as lived are actually dependent
upon each other, for somewhere lost in the facts is the existence of the essential living subject and his or her own historical and personal truths. By speaking, by telling the story, we give meaning to the facts and timeless life to the
subject. We give ourselves, ourselves.

CHAPTER 3

New Footing on Ancient Ground

Zitkala-Ša's *American Indian Stories* and
Leslie Marmon Silko's *Ceremony*

Reconciling Identity and Cultural Heritage:
Zitkala-Ša's American Indian Stories

No one is so eager to gain new experience as he who doesn't know
how to make use of the old ones.
MARIE VON EBNER-ESCHENBACH

For some of us, the thought of going home brings with it the notion that once there we will meet up again with a part of ourselves that still resides in the world of our youth. For those whose remembrances of home are filled with moments of self-discovery, definition, and affirmation, such encounters with the past are probably pleasant. They can find validation for—and ways of validating—who they are today. But what about those who left home before such moments could be articulated, while still in the process of determining who they are and where they fit in the world? These individuals, like John of *The Chaneysville Incident,* view home as the site of a struggle—a struggle between the past and the present. Far from being agreeable, then, the thought of going home is often accompanied by feelings fraught with contradiction. There is a longing to return, but there is also a fear of what will be found. Or, better yet, there is a fear of what the return will require if anything is to be found at all. This is the experience Zitkala-Šă and Leslie Marmon Silko give voice to in their respective works, *American Indian Stories* and *Ceremony.* For as the characters return home in search of themselves, tradition and acculturation collide, creating a fissure so wide between their past senses of self and their present states of being that the necessary bridge linking the two seems impossible to build. And, in fact, it is— until they realize that the ancient ways of knowing contain the very answers they need to reconcile the parts of themselves both old and new.

American Indian Stories begins with a series of autobiographical sketches through which Zitkala-Šă establishes a primary landscape—the reservation, a cultural reference—Native American, and an overriding atmosphere—transition, change.[1] The first six sketches in "Impressions of an Indian Childhood" depict her life as a child in a fairly chronological pattern, although time is not so much a matter of hours and days as it is a matter of the habits and traditions practiced during different times of the day and year. For instance, we learn that beadwork was often done in the morning and that food preservation was completed in autumn. This measuring of time—according to customs engaged in—helps Zitkala-Ša reveal a community sustained through cultural conventions and, what's more, a people attached by a history. The history, we learn, is contained in the legends retold almost daily during the evening meal, the formation and progression of which Zitkala-Ša marks as a most important ritual in itself:

> I loved best the evening meal, for that was the time old legends were told. I was always glad when the sun hung low in the west, for then my mother sent me to invite the neighboring old men and women to eat supper with us. Running all the way to the wigwams, I halted shyly at the entrances [. . .] It was not any fear that made me so dumb when out upon such a happy errand; nor was it that I wished to withhold the invitation, for it was all I could do to observe this very proper silence. But it was a sensing of the atmosphere, to assure myself that I should not hinder other plans [. . .] The old folks knew the meaning of my pauses [. . .]
>
> At the arrival of our guests I sat close to my mother, and did not leave her side without first asking her consent. I ate my supper in quiet, listening patiently to the talk of the old people, wishing all the time that they would begin the stories I loved best. At last, when I could not wait any longer, I whispered in mother's ear, "Ask them to tell an Iktomi story, mother." Soothing my impatience, my mother said aloud, "My little daughter is anxious to hear your legends."
>
> As each in turn began to tell a legend, I pillowed my head in my mother's lap; and lying flat upon my back, I watched the stars as they peeped down upon me, one by one. (13–15)

As Zitkala-Ša indicates here, legend preservation and ritualized living help the community maintain itself in the present while also preserving the company of the past.[2] The past lives on as both a thing remembered and a thing done; it is kept vital not only through legend dissemination, but also through a set of traditions—crafts, manners, and performances—learned through instruction, observation, and imitation. And because the very act of engaging in a tradition—like storytelling, for instance—keeps the past alive, it is the bedrock of life in this tribal community, even permeating the children's recreation time. As Zitkala-Šă explains, when the children are freed from their chores, they spend much of their time perfecting the skills of various traditions through role-playing. Where storytelling is concerned, she tells us the following:

> We delighted in impersonating our own mothers. We talked of things we had heard them say in their conversations. We imitated their various manners, even to the inflections of their voices. In the lap of the prairie we seated ourselves upon our feet, and leaning our painted cheeks in the palms of our hands, we rested our elbows on our knees, and bent forward as old women were most accustomed to do.
>
> While one was telling of some heroic deed recently done by a near relative, the rest of us listened attentively, and exclaimed in undertones, "Han! han!" (yes! yes!) whenever the speaker paused for breath, or sometimes for our sympathy. As the discourse became more thrilling, according to our ideas, we raised our voices in these interjections. In these impersonations our parents were led to say only those things that were in common favor. (21–22)

Zitkala-Šă obviously enjoys folklore play such as this. The tenacity of tradition gives her sense of self and life "an easy, natural flow" (39). And the narrative reflects this: it has a distinct coherence. But as we move to the second part of the autobiographical text, fragmentation becomes apparent.

We are warned of fragmentation's coming in the final section of "Impressions of an Indian Childhood," the section entitled "The Big Red Apples," which begins with the words, "The first turning away." Here fragmentation is foreshadowed, and its impetus is identified as encroaching acculturation. Zitkala-Šă explains:

> Within the last two seasons my big brother Dawée had returned from three years' education in the East, and his coming back influenced my mother to take a farther step from her native way of living. First it was change from the buffalo skin to the white man's canvas that covered our wigwam. Now

she had given up her wigwam of slender poles, to live a for-
eigner in a home of clumsy logs. (40)

Although she notices here the changes wrought as bit by bit native habits are
relinquished to eastern influences, Zitkala-Šă's childish naiveté allows her to
be enticed by the visiting missionaries' promises of the availability of fruits
and modes of transportation unimaginable before. Desirously she writes the
following:

> Judewin had told me of the great tree where grew red, red
> apples; and how we could reach out our hands and pick all
> the red apples we could eat. I had never seen apple trees. I
> had never tasted more than a dozen red apples in my life; and
> when I heard of the orchards of the East, I was eager to roam
> among them. (41–42)

So eager is she, that she ignores her mother's pleas for her to stay. She cannot
be moved to see that her romantic view of this other world is far removed from
its reality. Hence, her mother eventually grants her permission to leave, hoping, at the very least, that Zitkala-Šă will be educated and thus better equipped
for existence in a world and a time when "there will be fewer real Dakotas, and
many more palefaces" (44). Consumed by her fantasies, the naive child leaves
her community. And in so doing, she suddenly, albeit inadvertently, recognizes
the threat to her sense of self her choice has made real. She writes, "I was in
the hands of strangers whom my mother did not fully trust, I no longer felt free
to be myself, or to voice my own feelings" (45).

    In the next section, "The School Days of an Indian Girl," Zitkala-Šă
experiences—one after the other—the things that excited her into leaving.
Unfortunately, these experiences are filled with a sense of disillusion. The
pleasure she anticipated during the "ride on the iron horse" is negated by
"throngs of staring palefaces":

> On the train, fair women, with tottering babies on each arm,
> stopped their haste and scrutinized the children of absent
> mothers. Large men, with heavy bundles in their hands,
> halted near by, and riveted their glassy blue eyes upon us.
>   I sank deep into the corner of my seat, for I resented
> being watched [. . .] This embarrassed me, and kept me con-
> stantly on the verge of tears. (47–48)

When she reaches her destination, the rosy skied land she imagined shows its true lack of color, for it is barren and cold. Moreover, she soon learns the land is not the only thing bereft of warmth or hue—the people are as well. Hence, it is not long before disillusion is accompanied by an uncomfortable sense of alienation and the unconscious recognition of a covert code of difference.

In the sections "The School Days of an Indian Girl" and "An Indian Teacher among Indians," no longer is the movement of life accorded to custom or habit. Rather, life is depicted as moving through a series of struggles as Zitkala-Sǎ begins oscillating between two distinct worlds—one of outward structure, the other of ingrained tradition. Her details of her first day at the school clearly show us of what a world of outward structure consists. Not only is she bothered by the incessant noise of the place—"the annoying clatter of shoes on bare floors"—but she experiences confusion and discomfort at the lack of free movement in terms of action and behavior. The breakfast meal, for example, she describes as no less than a lesson in restraint and submission:

> A small bell was tapped, and each of the pupils drew a chair from under the table. Supposing this act meant they were to be seated, I pulled out mine and at once slipped into it from one side. But when I turned my head, I saw that I was the only one seated, and all the rest at our table remained standing. Just as I began to rise, looking shyly around to see how chairs were to be used, a second bell was sounded. All were seated at last, and I had to crawl back into my chair again. I heard a man's voice at one end of the hall, and I looked around to see him. But all the others hung their heads over their plates. As I glanced at the long chain of tables, I caught the eyes of a paleface woman upon me. Immediately I dropped my eyes, wondering why I was so keenly watched by the strange woman. The man ceased his mutterings, and then a third bell was tapped. Every one picked up his knife and fork and began eating. I began crying instead, for by this time I was afraid to venture anything more. (54)

Obviously, Zitkala-Sǎ finds such blueprint behavior difficult to abide by. However, her real struggles are defined differently, for they occur when outer structures impose upon and are meant to replace thoroughly ingrained beliefs and traditions. She asserts, it is not "eating by formula" that proves the hardest trial of her first day, it is having her "long, heavy hair" cut. Her mother had taught her "that only unskilled warriors who were captured had their hair shingled by the enemy [. . .] short hair was worn by mourners, and shingled hair by cowards!" (54). Hence, believing her hair to be an outer symbol of her inner character, she violently resists the shears. And although her resistance fails, this episode sets a standard for subsequent structural threats to culture, defining her chief mode of response as rebellion.

Detailing instances of rebellion, Zitkala-Šá highlights the significance of maintaining her cultural heritage. In addition, she highlights the importance of sustaining her spirit and individuality. Her chronicles expose how the school's rigid structure was not only meant to strip Native American students of culture in order to assimilate them, it was meant to strip them of their spirit and their own unique senses of self—two aspects of identity Zitkala-Šá refuses to part with, as we are shown many times. So steadfast is she in her resolve that something as simple as displaying her dislike for turnips becomes an affirmation, a grand expression of self. She writes, "I whooped in my heart for having once asserted the rebellion within me" (61). Liberating to be sure, such rebellious acts in the light of day are also her only way of coping with the fears that visit her during the night. As she tells us, her dreams are haunted by images of "the white man's devil," an "evil divinity" intent on capturing her while her mother sits idly by, doing nothing until the last possible moment, only then emerging "from her quiet indifference" to take Zitkala-Šá into her arms. Frustrated by her inability to escape the devil of her dreams, Zitkala-Šá seeks revenge when she wakes in the morning:

> Stealing into the room where a wall of shelves was filled with books, I drew forth The Stories of the Bible. With a broken slate pencil I carried in my apron pocket, I began scratching out his wicked eyes. A few moments later, when I was ready to leave the room, there was a ragged hole in the page where the picture of the devil had once been. (65)

Finding satisfaction in her actions, she thus vows to continue "[. . .] actively testing the chains which tightly bound my individuality like a mummy for burial" (67). And she will be true to her word. Still, after three years of schooling in the East, when she returns to roam "again in the Western country through four strange summers," she finds that her sense of self has become dangerously nebulous—clouded by generational gaps and cultural barriers.

> During this time I seemed to hang in the heart of chaos,
> beyond the touch or voice of human aid. My brother [. . .] did
> not quite understand my feelings. My mother had never gone
> inside of a schoolhouse, and so she was not capable of com-
> forting her daughter who could read and write. Even nature
> seemed to have no place for me. I was neither a wee girl nor
> a tall one: neither a wild Indian nor a tame one. (69)

As a result of all of this, her experiences at home during this time are tem-
pestuous, filled with unrest. She longs to ride the Dakota prairies with abandon, to discard shoes in favor of soft moccasins, but she is also desirous of
attending parties in hats, ribbons, and in close-fitting gowns like the other
eastern school-goers. On one occasion, believing Zitkala-Šă's troubled spirit to
be a result of complete acculturation, rather than the teetering on edge of two
cultures, her mother offers her an Indian Bible, telling her, "Here, my child
are the white man's papers. Read a little from them." The offering is meant to
comfort and to show her mother's understanding, if not her acceptance, of
what she thinks is her daughter's longing for eastern ways. But it only
increases Zitkala-Šă's anguish over and dis-ease with the worlds available to
her. She laments:

> I took it from her hand, for her sake; but my enraged spirit
> felt more like burning the book, which afforded me no help,
> and was a perfect delusion to my mother. [. . .] Now my wrath
> against the fates consumed my tears before they reached my
> eyes. (73–74)

In anger, she imagines running away, but her confusion drives her back to the
East instead:

> A few more moons of such a turmoil drove me away to the
> eastern school. I rode the white man's iron steed, thinking it
> would bring me back to my mother in a few winters, when I
> should be grown tall, and there would be congenial friends
> awaiting me. (74)

There, against her mother's wishes for her return again to the West, "to roam
over the prairies," to find her "living upon wild roots," she embarks upon a college career (76).

Laced with prejudice and bittersweet achievement, her return East and subsequent choice of continuing her education creates a deeper rift between mother and daughter, woman and culture. And yet it does not totally dispel her longing, her sense of connection with what she has left behind for the time being. We see this, for instance, after she wins an oratory contest for her college, a contest in which prejudiced students from the rival school show their true hearts.

> Leaving the crowd as quickly as possible, I was soon in my room. The rest of the night, I sat in my armchair and gazed into the crackling fire. I laughed no more in triumph when thus alone. The little taste of victory did not satisfy a hunger in my heart. In my mind I saw my mother far away on the Western plains, and she was holding a charge against me. (80)

Nevertheless, while it is illness that keeps her from continuing her college work, it is pride that keeps her from returning home. Not a complete disadvantage, her pride is what helps her find a way to begin harmonizing the self that resides with her mother and the self that remains in the East. It is what points her toward her goal of helping the "Indian race."

Fulfilling the goal of helping other Indians—by teaching in an eastern Indian school—is at first a test of her physical strength and then, as she fails this test and is asked to "return west to gather Indian pupils" for the eastern school (85), it becomes a test of her inner strength. For in this return to her community and reunion with her mother, she runs head on into the oscillation of her experiences thus far. Finding her mother and brother in dire straits, she demands to know the cause. Her mother tells her, "Dawée! Oh, he has not told you that the Great Father at Washington sent a white son to take your brother's pen from him? Since then Dawée has not been able to make use of the education the Eastern school has given him" (91). This answer angers Zitkala-Šă, but when her mother further details the story of her community's plight—the uselessness of their eastern educated youth because of the whites' unfair political and social practices—helplessness again sets in: how will she put her education to use in a world where one community remains suspicious of it and another strips her of the opportunity to use it? When her mother suggests they turn to the Great Spirit for guidance, Zitkala-Šă tells her, "Mother, don't pray again! The Great Spirit does not care if we live or die! Let us not look for good or justice: then we shall not be disappointed!" (92). Her mother, however, will not relinquish her spiritual beliefs or her cultural heritage—her hold on the world she has known. Instead, in an attempt to bring her daughter home as well—physically, spiritually, and culturally—she gives her another heavy dose of her community's reality, a reality filled with suffering, led by a generation whose experiences, not unlike Zitkala-Să's, have been laden with frustration and futility. Although Zitkala-Să feels the weight of her mother's words, the full gravity of her community's situation will not occur to her until she again returns to the school in the East. This time, with her mother's eye as guide, she will come to comprehend fully the covert creed directing life and education within Indian schools—a tenet, she tells us, which "included self-preservation quite as much as Indian education." After witnessing this doctrine practiced by a white male teacher upon an enterprising and promising Indian youth—through the constant reminder of the brave's status as a "government pauper"—she exclaims: "I burned with indignation upon discovering on every side instances no less shameful [. . .]" (95–96). Coupled with her limited strength, the school's fine-tuned power of deception makes help seemingly impossible for the situation in which she finds herself and her fellow Indians. Thus, she once more turns down the road of hopelessness. However, she is now able to trace the sources of that futility, finding the causal train leads, yes, to the white man's papers of promise, but ultimately back to herself:

> At this stage of my evolution, I was ready to curse men of small capacity for being the dwarfs their God had made them. In the process of my education I had lost all consciousness of the natural world about me. Thus, when a hidden rage took me to the small white-walled prison which I then called my room, I unknowingly turned away from my own salvation. Alone in my room, I sat like the petrified Indian woman of whom my mother used to tell me. [. . .] For the white man's papers I had given up my faith in the Great Spirit. For these same papers I had forgotten the healing in trees and brooks. On account of my mother's simple view of life, and my lack of any, I gave her up, also. I made no friends among the race of people I loathed. Like a slender tree, I had been uprooted from my mother, nature, and God. I was shorn of my branches, which had waved in sympathy and love for home and friends. The natural coat of bark which had protected my oversensitive nature was scraped off to the very quick.

Now a cold bare pole I seemed to be, planted in a strange
earth. Still, I seemed to hope a day would come when my mute
aching head, reared upward to the sky, would flash a zigzag
lightning across the heavens. With this dream of vent for a
long-pent consciousness, I walked again amid the crowds. (97)

Here, her inability to reconcile what she has gained with what she has lost
moves her to dreams of triumph via revenge. But it is through this fantasy and
self-analysis, this true inward turning, that she finds, as she so succinctly puts it,
"a new way of solving the problem of my inner self" (97). As she has learned, to
be an Indian educated in an eastern school is to be asked—no, required—to
relinquish her heritage in exchange for a farce, a farce made up of appearances
for appearances' sake and promises soon to be broken. It is identity without substance, education without opportunity. Hence, solving the problem of her inner
self becomes a matter of posing the question to herself and to others of
"whether real life or long-lasting death lies beneath this semblance of civiliza-
tion" Indian children in eastern schools are made to endure and enact (99).

We know, however, that this final question comes only through retrospection, only as she looks back and is able to see her past "from a distance, as
a whole" (98). These retrospective comments and questions end the autobiographical part of the text, and yet the narrative itself ends earlier—as she
resigns her position as teacher and enters an eastern city to follow her chosen
path of inquiry. She finishes her "life story," then, at a point of transition, when
her sense of self and time is still clouded and fluid.[3] Hence, it should not surprise us that as she truly begins her journey to her self, truly begins reconciling new traditions with old, we enter the realm of legend.

To make the transition from autobiography to legend more fluid,
Zitkala-Să begins the next section of the text with a story positioned in the
present—at the time of her reminiscent writing—a story that works as a prologue to the legend encounters recorded in the pages that follow. In "The Great
Spirit" Zitkala-Să documents the effects of her return to her native culture and
its attendant belief system. She chronicles the change this meeting has made in her
view of herself and the world around her. She speaks of sloughing off a religion
not her own and subsequently reconnecting to all living things in line with the
ancient beliefs of her people, a reconnection that gives a sense of balance to a
world full, as she knows, of difference, distinction, and hierarchy (107). Remembering the story of the Stone-Boy as she "roams the green hills" of her childhood,
her heart filled with the Great Spirit, she lovingly writes the following:

> Interwoven with the thread of this Indian legend of the rock,
> I fain would trace a subtle knowledge of the native folk which
> enabled them to recognize a kinship to any and all parts of
> this vast universe. [. . .] With the strong, happy sense that
> both great and small are so surely enfolded in His magnitude
> that, without a miss, each has his allotted individual ground
> of opportunities, I am buoyant with good nature. (102–3)

And then, after returning from her wanderings to her own cabin, she writes:

> [. . .] I feel in keen sympathy with my fellow-creatures, for I
> seem to see clearly again that all are akin. The racial lines,
> which once were bitterly real, now serve nothing more than
> marking out a living mosaic of human beings. And even here
> men of the same color are like the ivory keys of one instrument
> where each resembles all the rest, yet varies from them in
> pitch and quality of voice. And those creatures who are for a
> time mere echoes of another's note are not unlike the fable of
> the thin sick man whose distorted shadow, dressed like a real
> creature, came to the old master to make him follow as a
> shadow. (104–5)

So strong is her newly reacquired sense of the rightness of the world and her being in it that she easily rejects the conversion attempts of the "native preacher" who visits her that same day and defines her own spiritual concepts. Thus, in eloquent fashion, she ends this prologue-type piece with a promise and an assertion of her faith:

> I would not forget that the pale-faced missionary and the
> hoodooed aborigine are both God's creatures, though small
> indeed their own conceptions of Infinite Love. A wee child
> toddling in a wonder world, I prefer to their dogma my
> excursions into the natural gardens where the voice of the
> Great Spirit is heard in the twittering of birds, the rippling of
> mighty waters, and the sweet breathing of flowers.
>
> Here, in a fleeting quiet, I am awakened by the fluttering
> robe of the Great Spirit. To my innermost consciousness the
> phenomenal universe is a royal mantle, vibrating with His

divine breath. Caught in its flowing fringes are the spangles
and oscillating brilliants of sun, moon, and stars. (107)

Having now delineated her own reformation of thought, she moves backward
to reveal what is responsible for that change: her rendezvous with the legends
of her people.

The first legend Zitkala-Ša returns to, "The Soft Hearted Sioux," shows
what can happen when new beliefs collide with ancient customs.[4] While the
story illustrates the dangers of living according to a faith that prohibits actions
conducive to survival in the here and now, it does not argue for one brand of religion over another. Rather, it argues against any religion that prevents a living in
the world, so to speak. Steeped in the teachings of Christianity, which his nine
years away at the mission school have inculcated in him, the soft-hearted Sioux
is unable to perform the duties necessary to prevent the death of his father upon
his return to his community. Instead, he attempts to convert both his parents and
his people to his newfound faith in "that abstract power named God" (114). His
pleas for conversion are drowned out, however, by the Sioux's medicine man,
who, in questioning a faith that makes a man incapable of fulfilling the responsibilities of a son and a brave, convinces the community to disband, leaving the fate
of the ailing father in the hands of the converted, and thus inept, son. Days later,
his faith bringing neither food to his family nor health to his father, the young
man turns from all belief systems and behaves in a manner contrary to all customs. He butchers the prime member of a privately held herd of cattle and when
caught in the act, defends himself by murdering the animal's owner. All this ter-
rible turning away, the soft-hearted Sioux soon finds, is for naught, for his father
has died in his absence. Escape being hopeless, the young man turns himself in
and resigns himself to his impending execution. Still, he is only vaguely aware
that his father's death and his own demise have been brought on by his inability
to reconcile new beliefs with old ways of living—the lesson Zitkala-Ša learns
from her own trials. But if what Zitkala-Ša must do to live fully (as the legend suggests) is submit to a combining of new and old ways, she must have full understanding of both. And so, the legends that follow this first one work to remind her
of what the old ways consist of and, more importantly, what they require of her.

"The Trial Path," for instance, a story of love and murder, speaks, in
the end, to Zitkala-Ša of the importance of paying attention to the sacred tales
of her people, for contained within them are the essential modes of conducting
this life and surviving in the life hereafter. The grandmother of the story explicitly

voices the significance of such legends. When she notices that her audience, her granddaughter, has fallen asleep during her explanation of the tale's final action, she remarks to the silence surrounding her: "Hinnu! hinnu! Asleep! I have been talking in the dark, unheard. I did wish the girl would plant in her heart this sacred tale" (135). It is imperative that the girl "plant in her heart this sacred tale" because it tells of the ritual process through which her people "judge, punish, and expiate crime within the community" (Karcher, pers. comm.). If the family of the murdered man of this story, the grandmother's husband, had not had a way to deal with his murderer, the grandmother's lover, a bitter seed would have been planted in the hearts of all, souring all relationships by example. Moreover, it is crucial that the girl hear the tale to its finish, for while the legend itself deals with safeguarding the lives of the living, the grandmother's concluding remarks focus on how her people ensure the deceased make it safe and whole to "the next camp-ground" (135). The grandmother laments her granddaughter's inattention because she knows if one does not listen closely to such "sacred" tales, if one does not absorb such sacred knowledge, one runs the risk of not knowing how to traverse this world and the next.

Such ancient knowledge, however, is not all it takes to survive this life, as the next legend, "A Warrior's Daughter," illustrates. It must be coupled with something else equally essential to whole survival: inner strength. In "A Warrior's Daughter" it is Tusee's inner resolve that makes it possible for her to save the life of her lover when he is captured by an enemy tribe. Tusee has been raised to appreciate and rely upon the power within her. And so she does not hesitate to act when her lover's life is in peril. Although she beckons the Great Spirit, the foundation of her faith, to guide her, it is real human action she takes to bring the kidnapped warrior to safety. First, dressed as a member of the enemy tribe, she entices the young man responsible for her lover's torture away from the celebration arena and kills him. Then, donning the persona of an old woman carrying a child on her back, scouting the emptied party grounds, "searching for something forgotten," she frees her near-to-death lover. Moreover, when she finds him too weak to stand on his own, she readily accepts his weight:

> The sight of his weakness makes her strong. A mighty power
> thrills her body. Stooping beneath his outstretched arms
> grasping at the air for support, Tusee lifts him upon her
> broad shoulders. With half-running, triumphant steps she
> carries him away into the open night. (152–53)[5]

Had Tusee not been willing to task her own resources, her lover would have died and her community would have lost one of its bravest members. Hence, the legendary Tusee provides Zitkala-Ša with a role model. Her actions work to convey the message that each individual has the power within to make a difference not only in her own life but also in the lives of those around her. It is up to the individual to put that power to work for the benefit of many.[6] As the alternate ending to "A Warrior's Daughter" should indicate to Zitkala-Ša, passivity brought on by an ignorance of or an unwillingness to cultivate this vital resource can lead to demise—your own, your community's.

The fact that the belief in one's abilities can make a difference is an issue elaborated upon in the next legend, for this one deals with the good that results from the sister of self-confidence: the confidence of others. A legend very much like Zitkala-Ša's own story, "A Dream of Her Grandfather" is the tale of a young woman who, like her grandfather before her, works with the government for the welfare of her people.[7] One night the young woman dreams she receives a gift from her long-dead grandfather. Upon opening the gift, a sizable cedar chest, she finds not the stuff of the medicine man that was her grandfather, but

> [a] fantastic thing, of texture far more delicate than a spider's filmy web. It was a vision! A picture of an Indian camp, not painted on canvas nor yet written. It was dream stuff, suspending in the thin air, filling the inclosure of the cedar wood container. [. . .] It was all so illusive a breath might have blown it away; yet there it was, real as life,—a circular camp of white cone-shaped tepees, astir with Indian people. (157)

This vision also has a voice, that of the chieftain, a voice she hears proclaim to the people, "Be glad! Rejoice! Look up, and see the new day dawning! Help is near! Hear me, everyone." The words of the chieftain gather in the young woman's heart, and she is filled "with new hope for her people" (158).[8] With the girl's newfound optimism, the legend ends, but its import is meant to transcend the moment of transmission, for surely it works to posit the faith Zitkala-Ša's community has in her. And this certitude from others is as necessary to Zitkala-Ša's chosen path as is her own growing sense of self-assuredness and purpose; such support can only propel her on her way.

The road ahead, however, will not be easy. As the final legend shared with us, "The Widespread Enigma of Blue-Star Woman" indicates, it will be full of pitfalls, not a few of which can be traced to issues of identity—long a puzzle for Zitkala-Sǎ and here revealed as a conundrum shared by others. In this tale, as she fights to procure tribal land for herself, Blue-Star is asked to verify her identity. Such a question—formulated by the new American government—makes her do something she had never thought to do before: question her understanding of who she is. Steeped as it has been in the ancient customary beliefs of her people, her notion of self has always been an unwritten given, based on the natural order of things, an order that presupposes her right to tribal lands. She explains this concept and what it implies in the following manner: "I am a being. I am Blue-Star Woman. A piece of the earth is my birthright." The idea of having to verify who she is via written proof of her lineage is, as it should be, entirely foreign to her, for this is the way of the "white man's law" (159). Still, she questions her sense of self now because her beliefs pertaining to it do not hold water in the face of these newly written dictates.

Blue-Star Woman remembers when determining who one was, to whom one belonged, was not important. She recalls a time when recording one individual's heritage was of far less concern than keeping an unwritten record of occurrences connecting the whole tribe. She recalls the days when so complete was the belief that all were a part of something larger and not entities unto themselves, there was no need for family names.[9] Now she laments, "The times are changed [. . .] My individual name seems to mean nothing" (163). In light of this, she finds little comfort in her own assimilative achievements—drinking coffee, moving from teepee to log hut, reading and writing, her child attending school. She remains, instead, nostalgic for the old ways, so easily understood and so simply put by a past Indian leader to a president: "I am a man. You are another. The Great Spirit is our witness!" (164).

But the old ways of knowing oneself and others have been largely discarded by the next generation. As the Indian youths who visit Blue Star woman to discuss the issue of her identity and her claim to land make clear, identity is, these days, a shifting thing, depending upon what one wants. Unbeknownst to Blue-Star, what these young men want is part of the land she is fighting for, not to help her get hold of it herself, as they claim. Feigning concern for her well-being, they sit down to consume the little food she has, all the while intent on duping her into signing away half of her land and money to them, pawns of the government. In the end, their sweet promise of establishing her identity for her is enough to get her to agree that she would rather have "half of a crust of bread than none at all" (169). And this is what she gets, both literally (what is left of her food supply when the men leave) and figuratively (what is left of her land allotment when the government finally confers her identity as a tribal member).

Blue-Star is not, however, the only one injured by such treachery, for the land she is given, half of which will remain in the hands of the government, becomes a subject of dispute. The tribal chieftain, hearing that his "property was given to a strange woman" argues against the action. Instead of banding together with Blue-Star woman, as he once might have done, and peaceably sharing with her and others like her what is left of the land, the chieftain upholds Blue-Star's outsider status, maintaining, therefore, that the land cannot be made over to her. Such infighting is exactly as the new officials would have it, for it makes it easier for them to get more of what they want—the tribe's land—which is exactly what occurs. Wishing only to present his position, the chieftain is falsely accused of being a "bad Indian, singing war songs and opposing the government all the time," and jailed as a result. In exchange for his father's freedom, the chieftain's son agrees to pay his father's captors half of the tribe's remaining land. Accordingly, all member's of the tribe lose out. And, so, this last legend circles back to resound the call made in the first: hold on to what you know while you learn to negotiate a changing world; do not fail to put stock in the "ancient laws" that bind the people through a shared identity, for without them "a slowly starving race was growing mad, and the pitifully weak sold their lands for a pot of porridge" (174).[10]

Through the presentation of these legends, Zitkala-Šä illustrates the purpose and value of legends within her community and in terms of her own experience. In calling to mind the lessons learned yesterday, the legends have the power to shape the present day. Emerging, as they do, at the point in Zitkala-Šä's life when she feels her sense of self threatened, the legends become her means of seeing herself through the storm of doubt clouding her vision. Although each legend addresses a different aspect of the individual's relationship to her community and culture, as a unit they speak to the necessity of maintaining this relationship, for it provides the individual with a solid frame of reference to be called upon when, as in Zitkala-Šä's own experience, instability darkens the horizon.

Having learned this anew, Zitkala-Šä is finally able to articulate for herself—as she does in closing—the problems she sees now are not only her own, but those of all America's Indians. Still, it is her own lesson regarding the possibility of wholeness via community involvement and cultural engagement that resonates in the end, serving as both a reminder to herself and a bid to others.

William Bevis, in his essay "Native American Novels: Homing In," asserts that contrary to the "leaving plot" so popular in much white American fiction, "in Native American novels, coming home, staying put, contracting, even what we call 'regressing' to a place, a past where one has been before, is not only the primary story but also a primary mode of knowledge and a primary good" (580–81). While the "leaving plot" works Bevis refers to are—save for one—nineteenth century (*Moby-Dick, Portrait of a Lady, Huckleberry Finn, Sister Carrie, The Great Gatsby*), the "homing plot" (and Native American) works he studies in the essay are exclusively contemporary. Hence, perhaps I should not be surprised or disappointed that he briefly mentions Zitkala-Šá, whose work *American Indian Stories* "homes-in" on the very theme he discusses.[11] But I am, for when we compare her work with such contemporary works as Leslie Marmon Silko's *Ceremony*, we see quite clearly a similar message conveyed, a tradition carried over from one century to the next—a message that makes returning home not only essential but also more elaborate and complex than one might imagine.

Ceremony to Self: Healing through Folk Ritual in Leslie Marmon Silko's Ceremony

Looking back once, I saw the mountain and came away.
N. Scott Momaday

By returning home and reconnecting with her Native American heritage, Zitkala-Šá learns to embrace a vision of herself as a whole consisting of many parts. A complicated concept of self to be sure, the quest to discover it, accept it, and ultimately put it to good use has not become easier over time. As Leslie Marmon Silko's novel *Ceremony* illustrates, this search still requires what it did in Zitkala-Šá's day: understanding of and participation in those Native American cultural traditions specifically designed to help individuals define themselves and find purpose in life.[12] And these very things—a sense of self and a reason for living—are what Tayo, the novel's main character, lacks upon his return to his childhood home on the Laguna Pueblo reservation.

Tayo's experiences as a prisoner of war have all but shattered his will, and his knowledge of the stigma attached to his half-breed heritage has nearly destroyed his sense of self. Hence, much like Zitkala-Ša's coming home and in some ways similar to John's return in *The Chaneysville Incident,* Tayo's going back is marred by feelings of helplessness and isolation, manifested in a physical illness that leaves him too weak even to consider his own future. Instead, he attempts to take refuge in the past. But even there he finds himself plagued by the painful. His pleasurable memories of times spent with his Uncle Josiah merge with his horrific memories of the war, his cousin Rocky's untimely death, and his aunt's carelessly veiled disdain for him, and he sinks further into despair:

> He could get no rest as long as the memories were tangled
> with the present, tangled up like colored threads from old
> Grandma's wicker sewing basket when he was a child, and he
> had carried them outside to play and they had spilled out of
> his arms into the summer weeds and rolled away in all direc-
> tions, and then he had hurried to pick them up before Auntie
> found him. He could feel it inside his skull—the tension of
> little threads being pulled and how it was with tangled things,
> things tied together, and as he tried to pull them apart and
> rewind them into their places, they snagged and tangled even
> more. So Tayo had to sweat through those nights when
> thoughts became entangled; he had to sweat to think of some-
> thing that wasn't unraveled or tied in knots to the past—some-
> thing that existed by itself, standing alone like a deer. (6–7)

Tayo's need for a singular image to steady him becomes a hunger bordering on starvation, "a swelling in his belly, a great swollen grief that was pushing into his throat" (9). Accompanied as it is by a listlessness that makes him care little for his own life, this emptiness, like a thing with tentacles, threatens to hold him down in darkness. He remembers that he once believed that "if a person wanted to get to the moon, there was a way; it all depended on whether you knew the direc-tions—exactly which way to go and what to do to get there; it depended on whether you knew the story of how others before you had gone." He remembers that "he had believed in the stories for a long time, until the teachers at Indian School taught him not to believe in that kind of 'nonsense'" (19). And although he now knows that the teachers were wrong, that the stories had the power to hold him on a path, still he does not have the strength to resist "slipping away with the wind, a little more each day" (27). Recognizing his plight, his grand-mother, against the wishes of his aunt, sends for old Ku'oosh, the medicine man.

Tayo's experience with Ku'oosh represents the first step in his healing process, for along with the remedy Ku'oosh brings to restore Tayo's physical health he brings words that suggest the continuity of all existence and stories meant to remind Tayo of his own significance. From these words, from these old stories—like the Scalp Society story that interrupts the text—Tayo learns that "it took only one person to tear away the delicate strand of the web, spilling the rays of sun into the sand, and the fragile world would be injured" (38). This lesson of individual responsibility speaks to Tayo's own survival, but it is too much for him right now. Although Ku'oosh's Indian tea and blue corn-meal give Tayo back his strength, he cannot, just yet, muster the will to put the lesson to use in his own life.

Finding it easy "to stay alive now that he didn't care about being alive any more," Tayo begins using alcohol as a way to oblivion, swallowing "the beer in big mouthfuls like medicine [. . .] medicine for the anger that made [them] hurt, for the pain of the loss, medicine for tight bellies and choked-up throats" (39–40). However, unlike the other young men of the reservation who have just returned from the war, Tayo is unable fully to forget himself in drunkenness, violence, and promiscuity. As suggested to him by his remembrance of the story of Ck'o'yo magic, he understands such behaviors as part of a new but useless ritual, and he sets out to find a more productive and meaningful way back to himself.[13] His journey to wholeness leads him to memories that unlock his present state of mind and a tradition that holds the keys to his future.

Of the many things Tayo remembers, the most important memories have to do with his mother; with Night Swan, his Uncle Josiah's Mexican lover; and with Josiah himself. First, Tayo recalls not only what his mother's abdication of her heritage did to her—made her lost to herself and her people—but how it affected the community as a whole: it filled them with an anger that "could not be contained [. . .] but that it must leak out and soak into the ground under the entire village" (69). Then, he thinks back to what Night Swan had to say about his people, about all people:

> They are afraid, Tayo. They feel something happening around them, and it scares them. Indians or Mexicans or whites—most are afraid of change. They think that if their children have the same color of skin, the same color of eyes, that nothing is changing. [. . .] They are fools. They blame us, the ones who look different. That way they don't have to think about what has happened inside themselves. [. . .]

> You don't have to understand what is happening. But
> remember this day. You will recognize it later. You are a part
> of it now. (99–100)

And, finally, as Night Swan's remembered words open Tayo's eyes to the
changes around him and within him, he recollects something Josiah taught him
years ago about personal responsibility. Through the old story of the Greenbottle Fly, Josiah had moved Tayo to see that all people make mistakes; the
trick is learning something from them.[14]

Combining these remembrances, Tayo realizes that his mistake has
been his giving up on his own life. He tells his family he is ready to join the
living again. He is told, however, that the community elders believe he needs
further help; they want him to seek out old Betonie, the medicine man
Ku'oosh recommended. Tayo reluctantly agrees, fearing there is a more profound reason the elders want him gone: his malady has brought bad luck to
the Laguna pueblo.

What Tayo learns early on in his experience with Betonie is that his
malady is not the cause of his people's problems; it is something shared by his
people, by all people. Thus, contrary to what the white doctors urged him to
believe—"that he had to think only of himself, and not about the others, that
he would never get well as long as he used words like 'we' and 'us'"—he must
view his sickness as "only part of something larger" and find his cure "in something great and inclusive of everything," an ancient tribal tradition, a ceremony
(126).[15] Yet, there is a problem with the way the people conceive of ceremonies
today. Betonie explains:

> They think the ceremonies must be performed exactly as
> they have always been done, maybe because one slip-up or
> mistake and the whole ceremony must be stopped and the
> sand painting destroyed. That much is true. They think that
> if a singer tampers with any part of the ritual, great harm can
> be done, great power unleashed. [. . .] That much can be true
> also. But long ago when people were given these ceremonies,
> the changing began, if only in the aging of the yellow gourd
> rattle or the shrinking of the skin around the eagle's claw, if
> only in the different voices from generation to generation,
> singing the chants. You see, in many ways, the ceremonies
> have always been changing. (126)

With these words, Betonie urges Tayo to understand that inherent in ceremonial traditions is the notion of change and renewal. The traditional
ceremonies—the traditional ways of healing—were meant to change over
time, but the result was to be the same—healing and renewal. Defending his
own ceremonial alterations while also preparing Tayo to accept the task of
shaping of his own, Betonie elaborates:

> At one time, the ceremonies as they had been performed
> were enough for the way the world was then. But after the
> white people came, elements in this world began to shift; and
> it became necessary to create new ceremonies. I have made
> changes in the rituals. The people mistrust this greatly, but
> only this growth keeps the ceremonies strong. [. . .] [T]hings
> which don't shift and grow are dead things. [. . .] Witchery
> works to scare people, to make them fear growth. But it has
> always been necessary, and more than ever now, it is. Other-
> wise we won't make it. We won't survive. That's what the
> witchery is counting on; that we will cling to the ceremonies
> the way they were, and then their power will triumph and the
> people will be no more. (126)[16]

Because Tayo wants to get well, he wants more than anything to believe what
Betonie has told him. He wants to believe that healing can still be found in
ceremonies transformed by time and circumstance. However, just as in
moments of solitude Zitkala-Šǎ's sense of futility often got the best of her,
when left alone with his thoughts, Tayo's anger at the injustices his people
have experienced overrides his confidence in his teacher. Still in the stage of
levying blame for the past, he is as yet unable to accept responsibility for his
own future and the future of his people. Moreover, because he still sees his
half-breed status as cause for his own isolation and despair, he believes he is
incapable of being an instrument of recovery. But Betonie, comfortable with
his half-breed heritage, has another way of looking at the past. Paula Gunn
Allen writes the following in her essay "A Stranger in My Own Life: Alienation
in American Indian Poetry and Prose":

> Betonie accepts his heritage for the strength it gives him and
> looks to basic causes for the situation the whole world is in.
> Betonie is aware that alienation is a common sickness, not

confined to the reservation or its urban extremities, and he identifies "the witchery" as its source. (*Sacred Hoop* 141)

Betonie articulates this other way of thinking, which identifies a problem and seeks a solution, through simple logic and storytelling. And similar to what Zitkala-Šă learned from the legend "A Warrior's Daughter," Tayo comes to find through these two modes of instruction that his own and his people's destruction are not a given; the survival of both lies in his own hands as a tribal individual.[17] It is a matter of either giving up, turning away, or carefully attending to the transformations around and within oneself:

> There are balances and harmonies always shifting, always necessary to maintain. [. . .] It is a matter of transitions, you see; the changing, the becoming must be cared for closely. You would do as much for the seedlings as they become plants in the field. (130)

With Betonie as his exemplar and guide, Tayo chooses to tend to his own transformation. His choice indicated in his willingness to engage in a healing ceremony that will be, as Betonie urged it should be, as much of his ancestors' making as it is of his own.

American Indian ceremonials serve a combination of general and specific purposes. The general purpose of a ceremony has to do with tradition, and the specific purpose of a ceremony—because it depends on the circumstances calling for the ceremony in the first place—has to do with innovation. Because, foremost, Tayo is suffering from a sense of isolation from not only his community but also from all that exists, the general purpose—the traditional parts—of a ceremony must be attended to first. Betonie takes responsibility for the traditional parts of Tayo's ceremony, fulfilling the first of them by taking Tayo to the mountains just beyond the city of Gallup, the best place to reintegrate Tayo with all that surrounds him. As Paula Gunn Allen writes,

> The purpose of a ceremony is to integrate: to fuse the individual with his or her fellows, the community of people with that of the other kingdoms, and this larger communal group with the worlds beyond this one. A raising or expansion of individual consciousness naturally accompanies this process. The person sheds the isolated, individual personality and is restored to conscious harmony with the universe. (*Studies* 10)

That this harmony will occur becomes apparent upon Tayo's arrival in the Chuska Mountains, for within the first moments there, the feelings of futility begin to drop away.[18] There, in a place where

> the world below was distant and small; [. . .] dwarfed by a sky
> so blue and vast the clouds were lost in it. [. . .] He could see
> no sign of what had been set loose upon the earth: the high-
> ways, the towns, even the fences were gone. This was the
> highest point on the earth; he could feel it. It had nothing to
> do with measurements or height. It was a special place. [. . .]
> He felt strong. (139)

And with this newfound vigor, with this growing sense of being in and one with the world, Tayo is ready to begin the traditional next stage of a ceremony: dif-fusing the participant's attention, putting to rest the distractions of ordinary life, and redirecting and integrating emotions into a ceremonial context, "so that the greater awareness can come into full consciousness and functioning. In this way the person becomes literally one with the universe, for he or she loses con-sciousness of mere individuality and shares the consciousness that characterizes most orders of being" (P. Allen, *Studies* 11). To bring Tayo to this almost other-worldly state, Betonie employs many of what Allen tells us are "the composi-tional elements of ceremony" (*Sacred Hoop* 62). Using the "bear cure" on Tayo to bring his life back in order and to give it, once again, "direction, harmony, bal-ance, and happiness" (Harvey 257), Betonie has Tayo engage in ritual move-ments—including a walk through the five sacred hoops that open the way to healing.[19] While Betonie prepares this path and while he also takes Tayo along it, he intones a mythic prayer-story for Tayo, using "repetition and lengthy pas-sages of meaningless syllables," traditional devices meant to have, as Allen puts it, "an entrancing effect" (*Studies* 11).[20] And so they do: Tayo falls into a dream-filled sleep, from which he awakens feeling the way the ceremony would have him feel—as though "there were no boundaries; the world below and the sand paintings inside became the same that night. The mountains from all directions had been gathered there that night" (145). Through Betonie's ceremonial use of myth, Tayo begins to reconnect. Recalling the story-lesson that starts the novel, Betonie's actions, as Elaine Jahner writes in her essay "An Act of Attention: Event Structure in *Ceremony*," make clear to Tayo

> [t]hat learning the transmission process of myth involves learn-
> ing to bring the meaning of all the changes he has experienced

in life to the way he feels the stories. If he can bring the meaning of his actions to the way he feels the stories, then he will be
attentive enough to sense the subtle shifts and movements that
define the way the story takes shape through the people who
allow it to come into their lives. When the story comes into
lives, it sets the important boundaries because it shapes events
that relate past to present, prototype to immediate experience.
Through the ceremonies that Betonie performs for him, Tayo
realizes a little more about how to allow story to shape his experience as event so that both he and the story remain alive.
Through ceremony he begins to learn to feel the gathering of
meaning that occurs in the story.[21] (243–44)

Thus, Tayo rouses also believing he knows what he must do to truly find peace:
retrieve the speckled cattle his Uncle Josiah lost his life trying to save. But as
the specific aim of all ceremonies must go beyond an idea of individual peace to
the concept of community renewal, Tayo's ceremony will entail more than his
simply finding his uncle's lost stock. It will involve a long-term commitment to
ceremonial engagement. Recognizing the shape of Tayo's thoughts, aware that
Tayo was testing the results of the initial ceremony against "[. . .] the old feeling, the sick hollow in his belly formed by the memories of Rocky and Josiah,
and all the years of Auntie's eyes and her teeth set hard on edge," Betonie draws
an image in the sand and tells Tayo the following:

> One night or nine nights won't do it any more, [. . .] the cer-
> emony isn't finished yet. [. . .] Remember these stars, I've
> seen them and I've seen the spotted cattle; I've seen a moun-
> tain and I've seen a woman   [. . .] This has been going on for
> a long long time now. It's up to you. Don't let them stop you.
> Don't let them finish off this world. (152)

With these urgings, Tayo begins the part of the ceremony that will be of his
own making, the part of the ceremony that will bring him to a completeness
capable of embracing others.

Tayo, now alone, is not entirely surefooted. Hence, at the start of the
solitary portion of his ceremonial path, he swerves from it, brushing up against
Leroy and Harley and past behaviors that threaten to engulf him again. But
something about all of it reminds him of how ineffective "drinking and hell
raising" were, as ineffective as his own "sitting at the ranch all afternoon,

watching the yellow cat bite the air for flies; passing the time away, waiting for it to end." There was simply no way any of that could eradicate "all the past, all his life" (168). None of it could help him accomplish his mission. Only he could complete the "transitions that had to be made in order to become whole again, in order to be the people [our] Mother would remember" (170). Remembering *and* embracing this ceremonial tenet, Tayo returns to his ceremony again, watching "the sky every night, looking for the pattern of stars the old man drew on the ground that night" (178).

Finally, in the northern sky of late September, Tayo sees Betonie's configuration of stars, a sighting which coincides with his finding the woman of Betonie's vision. Tayo's time with this woman is brief but necessary, for it unleashes the kind of love that is essential to his journey—a love that is both urgent and tender, a love that furthers the process of Tayo's reunification with the land (mother) and its people (mothers) (P. Allen, *Studies* 127).[22] Filled with this emerging unity, Tayo greets the following morning by repeating the words of a song the people had for the sunrise:

> He repeated the words as he remembered them, not sure if they were the right ones, but feeling they were right, feeling the instant of the dawn was an event which in a single moment gathered all things together—the last stars, the mountaintops, the clouds, and the winds—celebrating this coming. The power of each day spilled over the hills in great silence. Sunrise. (182)[23]

And feeling, as he now does, awash with the new day's natural and simple power, Tayo sets out once more. Here, Tayo's experience is like that of the young woman in Zitkala-Ša's legend "A Dream of Her Grandfather." That is, just as the grandfather's vision-gift gave fresh hope to the young woman's life's work, Tayo's encounter with the woman of Betonie's vision renews his confidence in Betonie's vision, for "suddenly Betonie's vision was a story he could feel happening—from the stars and the woman, the mountain and the cattle would come" (186).[24] Once again he is intent on locating Josiah's cattle, determined that he will drive them home again, sure that "they would follow the plans Josiah had made and raise a new breed of cattle that would live in spite of drought and hard weather" (187).

During Tayo's search for the cattle, his feeling of oneness with the land continues to grow, and he moves further into a tribal sense of being.[25] He realizes that Betonie was right: hunting the cattle was good for forgetting "all the events of the past days and years. [. . .] It was a cure for that, and maybe for other things too." One of those other things was Tayo's strict chronological view of time, which is replaced while he hunts by a more traditional tribal concept of time. That is, he experiences time as timelessness:

> The ticking of the clock behind the curtains had ceased. [. . .] there was no longer any hurry. The ride into the mountain had branched into all directions of time. He knew then why the oldtimers could only speak of yesterday and tomorrow in terms of the present moment: the only certainty; [. . .] this present sense of being [. . .] This night is a single night; and there has never been any other. (192)

It is not surprising that Tayo's understanding of time shifts during his ceremony, for "there is plenty of time in the Indian universe because everything moves in a dynamic equilibrium and the fact of universal movement is taken into account in the ritual life that is tribal existence." Having, now, a more complete sense of himself "as a moving event within a moving universe," Tayo conquers doubt when it threatens him later by connecting with those other "moving events" of the land that will aid in his survival during the hunt, like the mountain lion, "the hunter. Mountain lion, the hunter's helper" (P. Allen, *Sacred Hoop* 147). In doing this, yet another dawning occurs inside him; he comes, at last, to know that his ceremony encompasses more than this moment's search, that "gathering the spotted cattle was only one color of sand falling from the fingertips; the design was still growing, but already long ago it had encircled him" (196).

Following the mountain lion's path, Tayo comes within sight of his uncle's herd, moving, as he hoped they would, "with the dim memory of direction which lured them always south, to the Mexican desert where they were born" (197). While he tails their southeastward movements, he feels a loosening in his muscles and chest, a falling away of the tension brought on by the burden of his self-imposed isolation:

> It wasn't as strong as it had once been. It was changing, unraveling like the yarn of a dark heavy blanket wrapped around a corpse, the dusty rotted strands of darkness unwinding, giving way to the air; its smothering pressure was lifting from the bones of his skull. (198)

This freeing feeling, however right and real, is nonetheless short-lived. For just as it comes to Tayo, fear replaces it: he spots two riders to the north. Knowing "the bill of sale in his shirt pocket would mean very little to armed patrolmen chasing a trespasser," Tayo tries to escape discovery (198). But his mare falls during the flight, taking her rider down with her.

When Tayo comes to, he is greeted by the two patrolmen he had been trying to avoid; his mare and the cattle nowhere in sight. One of the patrolmen wants to take him back to ranch headquarters, while the other seems to want to "forget the whole thing and let the Indian go" (200). As Tayo waits out their decision, he toys with the choices available to him: "He could secure the thresholds with molten pain and remain; or he could let go and flow back. It was up to him" (202). For a time, even after the men decide to abandon their plans for him and follow the tracks of the mountain lion instead, he slips between the cracks of his reserve. He entertains an old and destructive emotion—hatred.

> Not for what they wanted to do with him, but for what they did to the earth with their machines, and to the animals with their packs of dogs and their guns. It happened again and again, and the people had to watch, unable to save or protect any of the things that were so important to them. [. . .] [T]here must be something he could do to still the vague, constant fear unraveling inside him: the earth and the animals might not know; they might not understand that he was not one of them; that he was not one of the destroyers. (203)

What Tayo has to do, as he knows in his heart, requires first an understanding that hatred is not productive and then an action spawned by a loving commitment to the world of which he makes himself a part. What he has to do is complete the hunt; what he has to do is continue on with his ceremony. And so he does. Guided by a hunter he meets along the way, he returns to the woman who taught him of love's healing power. He also finds his mare and, finally, his Uncle Josiah's cattle, for both did what came naturally to them; they came down from the mountain and into the arroyo, into the woman's livestock trap. With the knowledge that these things are safe and secure, Tayo is able to return himself home.

Once the cattle have been retrieved and Tayo is safe at home, except for his Aunt who remains distrustful of "the peace they had in the house now," the larger part of Tayo's family considers his ceremony a success and, therefore, completed. As a matter of fact, his grandma cannot help repeating the comment, "So old Betonie did some good after all" (215). Tayo, however, has another understanding of what others see as his accomplishment. He knows that completeness is a ceremony in continual progress, something that must be attended to always. Thus, he moves from the family home to Josiah's ranch, where his newly found sense of inclusion is always already reflected in the landscape surrounding him. At the ranch, his past dreams of "terror at loss, at something lost forever" are refigured as "nothing lost at all." There he validates what he has learned: that one must develop a nurturing love for the self and for all that surrounds the self, for only this kind of love prevents and transcends loss.[26] What he knows now is that

> all was retained between the sky and the earth and within him-
> self. [. . .] The snow-covered mountain remained, without
> regard to titles of ownership or the white ranchers who
> thought they possessed it. They logged the trees, they killed
> the deer, bear, and mountain lions, they built their fences high;
> but the mountain was far greater than any or all these things.
> The mountain outdistanced their destruction, just as love had
> outdistanced death. The mountain could not be lost to them,
> because it was in their bones; Josiah and Rocky were not far
> away. They were close; they had always been close. And he
> loved them then as he had always loved them, the feeling puls-
> ing over him as strong as it had ever been. They loved him that
> way; he could still feel the love they had for him. The damage
> that had been done had never reached this feeling. This feel-
> ing was their life, vitality locked deep in blood memory, and
> the people were strong, and the fifth world endured, and noth-
> ing was ever lost as long as the love remained. (219–20)

The kind of mother-love given credence to here is the kind of love proffered and received in the relationship Tayo and Ts'eh develop after meeting again in the mountains behind the ranch. But it is not the kind of love most others, as yet, understand. The messages from the Laguna conveyed to Tayo at the ranch indicate this. Robert tells him:

> They want you to come home. They are worried about you.
> They think you might need the doctors again. [. . .] Old man
> Ku'oosh and some of the others are wondering too why you
> haven't come. They thought maybe there might be something
> you should tell them. [. . .] And Emo has been saying things
> about you. He's been talking about how you went crazy and

are alone out here. He talks bullshit about caves and animals.
[. . .] You know how people are about things like that. White
people are that way too. The Army might send someone to
take you back. [. . .] Maybe if you came back for a while. You
know, so they could see that you are all right. So you could talk
to them, and then they could see what a liar Emo is. (228)

Tayo is deeply moved by the knowledge that his behavior elicits suspicion and
doubt at home. Yet it is the visions Ts'eh has of those who will come looking
for him—the army people because Emo called them and the old people
because they cannot agree on who he is—that make it clear to Tayo he must
return to Laguna to share the effects of his ceremony.

Along the way back to Laguna, Tayo runs into Harley and Leroy, and
his encounter with them tests his trust in his newfound view of himself and the
world—a view that has given him strength and purpose. Believing, for a
moment, that for those at home to accept him, for the army people to leave
him alone, he must present himself as one of the group, "just another drunk
Indian, that's all," Tayo joins up with his old friends. But when he realizes that
Leroy and Harley were sent to betray him, he comprehends why, for a second,
"he had lost the feeling Ts'eh had given him, and why he had doubted the ceremony: this was their place, and he was vulnerable" (243). He remembers he
cannot allow fear to paralyze him; he must resolve to propel himself forward.
Leaving his so-called friends behind, Tayo sets out again alone.

As a solitary traveler once more, Tayo comes to an even fuller understanding of his own ceremony. Just as Zitkala-Ša eventually came to a place
where she "could see clearly that all are akin" (104), when Tayo arrives, finally,
at the place where "the pattern of the ceremony was completed," he knows
that the ceremony itself must always already go on. He knows that "the story
was still being told. He was not crazy; he had never been crazy. He had only
seen and heard the world as it always was: no boundaries, only transitions
through all distances and time" (246). Moreover, and again like Zitkala-Ša, he
accepts that it is his job now to teach his people. He must pass on to them what
Betonie taught him: that the new ceremonies were not like the old ones, that
his ceremony was and is theirs as well. It is a necessary healing both old and
new, as American Indian Stories and Ceremony work together to illustrate,
both yesterday and tomorrow: timeless.

CHAPTER 4

What I Learn from You Goes with Me on the Journey

María Cristina Mena's "The Birth of the
God of War" and Roberta Fernández's
Intaglio: A Novel in Six Stories

Grandma's Show and Tell: The Sum and Substance of Story-
telling in María Cristina Mena's "The Birth of the God of
War"

A woman who has no way of expressing herself and of realizing
herself as a human being has nothing else to turn to but the own-
ing of material things.

ENRIQUETA LONGAUEX Y VASQUEZ

My childhood overflowed with times spent listening to my grandfather tell stories of family members or sitting with my grandmother as she flipped through
photos of relatives and close family friends. My adult years follow a similar pattern, although now the stories are often told in the letters my grandparents
write to me, the photos observed via e-mail, or the copies of negatives sent to
me by my stepmother or my aunt. I have learned a great deal from all this folklore activity, namely that it is through these different folklore forms that we—
the members of my family, myself included—put our lives together. Through
the various forms of folklore,

> [w]e order our lives into eras, and organize and dramatize
> incidents within them. [. . .] Many of the episodes in a fam-
> ily's past are exciting and memorable; still, much of their
> magic derives from the forms in which the past is
> expressed—stories, photographs, celebrations. They hold
> secrets—about the past, of course, but also about the way we
> choose to think of ourselves, about the dreams we project
> backwards on our ancestors concerning what we would like
> them to have been, and what we need from them now.
> (Zeitlin, Kotkin, Baker 8)

In other words, we cherish the folklore form as much as we do the content for
a very specific reason—through the form we find ourselves. This idea has been
given significant thematic weight in the works studied thus far. It also lies at the
heart of the Mexican American works focused on in this chapter: "The Birth

of the God of War," by early-twentieth-century short-story writer María Cristina Mena, and *Intaglio*, by contemporary author Roberta Fernández. Thus, just as in the other writings of this study, here, too, we come to see the healing potential and personal growth capacity of working within tradition.

In the introduction to this study, I discussed the fact that folklore is one of the ways people express attitudes, ideologies, concepts of self and others, values, etc. It is also, as the tales told by Uncle Julius in Chesnutt's work indicate, a way people communicate "aspects of culture which are seldom or never stated in other ways." For women, in particular, folklore is often used to "tell us things that social strictures or psychological repression prevent women from otherwise saying—things at variance with the official idea of culture" (Jordan 26–27). Folklore was utilized for this purpose by the members of the Grasse Quilting Circle. And it is put to task for similar reasons by both the author of "The Birth of the God of War" and the characters within the story she presents. Mena and her characters use folklore—specifically the storytelling tradition—to convey an image of women in contrast with the "familiar Hispanic ideal of modest and submissive behavior for women" (26–27).[1] As a result, the tradition is revealed as the vehicle to this more fulfilling way of being.[2]

Because of Mena's choice of titles, one might be fooled into thinking that her central creative concern in this piece is to share with readers the ancient Aztec myth of the god of war.[3] But "The Birth of the God of War" is truly a story within a story. Although the actual myth of Huitzilopochtli (the god of war) takes up a large portion of Mena's text, it still only functions as an example of the many tales the narrator's grandmother shared with her. The real focus of this piece is the narrator's *mamagrande* and the tradition through which she hands down the myth. That this is the case becomes apparent in the first paragraph of Mena's story:

> When I had been attentive and obliging, my grandmother would tell me stories of our pristine ancestors. She had many *cuentos* by heart, which she told in flowery and rhythmic prose that she never varied by a word; and those epic narrations, often repeated, engraved a network of permanent channels in the memory-stuff of one small child. Indeed, the tales of *mamagrande* were so precious to me that I would pray for afternoons of shade, which were the propitious ones, and I almost hated the sun, because when it baked our patio my

grandmother would not occupy her favorite hammock, nor I
my perch near by, on the margin of the blue-tiled fountain.
And I invented a plan by which I could earn a reward. (45)

To be sure, as indicated here, the tales shared with the narrator when she was
a child were of the utmost importance—cherished things, no doubt. But in the
process of recalling the reverence she had for these tales, the narrator
identifies two other things as equally precious, for without them there would
not have been tales to begin with. Those two things were the person doing the
transmitting—the storyteller, the narrator's mamagrande—and the occasion
for transmission—the storytelling session. So beloved were these things that,
as the narrator admits, if the weather did not oblige, she would resort to covert
means to engage her grandmother in story time. She tells us:

> Her cigarettes, which were very special, came from the coast
> once a month, packed in a cane box. Tapering at one end and
> large at the other, in wrappings of corn-husk, they were fas-
> tened together in cone-shaped bundles of twenty-five, and tied
> at apex and base with corn-husk ribbon. Now, I knew that
> *mamagrande* disliked to untie knots (she had often called me to
> unknot the waxed thread of her embroidering), so I would pri-
> vately overhaul her stock of cigarettes, making five very tight
> knots at each end of each cone; and then at the golden hour I
> would watch from behind the flower-pots on the upper gallery
> for her tall figure in spreading black silk, with her fan in her
> hand and her little gold cigarette-pincers hanging at her waist.
> When she appeared, I would wait breathlessly for the business
> of her getting settled in her hammock, and suddenly calling me
> in a sweet, troubled voice to release a cone of cigarettes;
> whereupon I would run down to her and untie those bad little
> knots with such honeyed affability that she would proceed to
> recompense me from her store of Aztec mythology. (45)

Once the child has the teller situated in a story session, one might think the
crux of her work done; all she has to do now is sit back and enjoy a narrative
or two. However, according to the narrator's description of the types of tales
and the ways those tales were shared with her, more than her imagination is
required when her grandmother embarks on storytelling. Her whole attentive

self is necessary, for the relationship between what the narrator's mamagrande is saying and what mamagrande is doing is of essence here.

In telling this story of her grandmother's storytelling, the narrator points out not only the significance of the stories she is told, but also the relevance to her own life of her grandmother's storytelling. That is, she highlights what Richard Bauman calls the "performance event." In his work *Story, Performance, and Event*, Richard Bauman tells us that "narratives are keyed both to the events in which they are told and to the events that they recount, toward narrative events and narrated events" (2). Therefore, he urges us to view oral narrative moments as performances and performance itself

> [. . .] as a mode of communication, a way of speaking, the essence of which resides in the assumption of responsibility to an audience for a display of communicative skill, highlighting the way in which communication is carried out, above and beyond its referential content. From the point of view of the audience, the act of expression on the part of the performer is thus laid open to evaluation for the way it is done, for the relative skill and effectiveness of the performer's display. It is also offered for the enhancement of experience through the present appreciation of the intrinsic qualities of the act of expression itself. Performance thus calls forth special attention to and heightened awareness of both the act of expression and the performer. (3)

The narrator's close attention to processual details—she provides all the steps involved in preparing for and carrying out the event—and her vivid description of her grandmother's behavior during this storytelling moment—she lovingly clarifies how her grandmother looks, sounds, moves as the event unfolds and the story is told—marks it as a portion "of the flow of behavior and experience that constitute meaningful contexts for action, interpretation, and evaluation" within their culture (Bauman 3). Moreover, it illuminates the fact that there are good reasons for her being asked to give text and performance equal measures of her attention. Like Jack of *The Chaneysville Incident*, in telling a story, the grandmother seeks to procure the child's full attention, for she is just as intent on entertaining her granddaughter as she is dedicated to educating her—both in the mythological history of her people and in the art of oral storytelling.

Providing the child with her people's myths is important to the grandmother because as the repository for and transmitter of these stories she knows full well the import of them. She knows this body of material, by its very nature, is intrinsic to the child's growing sense of herself and the world. She knows it is through myths that we "make our experience intelligible to ourselves [. . .] give philosophical meaning to the facts of ordinary life," and determine the value of our experiences. Moreover, we represent ourselves to others through myth, convey our understanding of ourselves in the world, and define our beliefs and attitudes (Schorer 355–56). Hence, the Aztec myth shared with the narrator on the occasion remembered here does more than simply detail the immaculate conception and miraculous birth of Huitzilopochtli, the god of war, "protector-genius of the Aztecs" (Mena 49).[4] Worked into the imaginary elements of this myth is the foundation for the child's own belief system and a lesson in its interpretation and valuation.[5] As the myth enacts the system being put to positive use, the child gains a better understanding of its purpose and an appreciation of its worth in her own life. Still, as indicated earlier, myths are valued for more than just the lessons they contain. They are also valued for the function they serve in the life of the teller—as self-defining mechanisms. Therefore, the grandmother strives to pass on not only the myth's lessons but also the myth's telling. For what better way to the self can she give the child than the one she knows best—the way of storytelling.[6]

According to Ralph Ellison's remembrance of his own search for self-experience, one of the things we search for when we are chasing down an understanding of self is a connection to something, typically a connection to our past and our people.[7] That connection can be made, in part, through the stories told to us by family or community members who know of what they speak.[8] But, as I know from my own experience, that connection truly becomes complete when we learn to tell such stories ourselves. To tell these stories, I have found, is to insert yourself into them, to become a part of the people, places, and experiences your words bring to life. In the end, moreover, as John of *The Chaneysville Incident* discovered, it is to find yourself. Américo Parades, a leading scholar in folklore and Chicano studies, suggests that for minority groups such as Mexican Americans, whose "basic sense of identity is expressed in a language with an 'unofficial status,' different from the one used by the official culture" such immersion in tradition is essential when identity is in question. He insists "that while in Mexico the Mexican may well seek lo mexicano in art, literature and philosophy, or history—as well as folklore—the

Mexican American would do well to seek his identity in folklore," in both the folklore's content and its performance (1).[9] This tenet is underscored throughout Mena's work; it is what the narrator learns from her grandmother's example and the message she ultimately passes on to her own listeners. In Mena's story, the narrator presents her mamagrande as a thoroughly contained individual, and because her mamagrande is portrayed always through her storytelling techniques, a bridge is built linking the achievement of such self-actualization to the tradition in which her mamagrande is engaged.

As the narrator shows us, through storytelling her mamagrande maintained a thorough and gratifying connection to her people's past. As a matter of fact, of the many aspects of the art communicated, the narrator was especially affected by her grandmother's conveyance of what she felt was an almost uncanny intimacy with her subject matter. So good was the grandmother at this that as a child the narrator could not imagine the stories as ancient myths. She felt, instead, as though they were occurrences of a more recent reality:

> It was not mythology to me; no indeed. I knew that *mama-grande* was marvelously old,—almost as old as the world, perhaps,—and although she denied, doubtless from excessive modesty, having enjoyed the personal acquaintance of any gods or heroes, I had the dim feeling that her intimate knowledge of the facts connected with such unusual events as, for instance, the birth of Huitzilopochtli, was in its origin more or less neighborly and reminiscent. (45)

Because of the grandmother's aptitude for intimacy, the child felt a kind of proximity by proxy—a familiarity with the events and characters of the tales shared with her via her mamagrande's ability to convey a connection of her own. Such intimacy is not to be trivialized, for it allows the child to feel a part of something larger, a part of her own heritage. And feeling a part of her heritage makes her also feel responsible for it. This is evidenced in part by the fact that she has remembered the story and is now sharing it with us. But she also shows her commitment to this responsibility in her comments on the best way this should be done—the storyteller's way, the way of her mamagrande.

The first comment she makes regarding this has to do with where and how the story starts. After briefly identifying Huitzilopochtli as a god more honored than "any other deity ever set up by man," she goes on to tell us how to pronounce his name (Weet-zee-lo-potch-tlee) and the name of his mother,

Coatlicue (Kwaht-lee-quay); but then she suddenly breaks in on these introductions, as if catching herself in a mistake. And so she has, for as she admits, her grandmother did not commence in such a way. Her grandmother started at the beginning, "[. . .] in a hushed voice, with a wave of the hand that would make the blue smoke of her cigarette flicker in the air like a line of handwriting" (45). Her grandmother started with an introduction quite different from the narrator's mistaken one, an introduction that urged the child to listen to the world from which the myth springs—the natural world around her[10]—for it, too, has a story to tell:

> The forests have their mysteries, which are sung in their own language by the waters, the breezes, the birds. [. . .] Nature weeps and laughs, sings and cries, and man listens to that weeping and that laughter without knowing the cause. When the branch of the tree inclines itself under the weight of the wind, it speaks, it sings, or it cries. When the water of the forest runs murmuring, it tells a story; and its voice may be accordingly either a whisper or a harsh accent. Listen to the legend of the forest; listen to it as sung by the birds, the breezes, the waters! (47)

Having retraced her steps back to the real start of the story and, in the process, having urged her own listeners to turn an ear to the natural world, the narrator continues on with the tale as it was told to her. However, she breaks in on the story on numerous other occasions to highlight special aspects of her grandmother's storytelling. Of these stylistics, one she points out because she believes herself incapable of replicating it, the others she focuses on simply because they made the stories come to life for her and, in chronicling them, she hopes her rendition will do the same for her own listeners.

In telling a story, the narrator's mamagrande used words to create images that were full and rich, images that resonated in the child's mind long after the story closed. The narrator, however, feels that having to translate the story from Spanish to English makes her incapable of such an accomplishment. Thus, after telling her readers, "Alas! the sonorous imagery of those well-remembered phrases loses much in my attempt to render them in sober English," she merely summarizes the events of the moment and hastens on with the story. But later it appears she finds this modus operandi sorely lacking. For when she runs up against the problem again, she decides it is better to construct certain phrases in both languages because the Spanish version "seems to carry more of the perfume that came with those phrases as I heard them by the blue-tiled fountain" (47).[11] She also, shortly thereafter, strives to make clear that while her grandmother's use of the native tongue had much to do with the story's effects on the child, it was not the language alone that made the events in the story vivid. It was also the special way her mamagrande had of infusing words with meaning and emotion that made the story spring to life in the child's imagination, which is as it should be. Whatever the medium used to communicate experience (in this case, a myth), "its ability to engage the mind and arouse emotions greatly depends upon the sensitivity and artistry of the narrator. A good narrator may engage [an] audience totally, directing or redirecting their thoughts, emotions, and perhaps their future behavior as well" (Oring 122). Apparently, the narrator's grandmother was one *good* narrator, for after repeating the words her mamagrande used to describe a scene of particular import in the tale, the narrator exclaims, "How expressive, in the mouth of mamagrande, was that desperate reconnoiter, and how plainly I could see the beast's yellow gaze 'walking' from object to object" (47). Enthusiastic reflections such as this do more than pay homage to her mamagrande's craft, however. They also help her begin establishing a storytelling method of her own that will both satisfy her personally and help her fulfill her obligations as storyteller.

The storytelling procedure the narrator is developing is directly related to the tale she is telling. And as the tale she is telling is both the same as and decidedly different from the one her mamagrande shared with her, her mode is both in keeping with and markedly distinct from her grandmother's. What is happening here to both the myth and the narration of the myth is in keeping with what Elliot Oring, in his work *Folk Groups and Folklore Genres*, has to say about the nature of folk narrative. He tells us that just as there are many types of folk narratives (the myth being only one), individual tellings of the same narrative differ:

> 1) Folk narratives tend to exist in multiple versions. No single text can claim to be the authoritative or "correct" one. Rather, different narrators perform narratives differently in different circumstances. A folk narrative, in other words, must be re-created with each telling. 2) As a result of this process of re-creation, the folk narrative reflects both the past as well as the present. Narrators must draw upon past language, symbols, events, and forms which they share with their audience for

their narrations to be both comprehensible and meaningful. Yet because each narration is a creation of the moment, it crystallizes around contemporary situations and concerns, reflecting current values and attitudes. A folk narrative is something of a renovation; the past is made to speak in the present. 3) A folk narrative reflects both the individual and the community. The narrator shapes the narratives he re-creates in accordance with his own disposition and circumstances. Yet his creativity is not unlimited. His narrations depend upon a measure of community acceptance. The recreation of a narrative relies upon a negotiation between the narrator and his audience. The narrator's individuality must find outlet in a narrative acceptable to the community if he is to be confirmed in his role as narrator and if he is to be permitted to perform again in the future. (122–23)

The narrator's assertions of her own individuality come through most clearly on those occasions when she takes a bit of poetic license in the sharing of her grandmother's tale. For instance, while relating a battle scene in the story, the narrator decides not to give the particulars of the battle's outcome, opting, as she puts it, "in mercy to the reader" to "leave the end of that ferocious conflict to the imagination" (47). This personalized style is significant on two levels. First, it is the narrator's distinctive way of actively engaging her listeners' minds. More important, however, it is her way of making the story her own, establishing herself as the teller, so to speak, of *this* tale, which is a weighty issue for her. Situating herself as teller helps her mark a clear line of demarcation between the tale her mamagrande told her and the tale she is creating now, pulling our focus to the latter. As I mentioned earlier, unlike her grandmother's tale, the narrator's has more than one story line. It is not only Huitzilopochtli's story, it is the storyteller's, her mamagrande's; it is a tale of tradition. Therefore, rather than simply reciting events in the story verbatim according to her mamagrande's version, the narrator often also includes a description of *how* her grandmother presented particular portions of the tale. One place where she does this is just after the death of Camatzin—the great hunter—and the return of his body to his wife, Coatlicue. Here she breaks in on the story line before proceeding, in order to tell us a bit about her grandmother's craft, highlighting as well those aspects of her cultural heritage she finds pertinent to this tale:

After a moving description of that first night of bereave-
ment—a description in which the mystic voices of nature
sounded their significant notes, my grandmother would pro-
ceed to recite in measured rhetoric the spiritual stages by
which Coatlicue found consolation in religion. For the
Aztecs, apart from and above their hero demigods, to one of
whom this saintly widow was destined to give birth, wor-
shipped an invisible Ruler of the Universe. (48)

The narrator apparently feels her grandmother's attention to detail is an aspect
of the storytelling experience important enough to be shared and highlighted.
So, too, as we also see in this example, is the passing on of those bits of cultural
history the story gives rise to. These aspects of mamagrande's storytelling are
so consequential, in fact, that the narrator again and again describes "how my
grandmother told it" as she relates the tale to us, making increasingly evident
not only the dual story line, but also the idea that there is much to be learned
from mamagrande's example.

As the story draws to a close, we see that the narrator has learned a
great deal. Although she continues to refer to her grandmother's detailing up
until the story's end, she now adds her own as well, elaborating where she sees
fit to do so. Moreover, she creates her own conclusion, closing not when "The
Birth of the God of War" is finished, but when she is done telling the tale of her
mamagrande. Doing so with a confidence in her abilities only glimpsed heretofore, she successfully merges the voices of this piece. A collaboration of sorts
takes place and the resultant story becomes richer as a result, layered, so to
speak, which is what should happen to all well-told stories over time and with the
passage from generation to generation. Voices overlap, new details are added
while others are omitted, and the story metamorphoses to fit the objective of the
present telling. In this case, as we know, the narrator's objective has been
twofold: to share her grandmother's tale and to tell the tale of her mamagrande,
the storyteller. Thus, just as we witness the story's transformation, we witness the
narrator's emergence into her role as storyteller. Moreover, it is a role in which
she truly finds comfort, for it helps her maintain a connection to her mamagrande and to those things that center and define us, as she has learned from her
mamagrande's example: our personal pasts, our community's beliefs, our remote
histories, and what embodies these very things—our valued traditions.

Staying linked to the storytelling tradition permitted María Cristina
Mena to survive as an artist, to affirm the "central role women play in cultural

production," and, ultimately, to posit this time-honored tradition as a mode of self-definition and survival for the Mexican American female community (López 40). Still, storytelling is but one of the many folk traditions available to the Mexican American woman who seeks a way of knowing and expressing herself. As contemporary author Roberta Fernández illustrates in her work *Intaglio: A Novel in Six Stories,* many other cultural traditions are also utilized for this purpose. I close with Fernández because her work points to a number of traditions that facilitate self-definition. And what the narrator is meant to learn, we learn as well: many folk traditions—storytelling, needlework, dance, ceremony, ritual—allow people to interpret and negotiate the world for themselves; furthermore, it is up to the individual to recognize this valued aspect of folk traditions—as the women in the stories teach the narrator—and then choose the tradition that most fully suits her vision and aids her on her journey to wholeness.

Oh, the Many Ways to Find Me: One Search, Many Traditions
in Roberta Fernández's Intaglio: A Novel in Six Stories

Women [. . .] often [. . .] need to return to their past, to the women
who were part of that past, to girlhood when a self existed that was
individual and singular, defined neither by men, nor children, nor
home, almost as though with layers of roles and responsibilities they
have covered over a real person and must now peel back those layers
and reclaim the self that was just emerging in adolescence.
MARY HELEN WASHINGTON

Roberta Fernández's *Intaglio: A Novel in Six Stories* traces the coming of age of a young girl on the Texas-Mexican border. However, just as Mena's work had a dual focus, there is a double center to *Intaglio.* In equal measures, our attention is drawn to the story of a maturing girl and to the stories of the tradition-defined women who inhabit her world. This occurs because as the narrator seeks to distinguish herself, to find her own place in the world, and to choose a suitable mode of self-expression, she turns for guidance to the women who surround her. And her story soon becomes theirs as well. Or, more specifically, her story soon becomes a story of traditions. For each encounter she has reveals to her a woman engaged in a folk tradition that not only serves her cultural community, but also sustains and centers her as an individual.

As the title indicates, *Intaglio* is one piece comprising six parts, sub-titled according to the names of the women in whose company the narrator spent meaningful time. By and large, as the narrator tells each woman's story via her own experience with the woman, she spotlights the particular tradition in which that woman works. However, in the novel's first story, "Andrea," our narrator, Nenita, encounters not one, but *three* family traditions—scrapbook-making, dancing, and storytelling—that buttress each other; through her mother's photo scrapbook of her cousin Andrea's dance career, the narrator is initiated into the ritual of storytelling.[12] Just as these traditions are, to a certain extent, dependent upon each other for vitality, the women are, to a large degree, reliant upon the traditions to link and identify them as family members and to define and support them as individuals.

The kind of tradition-dependent identity negotiations we have here are in keeping with family folklore use in general. In her essay "Family Traditions and Personal Identity," Barbara Allen tells us that while "family traditions are used and/or function to bind individuals to their identity as members of a family," there are actually two kinds of identity "involved in the use of family folklore: that of the individual as a family member and that of the individual as an individual."[13] Moreover, Allen explains:

> Family traditions seem to fall into two categories. The first comprises traditions that emphasize the historical aspect of family life, such as stories, oral genealogies, the use of family names and sayings, and the collection and preservation of photographs, heirlooms, and souvenirs. The second group of family traditions includes customs associated with the cycle of family life, such as reunions, the celebration of holidays and other special occasions, and rituals like nightly group prayers or bedtime storytelling. (1)

Bringing together both historical (the scrapbook and the accompanying stories) and customary family folklore (the storytelling sessions themselves), the women of *Intaglio's* first story establish the two complementary identities mentioned above. Their "conjunctive use of different kinds of family folklore" serves at once to recognize each woman's identity as an individual and to affirm her continuing identity as a mother, daughter, aunt, or cousin (B. Allen 4). The scrapbook, for instance, is the family folklore form Nenita's mother, Clarita, brings to the group. The process of scrapbook-making eased her longing for family members far away; it was a creative act linking lives. Clarita explains to Nenita:

> You can't begin to imagine how much I loved touching all the material that kept coming in. Year after Year. Sometimes when I was down in the dumps, the mailman would surprise me with a thick package. I never knew when it would arrive. [. . .] For hours and hours we'd look at the pictures, imagining what her [Andrea's] life must have been like. (19)

The scrapbook was also Clarita's way of bridging history and destiny: a mode of maintaining a vital connection to the past while also shaping the hopes and dreams of the future. Nenita asserts:

> Mother was right. [. . .] She's always said that for us this album has taken on a life of its own. Because of her incredible patience in putting this book together, it will always be more than just a set of inanimate images, more than a record of Andrea's career. Mother has said it will always be the repository for our own dreams and aspirations, of the past as it was and as we would have liked for it to have been. (30)

The mother's interpretation of the scrapbook points to its dual purpose as a connecting record and a wishing well. But, above all, as Nenita learns years later when the scrapbook is irretrievably lost, the scrapbook was Clarita's method of ordering her world, a means of placing herself permanently in it, her "own special way of expressing herself" (40). Opening the scrapbook to her family is like offering herself. Hence, more so than for the pictures of Andrea it contained, Nenita should remember it for its example.

The lesson contained in the scrapbook is one the other women who make up the narrator's household—her mother's sisters, Julianna and Griselda—know well, for they, too, engage in a tradition that connects lives and defines individuals. Ironically, it is the scrapbook that facilitates the aunts' mode of self-expression: storytelling. This becomes clear when the scrapbook is taken out on the eve of a visit from Andrea and her sister, Consuelo. As the women leaf through the pages of the scrapbook, birth order roles are assumed and each, in turn, accepts responsibility for taking up a story strand. Nenita and her sisters as listeners encourage the story's continuation through questions and interest.

Although Clarita has arranged the scrapbook chronologically, the aunts' story contributions dictate when pages get turned and which ones get attention, shaping the history conveyed. Via the scrapbook, storytelling sessions take place with surprising regularity, teaching Nenita a ritual through which individuals are given voice.[14] The stories themselves identify the women as members of a family, but they also refer Nenita to yet another self-defining tradition: dance.

The stories the women tell about Andrea's dance career only touch on the importance of dance to Andrea's life. The second in line of four generations of dancers, Andrea is the continuation of a family legacy. And yet this is not what Andrea's dancing is most valued for. Its marketability matters more. Her talent is viewed as a way out of the workaday world and into the romantic life of stage and stardom. Through the scrapbook images and the stories they produce, Andrea becomes a larger-than-life star, her dance taking a backseat to the extravagant character smiling for the camera. Hence, when Nenita finally meets Andrea, she finds the person in real life pales in comparison to the woman of her imagination. As Nenita tells us, "[. . .] I felt uneasy facing the stranger in the clean-cut white dress. Andrea's smile did not exude the least bit of the flamboyance I had learned to associate with the figure of the picture book" (24). But when the scrapbook is brought out and Andrea is urged to peruse it, to explain why she "gave up the theater," the difference between the pictures and the person is explained. The pictures mean very little to Andrea, as she tells Nenita: "I'm really quite unattached to them. I suppose that's why I sent them to your mother" (29). For Andrea, what mattered at the time the photos were taken—the dance—is what the photos do not communicate. All the photos convey is the beauty of the dancer and the dance costume, not the purpose of dance to Andrea's life. When Nenita runs from the room and returns decked out in her own dance ensemble, hoping for Andrea's approval, Andrea moves Nenita's focus away from the performer and onto the performance: the purpose of the dance.

> It's not what you wear that's important. What counts is not
> the costume but the dance. It's in the movement of your
> arms, the control of your torso, the limberness of your legs.
> That's what really counts. Just like in life. It's also very impor-
> tant to adapt to your surroundings. *Por desgracia* your outfit
> comes undone. What do you do then? Your castanets are
> stolen right before you go on stage? You must adapt to the sit-
> uation on the spot. That's what makes the difference, not

your appearance. *Tú sabes, el hábita no hace al monje.*
Clothes don't make the person. (29)

Here Andrea defines life in terms of dance. Dance, as she explains it, is not a
way to make a living, but a way to live.[15] Nenita learns that like her mother's
scrapbook and her aunts' storytelling sessions, Andrea's dancing served a dual
purpose. While carrying on the family dance legacy, she was able to reaffirm
her continuing identity as a member of the family. And the dancing itself provided her with a centering practice, a way of negotiating her world, and a
means of fashioning herself as an individual.

The initial chapter's blending of traditions makes the point early on
that there are a number of traditions that facilitate a sense of self, but it also
suggests the significance of the individual's relationship to the tradition: a suggestion the following chapters, with their "one woman, one tradition" themes,
elucidate more fully.

In the next chapter, "Amanda," as Nenita describes her fascination
with this woman and her art, the idea of creative expression as a means
through which individuals define themselves is furthered explored. To begin,
we see how Amanda's needlework, like the traditions of *Intaglio's* first chapter, centers and defines. As Virginie witnessed of Mary in *The Minister's Wooing*, with needle and thread Amanda enters an austere world of
self-containment, "reassuringly permanent in the uniform she had created for
herself" (48–49). Working on many outfits at once, rather than on one start to
finish, allows her to suit the tradition to her disposition—expressing the many
parts of herself at one and the same time. Thus, her art becomes her and she
becomes her art, reflected again and again in the "dresses everywhere, hanging from the edge of the doors, on a wall-to-wall bar suspended near the ceiling and on three or four tables where they would be carefully laid out" (49).
In much the same way the tradition serves the women of both Stowe's and
Otto's works, needlework provides Amanda with more than just an outlet for
herself; it supplies her with a vehicle through which the transformation of herself and others becomes possible. Hence, the word that begins the chapter,
defining the art and Nenita's particular experience with it, is *transformation.*
Of Amanda, Nenita tells us:

> Transformation was definitely her specialty, and out of geor-
> gettes, piques, peaux de soie, organzas, shantungs and laces

she made exquisite gowns adorned with delicate opaline
beadwork which she carefully touched up with the thinnest
slivers of iridescent cording that one could find. (47)[16]

A combination of three Mexican (and traditionally female) folk crafts—
garment creation, embroidery, and beadwork—Amanda's handiwork draws
customers far and wide, from every rung on the economic ladder. Taking the
simplest pattern from a magazine or the most difficult design from fantasy,
Amanda enters into the arrangement, re-envisioning herself as she re-creates
her customer's own self-image.[17]

The transformations Nenita witnesses at Amanda's hands only add
validity to the rumors Nenita hears of Amanda's "dabbling in herbs." And the
possibility that Amanda is an *hechicera,* or enchantress, draws Nenita more to
her until, finally, she begs Amanda to aid her in her own transformation.
Amanda makes Nenita the special outfit she imagined for herself—a hooded
black cape, elaborately decorated with incandescent raven-colored chicken
feathers, cats' paws, and sparrows' bones—and Nenita revels in the uniqueness of it, and the feeling of freedom her vision melded with Amanda's talents
of transformation provides:

> For a long time I sat on a lawn chair, rocking myself against
> its back, all the while gazing at the moon and the familiar sur-
> roundings which glowed so luminously within the vast uni-
> verse while out there in the darkness, the constant chirping
> of the crickets and the cicadas reiterated the reassuring per-
> manence of everything around me. (55)

Unfortunately, the sinister outfit is rejected by her family, and Nenita is forced
to put it away before she has a chance to understand its significance, just as
time and growth force her to "put away" her fascination with Amanda and her
tradition before she has a chance to comprehend their relationship.

Years later, however, when Nenita comes upon the packed cape while
scavenging through old boxes to relieve boredom, she realizes why her mother
had not burned it as she had promised; the cape was Amanda's "expression of
genuine love." And so she explains:

> [. . .] I placed the little cape among my collection of a few but
> very special possessions which accompanied me everywhere I

went. I even had a stuffed dummy made, upon which I would
arrange the cape in a central spot in every home I made. Over
the years, the still-crisp little cape ripened in meaning, for I
could not imagine anyone ever again taking the time to create
anything as personal for me as Amanda had done when our
worlds had coincided for a brief and joy- ous period in those
splendid days of luscious white gardenias. (56, 57)

Here Nenita alludes to what she will come to grasp completely when the cape,
like the scrapbook before it, is lost for good: the necessary ingredient that
made not only the cape but also the sum of Amanda's work so special—"the
enchantment which her hands gave to everything they touched [. . .]"—the
expression of self, a gift unlike any other (58).

Such a gift comes in as many forms as there are individuals, as Nenita
illustrates in the next chapter, "Filomena." For where Amanda's gift of self is
embodied in fabric, Filomena's is embodied in ritual. Filomena is a less
flamboyant character than the women introduced thus far, and yet it is just this
which attracts Nenita. As Nenita explains, "No doubt it was this simplicity of
manner that gave her a certain agelessness and enigmatic wisdom. [. . .] Filomena moved in slow steady paces [. . .] deeply rooted and steadfast" (64). Filomena's stoicism works on Nenita like a magnet, and Nenita learns from Filomena
the rituals that make a peaceful spirit possible in the face of pain and loss.

Filomena and Nenita come together after the loss of Filomena's husband, Martín. After his death, as Filomena's meager finances force her to send
her oldest son, Alejandro, away to school and her younger two children to live
with relatives in Michoacán, she is compelled to channel her "quiescent mater-
nal feelings" elsewhere, and Nenita becomes the recipient. During this time,
Filomena introduces Nenita to her own brand of spirituality, which includes honoring a pantheon of saints and participating in a variety of folk-religious rituals
and festivals.[18]

When Alejandro, who had become over the years like a big brother to
Nenita, graduates from high school, he returns home to help support his
mother and his siblings, who refuse to return from "the land of their ancestors." During his stay, he presents Filomena with two gifts: three white
wrought-iron birdcages, which he fills with a variety of birds, and one single
cage containing a parrot named Kika. Alejandro presents these gifts so that
Filomena "would never again be alone during his absence" (67). Joining voices
each morning, the birds fill the house with sounds and life. And, as Alejandro

hoped, it is these creatures who keep Filomena company after Alejandro is sent off to war, never to return alive.

When the family learns of Alejandro's death, Nenita goes into deep mourning, a grief filled with denial and bitterness. She agrees with the neighbors who "shook their heads and said that fairness had betrayed herself when she had dealt with Filomena" (70). Hence, she is surprised to see at the funeral that, unlike the other mourners, Filomena responds to Alejandro's death

> [. . .] with equanimity, for she only cried a little, both before and after the funeral, and then during the sounding of the taps. After that, she retired to her little room where once again she sat in front of her altar for long hours, praying for the souls of the three men in her family whose lives had been prematurely snuffed out in distant wars. (70)

During Filomena's mourning period, which lasts a month, Nenita learns from the other women in her family the source of Filomena's strength: the engagement in spiritual rituals largely of her own making that support her belief in the life of the dead, her resolve to keep the memories of the dead alive, and her unfaltering hope that she will meet them again. Nenita realizes she can learn from Filomena, and, when her mother allows her, she returns to her old habit "of spending late afternoons" with Filomena.

On her first return, she finds Filomena's *altarcito* (an altar she creates in her own home to honor her father, her husband, and her son) much changed, reassembled and expanded. The biggest difference, however, is the addition of the birds, whose cages now hang above the altar, "seemingly to include the birds' warbles and the parrot's noisy voice as a part of her offering" (71). This addition so moves Nenita that she makes her own offering and then joins Filomena daily in prayer, "while the birds chirped softly" above them. Her inclusion and involvement in Filomena's ritual makes her own prayers like Filomena's: "no longer murmurs of petition; instead, they had become statements of resolution: 'Thy will be done on earth as it is in heaven'" (71).

Like the altarcitos of real-life Mexican American women, Filomena's altarcito creation and use represents "[. . .] a personal, private, and most importantly, a creative source of religious experience" (Turner 309). And while this tradition is Filomena's way of expressing herself and managing her innermost emotions, it is also a means to a deeper relationship between Filomena and Nenita. This relationship, like those Nenita shares with the

other women mentioned thus far, is suffused with lessons about her community's cultural traditions and the self-sustaining work they provide.[19] We see
that this is the case soon after Nenita's involvement in Filomena's daily rituals
begins. For Filomena invites Nenita to go with her to her ancestral home,
Michoacán, to "participate in the traditional Tarascan rituals of the Day of the
Dead," as well the "observances on the island of Janitzio," traditions from
which Filomena feels Nenita could benefit.[20]

The rituals Filomena's family engage in are intricate and elaborate,
and through her participation Nenita comes to a better understanding of the
value of ritual. Through these folk-religious practices she learns life is sustained in death, the past remains alive in the present, and bonds are made that
will hold people together regardless of time and distance. Moreover, while
absorbed in these traditions she experiences a kind of inner calm, a centering
peace. She proclaims, "My parents were right; I was definitely undergoing a
spiritual cleansing" (74). And to affirm and further articulate this aspect of
Nenita's encounter with tradition, Filomena declares: "Here we all find what
we are looking for" (76). At the time, Nenita understands Filomena's "here" to
mean in Janitzio. But when she finds she is able to recapture the essence of the
ceremonies at home by opening "up to the gift of faith as she had done in Janitzio," she sees that Filomena meant "here" in your traditions (77).

Ten years later, life begins to test Nenita's faith in this lesson:

> I had been feeling very uncomfortable in one of my first
> graduate classes at the university. A middle-aged professor-
> poet [. . .] taught his literature class with a degree of cynicism
> that made me uncomfortable. His total rejection of spiritual
> epiphanies bothered other members of the class as well, and
> so we had started to meet on our own to comment more
> freely on some of the writers we were reading. Even with our
> more open discussions in the small group, I still felt I was los-
> ing my old sense of identity. At times I even felt that many
> new images were being imprinted on me and that I had not
> even had the chance to approve or reject what was happen-
> ing. [. . .] The contrast between the past and the present was
> so immense that I began to question whether things had
> really been the way I was remembering them. I knew then
> that I needed to go home. (81–82)

Unfortunately, her visit home is clouded by Kika's death. This time Filomena's peaceful acceptance of loss infuriates Nenita, and she leaves with a greater sense of sadness and confusion than she felt when she embarked on her return.

Back at school, her conflicting emotions lead her to reject what she had learned from Filomena about personal ritual and inner peace, and turn instead "to the ideas of writers I admired for asking the right questions about being and about giving meaning to one's life through action: Sartre, Camus, Sabato, Beckett." She remains unable to find meaning and purpose in her own life, however, until she reads Flaubert's *Trois contes*.

This story about "the faith of a simplehearted maid" reminds her of Filomena, and thus she moves away from abstract thinking and toward an involvement with "tangible and communal action."

> I found a real sense of authenticity through new contacts in many different projects but it was in the community arts that I found my most meaningful outlet. For a long time I participated in colorful exhibits in the parks, poetry readings in community centers, sales of folk crafts, coordination of children's folkloric dances. I felt that these activities connected me back to the stimulating creativity of the people who had served as my mentors as I was growing up, at the same time that they satisfied my new needs to move away from an alienating individualism towards a public collectivism much more in keeping with the experiences of my youth. (84)

The women of her extended family provided her with examples of self-fulfillment through tradition engagement. Here she attempts to apply their examples to her own life in order to reconcile the parts of herself residing in different places—one still at home, one out in the world. Her success in this venture is short-lived, however. For where each of her female relatives fully immerses herself in one tradition, Nenita merely dabbles in many. Moreover, she is among people who take on their crafts mainly for their product's monetary value. This becomes especially clear to her when she runs across a young woman selling earrings fashioned to resemble the "folk altars that many contemporary artists were assembling and exhibiting in galleries and museums" (84). About the earrings, Nenita tells the woman, "I find them to be very insensitive to the spiritual beliefs of the people in the *pueblos*. I have a dear friend who would probably feel pretty sad at seeing you make light of her deeply felt respect for religious icons. It's terribly personal with her." Nenita's comments address the issue that so disturbs her: culture without context, pop art out of serious tradition. The artist, however, argues that because she never had any direct contact with the traditional religious sentiments Nenita speaks of, the earrings are her way "of showing respect," her way of "giving tribute to that experience." At this, Nenita, to her own surprise, buys a pair of the earrings. Later, as she conjectures over what Filomena would think, she feels ashamed of her purchase, concluding that "only someone from this centerless city could have come up with these gaudy creations" (85).

This meeting ends Nenita's experience with tradition in the city and marks a new time of crisis. That night, she wonders how she can draw strength from the altars of her childhood when those experiences seem so far out of reach, separated by both time and distance. And then Filomena's lesson comes back to her. She must make an altar of her own, and for herself. Nenita realizes, just as Tayo of Silko's *Ceremony* came to learn during his own search, that simply because the place of the tradition is left behind does not mean the tradition itself must be. Therefore, placing a drawing of Kika (whose death began her initial crisis with her own spirituality and the traditions upholding it) into a glass jar, she decides the earrings will serve a purpose after all, and she puts them in the jar as well. Then, she goes in search of a place for her altar, finding it among the eucalyptus trees growing in a grove just beyond the city limits. As she buries the jar, she hears the familiar whisper of voices chanting: "*¡Flores para los muertos! ¡Flores para los muertos!*" (86).[21] Having created and completed her own version of Filomena's ritual, and with the voices from home sounding behind her, she is able to return to the city, the pieces of herself coming together again.

What Filomena teaches Nenita about self-fulfillment through folk-religious ritual is joined by what Nenita learns about the *sabio* traditions from Leonor, the woman of the novel's fourth story. Although these two women seem to engage in completely disconnected brands of spirituality, there is, as Nenita comes to find in her experience with Leonor, one binding element—the personal centering and self-definition they provide.

As Nenita entered adolescence, she would spend part of each summer with her best friend, Aura, and Aura's grandmother, Leonor—Amanda's sister. Nenita explains that she claimed Leonor as her surrogate grandmother, drawn by her outgoing personality as well as by her "streak of the meditative and the ethereal" (95). Leonor puts her faith in her knowledge of the cards, a tradition she inherited from her grandfather. The strength of her faith supports her, she tells Aura and Nenita, and is directly related to the significance of her having been chosen as the one to carry on the tradition:

> My cards have served me well ever since Papá Antonio gave them to me all wrapped up in a purple silk cloth when I was thirteen. At that time, Amanda and I were the only ones left at home. Mamá Chela showed her how to read tea leaves and Papá Antonio passed on his knowledge of the cards to me. I've respected their advice ever since then. [. . .] It was the tradition to pass on the knowledge to only one child in each generation. Papá Antonio's mother taught him when he too was thirteen, way back around 1840. He chose Tía Concha, his fifth child, to carry on the knowledge but she died in 1913. She was fifty-six and for some reason which I never understood she had not passed the knowledge on to any of her children. At that time Papá Antonio was already very old but he picked me as the one who would carry on the tradition. Over and over we went through the interpretations until he was convinced I understood the wisdom they reflected. Then, a year later he died. It was 1915 and he was eighty-seven. (96–97)

The tradition, according to Leonor, is no small gift and Nenita is mesmerized by Leonor's steadfast commitment to it and her solid convictions regarding its value in her own life. Thus, one night Nenita and Aura willingly forego a party in order to be a part of Leonor's soothsayer rituals.

Together the girls prepare themselves for their meeting with Leonor. Like Filomena's preparations for the ceremony honoring the dead, this night's preparations involve following a sequence of actions in strict order. Nenita points out:

> Aura and I had strict orders to rest in our room. Leonor could not have been more emphatic about the exact sequence we follow in preparation for our meeting with her. [. . .] [W]e washed our hair with the chamomile rinses Leonor had prepared for us, then sat on the porch next to our room letting the hot evening breeze dry it slowly. Later we brushed, then braided each other's hair into a single thick braid. By then our stomachs were begging for nourishment but Leonor had insisted on our fasting all evening.

> Soon we heard the bells of the church sounding nine
> o'clock. Right away we put on our long white slips, then the
> white nylon dresses with gold trim at the neckline and wrist-
> bands. [. . .] Finally, just before we left the room, we
> arranged a garland of gardenias on each other's head. (99)

These ritualized actions are just the beginning of an encounter with tradition
that, the girls are told, will be far more profound than their first communion.
And it is, for on this, the night of the summer solstice, Leonor guides the girls
through the journey of their lives.

Although the predictions Leonor makes that night do eventually come
to pass, it is what Nenita learns from Leonor about individuals and tradition
that truly matters in the end. During the ritual of the future, Nenita learns that
traditions center individuals by calling attention to detail. The ways of this tradition, like the ways of Andrea's dance, for instance, are the ways of living.
That is, as Leonor tells her, you must "think carefully about the questions you
want to have answered, without the proper question you cannot arrive at the
answer you need. Wording the questions is your most important challenge."
Nenita's experience with Leonor calls to mind the essence of her experiences
with the women of the preceding chapters, especially those with Amanda and
Filomena. For here, too, working in tradition is identified as a means of self-
expression, fulfillment, and transformation. Reinforced as well is the idea that,
like the individuals who engage in them, traditions require their own transformations. As Leonor tells Nenita at the end of the solstice ceremony, "transformations constantly regenerate our life. Remember that nothing is ever truly
lost. Whatever disappears or dies simply becomes transformed into something
new. With this guidance you can make your way on your journey" (101–2).

In calling to mind the lessons of the previous stories, *Leonor* reminds
us that each story of the novel is meant to circle back to the others—by elaborating in some way the lesson learned therein. Nowhere, however, does this
become more clear than in the story that follows Leonor's, the story of Esmeralda. For surely, this woman's story highlights one of the things the combination of stories is meant to reveal: a female community existing within the larger
community of men and women. Moreover, and like the female communities of
Stowe's and Otto's texts, this is a community engaged in traditions, many of
which the women have developed for their sole use and benefit.

In order to emphasize the existence of and very real necessity for a
female community and culture, the story of Esmeralda, whose real name is

Verónica, forefronts a number of gender issues. To begin, it illustrates that beauty is a double-sided magnet—it attracts both wanted and unwanted attention. For women in particular this is a frightening conundrum; for although beauty opens doors, danger to women's lives lurks behind many. This is Vernonica's experience. Her beauty lands her the job she so desperately needs—a ticket taker at the local theater—but it also invites the type of flattery and attention that results in objectification, as Nenita explains: a flattery "more self-indulgent than well intentioned towards the silent, bewildered young woman inside the glass enclosure" (113). From this display case, Verónica gains the attention of Santiago Flores, a local customs newspaper reporter. In his chronicle, Flores dubs Verónica "Esmeralda," claiming "no name becomes her more." Although the name itself may be beautiful, the effect of Flores's commentary is not. His remarks eroticize Verónica, making her less a person than an object on display—so much so, in fact, that as Nenita recalls, "no one seemed to care who she really might be. She had become a public figure of sorts, sitting for hours each day inside her rounded glass house. The crowds [. . .] presumed she would be flattered by the exoticism they projected on her" (113).

The danger inherent in such attention is well known by the women of this extended family, who ask Nenita to accompany Verónica home at the end of her shift each day. Yet it is missed by the male relations, whose social counterparts are the very perpetrators of such danger. Instead, the men of the family insist that Verónica enjoys the attention, ignoring her pleas of humiliation. Moreover, when she reveals her fear of physical harm, they insist the attention is innocuous. Returning home one day after fending off the attentions of two boys, Verónica is told by her cousin, Orión, to "[. . .] loosen up a bit. They just thought you were pretty and wanted to catch your eye. It was their way of complimenting you" (116). Unfortunately, Orión's interpretation of the boys' behavior could not be further from the truth. The next day, regardless of Nenita's attempts to help her, Verónica is kidnapped by the boys and viciously raped. When she is returned to her home, she is beaten and bewildered. Her spirit is completely broken, for this is not the first time Verónica has encountered the danger of being female in a world dominated and interpreted by men.[22]

Prior to Verónica's coming to live with Leonor, she had lived with her mother's cousins: Iris and Alfredo. While there she experienced her first love. And yet, because of the sexual double standard applied to men and women, she was unable to act publicly on her feelings. Hence, she arranged a secret meeting with her lover, a meeting prematurely aborted by Alfredo's secret witness.

Upon finding out about Verónica's as yet still innocent affair with one of his workers, Alfredo stamped her a whore and insisted upon her removal from his household before he claimed her body himself. Verónica, shamed and exposed "for no reason at all," was then sent from house to house until she finally came to stay with Leonor, where she experienced a humiliation far worse (121). The combination of the two leave her bereft of the will to live. That is, until the community of women of which she is now a part comes to her rescue through folk traditions that in joining women together return her to herself.

In this part of Verónica's story, Nenita watches as the women of her extended family collaborate in order to save the life of another. At first, their joined traditions are strictly medicinal, meant to mend the body, to give it strength enough to support the healing of the spirit.

> [E]veryone took care of Verónica. Leonor meandered through her herbal patch, carefully selecting sprigs of different properties to prepare into teas and ointments. Blending either *yerba del oso* or *maravilla* with baby oil, she'd pass the ointment on to Isela who would rub it for hours into her daughter's skin, inducing her to sleep profoundly for long stretches of time. After Verónica woke up, Cristina would soak her in hot minted baths, mixed with either *romerillo* or *pegapega*. Amanda insisted on stating that "Verónica had experienced a great fright." To alleviate her from its effects, she ran palm leaves up and down Verónica's entire body, then burned creosote in clay urns next to her bed. (124)

When the folk healers begin to see the successful results of their ministrations, evidenced in the return of Verónica's physical health, they begin the healing of her soul.[23] Making her "concentrate on the moment," they force her to tell the story of her rape over and over, crying with her, until she has virtually cried out the source of her own sorrow. Then, they conduct a "wailing session," a time when the women cry "together for the sorrows of all the women in the family" (125). A folk custom to be sure, a wailing session consists of each woman's taking a turn revealing her deepest pain. Because the experience each woman conveys is an experience the other women can relate to—the inability to help a loved one, abuse from men, secret loves and lost loves, the ravages of war— no woman cries alone. But the session is meant for cleansing not for wallowing, as Verónica's experience with this wailing session proves. After listening to the others' stories, she once again tells her own, speaking "in the name of all the women and girls who had experienced sexual violation" on the same day she had. She insists, however, that for herself the wailing stop, proclaiming, "I do not want to become a victim." This is the resolution the wailing session was meant to bring about. As Leonor tells her, "In the end, that is how we hoped you would feel" (127).

Following the wailing session comes the sharing of great joys, "sheer happiness," as Mamá Cristina explains, "even *picardía*," open sexual expression. This is a treat for the women, a time and a place where they can freely express their enjoyment of their own sexuality. Moreover, this storytelling session illustrates how women's folklore "tells us things that social strictures or psychological repression prevent women from otherwise saying—things at variance with the official ideal of the culture." For the older women of the family, the combination of traditions works as a vehicle for teaching "aspects of a culture which are seldom or never stated in other ways" (Jordon 27). And where Nenita and Verónica are concerned, the traditions become a part of their own survival mechanisms, their knowledge of them making them members of a community of women in which the whole female self is the center of attention.

Through Verónica's experience, Nenita learns a new way to negotiate the world. Thus, "Esmeralda," like the other chapters, is a story that teaches Nenita a lesson about folk traditions: there are those designed to facilitate whole survival. And yet, it is her own retelling of her encounters with tradition that emphasizes their restorative aspects and keeps them alive in her heart. Hence, it should not surprise us that the storytelling tradition is, once again, the focus when we arrive at the novel's final chapter, "Zulema."

Zulema's entire life is shaped by storytelling. First, it is the story she is told the morning after her mother dies in childbirth. To save Zulema and her brothers from heartache, the family tells them that their mother has gone away to take care of her sick sister, Carmen, and that she will return when the war has ended. Although the truth is meant to be told eventually, as the years pass, reality and fiction become virtually indecipherable, and the adults decide "it would be much more difficult to adjust to a new reality than to live with the pattern that had been set" (150). Nevertheless, during these years Zulema, in order to deal with her mother's absence and to quiet her own belief that her mother will never return, begins to tell her own stories. Her stories are Sleeping Beauty–type tales minus the happy ending. In these stories, the revolutionaries strip the prince of his crown and make it impossible for him to find

Sleeping Beauty, who remains forever lost in the woods. Zulema tries to share her stories with her brothers and then her father, but they did "not like her plots because they considered her endings to be strange, even morbid at times" (143). No one truly understands that her stories are her way of dealing with reality; hence, she is fated to keep them to herself for years.

When Zulema finds out the truth about her mother's death, she withdraws into herself completely, skipping school and spending hours in silent meditation. But when her truancy is brought to the family's attention, the women of the family (as we saw them do for Verónica) come together to help her. They begin by teaching her a variety of traditionally female folk crafts that keep her hands busy while her heart mends. Mariana, her aunt, teaches her the "secrets that went into cooking traditional dishes"; Doña Julia, a close neighbor, considered part of the family, teaches her to crochet; and the other women entreat her to join their quilting group (145–46). These folk crafts keep her occupied through her period of mourning and help her come to grips with her mixed emotions over her mother's death and the family's secreting it from her.[24]

Shortly after this period of recuperation through tradition instruction and involvement, Zulema marries and begins a family of her own. As the years accumulate, she attempts to interest her own children in her stories, but "all four thought the stories were silly and repetitive." Again, she is forced to keep her stories to herself. That is, until she finds an audience in Nenita, the only one "making requests for recitations about her extravagant characters," the only one who let "her tell the stories the way she wanted" (143). And with Nenita as audience, the stories pour forth, for as Zulema tells Nenita, "Telling stories. That's what I've enjoyed the most" (146).

When Zulema dies, Nenita holds her own private ceremony for her, putting to use what she learned from Filomena about personal ritual and healing. Then, employing Amanda's example, Nenita sews her inner emotions into the silk lining of Zulema's coffin. Stitching it with tiny *milagros* and shiny red ribbons, and making Zulema a halo of sorts out of marigold bouquets, Nenita transforms the coffin into a work of art. Finally, paying tribute to the woman whose very life epitomized the whole of Nenita's lesson on storytelling, a lesson that began in the novel's first chapter, Nenita places three blank records beside Zulema, telling her, "*Llénalos con tus cuentos favoritos.* [. . .] Fill them with your favorite stories" (153). In addition, when she leaves the church, she goes home to begin the task of telling her own, filling in the pages of the journal her aunts Mariana and Zulema gave her the previous year.

Two days later, Nenita shares her journal of stories with her sister, Patricia, who tells her, "I'm not sure what you are trying to do, but what you have here is not at all what really happened" (154). Patricia weighs the value of the stories by their accuracy, but Nenita knows now where their true value lies. Their value does not reside in their proximity to the actual, but in their ability to help individuals interpret that reality. Thus, she tells her sister, "You know, each of us tells it as we see it" (154). Like her mother's memory book, Nenita's own journal is a combination of past and present, a place where what she has learned is not only remembered, but also becomes part of what she reaches out to in her own future. This is what Nenita's aunts intended, for they inscribed the journal with the words, "Make this a memory book of your very own dreams and aspirations" (148). Moreover, this is what she has been taught by all the women inhabiting her stories. Grounded in their respective folkways, these women illustrate for Nenita, as the mamagrande did for the narrator in Mena's story, that tradition brings you back, tradition takes you forward—alive, well, whole.

Conclusion

What's This Got to Do with Me?

*Folklore and the Search for Self: A Door to the World in the
Literature Classroom*

No journey carries one far unless, as it extends into the world
around us, it goes an equal distance into the world within.

LILLIAN SMITH

It is almost summer and, once again, I have been asked to teach the Contemporary American Novel course at the community college down the road. I have, of
course, agreed to do so, eagerly anticipating how different it will be this time
around—different and yet the same. It will be the same because, like the pro-
fessor whose course I took over a few years ago, I, too, want to focus my students
on contemporary literature's portrayal of the "search for self." It will be different
because this year I have the freedom to choose the readings for the course. And
a change in what we read will ultimately mean a change in what we find. That
may seem elementary. However, if the texts I choose reveal a different understanding of the "search for self"—one that makes a connection between cultural
heritage and that search, as the texts of this study do—then that change is of the
utmost importance. It offers my students a broader learning experience.

A study of the "search for self" theme in contemporary literature begs
at least a brief discussion of how the search has been presented in American
literature over time, giving teachers of contemporary literature the opportunity to put students in touch with earlier works. It offers a chance to illustrate
what I have attempted to prove here: that contemporary authors are not so
much creating a "new" message as they are carrying on a legacy. When we look,
for instance, at Whitney Otto's work in light of Harriet Beecher Stowe's, we see
there is, indeed, an American literary tradition that makes the achievement of
self a matter of community and culture rather than of isolation and industrial-
ization. Moreover, we have evidence that what was written long ago still applies
today—as both the nineteenth- and the twentieth-century authors of this study
provide models of American life wherein the road to success leads back to a
communal life structured by folkways, which is likewise depicted as a complex
and intricate manner of living.[1]

Choosing contemporary works that posit a bond between cultural heritage and a sense of self also means an investigation of those folklore traditions marked as a means to achieving a sense of self that is whole instead of fragmented, connected instead of drifting.[2] This study is based on the discovery that simply identifying the presence of that bond is not enough. Merely to point out the fact that engagement with tradition is a part of, say, Tayo's journey to self is to ignore the relevance of that particular tradition to the community of which Tayo is a part and its thematic significance in the text. In order to comprehend truly the link made between tradition and a sense of self, students and teachers alike must understand the tradition(s) identified. Examining the folklore of the distinctive groups presented in the texts helps fulfill this literary responsibility. Through a folklore and literature study such as the one herein, new light can be shed on the lives portrayed within the text and through the text. We can get a better handle on how different groups of people negotiate the world, what behaviors and practices they rely on to make this possible. Essentially, we are encouraged to do more in-depth explorations of similarity and difference.

In highlighting a shared message regarding the achievement of a sense of self—that it is directly linked to an acknowledgment of and engagement in folk traditions—this folklore and literature study creates a bridge spanning over 100 years of American literary thought and covering the distance so often maintained between distinct cultural groups. But a shared message is not the only thing the texts of this study have in common. For example, although the traditions marked as vehicles to self typically differ from folk group to folk group, this is not always the case. The works by Chesnutt and Bradley, Mena and Fernández, and Zitkala-Šǎ, for instance, illustrate that the oral tradition is similarly used by African American, Mexican American, and Native American communities to define individuals and (re)connect them to the community at large.[3] And when we combine the efforts of Stowe and Otto with those of Zitkala-Šǎ and Fernández, we see that women of many cultures use needlework as a means to self. Moreover, and while it has not been a major focus of this study, on occasion the folk traditions spotlighted also serve as structuring techniques. As I pointed out in chapter 1, both Stowe and Otto put their texts together according to the tradition through which their characters come to better know themselves: the tradition of quilting. And certainly the form of Silko's *Ceremony*—which is a slow confluence or merging of myth and reality—is meant to reflect one of the most important aspects of Tayo's own ceremonial journey: the disappearance of boundaries.[4] Finally, the texts come together to show us that the struggle to know ourselves is neither new nor is it unique to any one folk group; it is a centuries old battle waged by members of all groups. And it is just this similarity that brings me to a discussion of the differences between the texts. For as the texts as a unit also show us, what initiates the struggle differs for each character. That is to say, each character has a culturally specific experience *in* the world that either threatens or impedes her or his achievement of a whole sense of self.

For the nineteenth-century characters, this experience occurs while they are still connected, if not completely grounded, within their cultural community. Hence, although it entails a good deal of confusion, there is little doubt as to how they can work through their questions about who they are or where they fit in the world. They always already know: they should turn to the traditions they live by daily. The contemporary characters, on the other hand, have this experience outside that community, after they have, as a result of their having, or simply because they *are* separated from it. Parted from the stability of community and tradition, their senses of self are left open to the influences of others. A danger to be sure, this situation presents a set of questions best articulated by Kesay E. Noda, who, in the essay "Growing Up Asian in America," writes the following:

> How is one to know and define oneself? From the inside—within a context that is self-defined, from a grounding in community and a connection with culture and history that are comfortably accepted? Or from the outside—within terms of messages received from the media and people who are often ignorant? Even as an adult, I can still see two sides of my face and past. I can see from the inside out, in freedom. And I can see from the outside in, driven by the old voices of childhood and lost in anger and fear. (122)

Looking "outside in" as they are, by and large, the contemporary characters try to define themselves according to the ever-changing concepts of gender and ethnicity. But individuals who seek self-definition in this way are bound to find their idea(s) of self subject to shift given the whims of others. And it is this constant shifting of conceptualizations that sends each contemporary character into a tailspin. Finn, of *How to Make an American Quilt*, struggles with the fluctuations in what it means to be a woman. Loaded down with too many ideas of what she should be, and conflicting ones at that, her sense of self clouds over. Set adrift, so to speak, she begins dillydallying through life, unable to chart her own course. John, of *The Chaneysville Incident,* grapples with the notions of what his relationship with his African American history should be. Dissatisfied with the options others offer him—reject that history or be a champion of it— John decides simply to ignore it. The resultant dis-ease he experiences nega- tively affects his personal relationships and makes it impossible for him to move forward. Burdened by painful memories of war and childhood, memories in which his half-breed status shaped his relationships with others and thus his understanding of self, Tayo, of *Ceremony,* plainly shuts down. With the load of the past and the perceptions of others fixed on his back, he sinks into a state of ennui that almost consumes him. And even though Nenita, of *Intaglio,* spent her childhood surrounded by a Mexican American community defined through folklore, when she goes away to college, she experiences a momentary lapse in her knowledge of herself and her faith in Mexican American traditions. So strong are the inducements to trivialize her heritage that she begins to move away from all she has known and finds herself virtually empty handed.

The situations delineated in the pieces of fiction chosen for this study have their basis in reality. And for me, a teacher and student of literature, this is the true value of my work. Real-life evidence of such conundrums abound. As I know from personal experience, most of us question who we are at some point in time. And like the characters of this study, most of us find "outside in" definition an endeavor resulting in loss. So where do we go for answers? Well, according to what I believe the novels of this study tell us, we should return to our cultural communities and to those traditions that have served so many for so long.

Unfortunately, the problem is that we are increasingly apt to refute the notion that literature is but a mirror on the world, and thus *therein* can be found messages for living; and we are even more resistant to the idea that folk- lore is anything beyond a bunch of baskets set on display at the farmer's mar- ket, that this is actually a way to define ourselves. Yet even if we accept that literature speaks to real life, even if we agree on folklore's relationship to iden- tity, I don't want to suggest that the authors of this study (or any others who do similar work, and there are many) offer folklore as a quick panacea for the ills of self-definition.[5] My investigation of the traditions presented in the texts and how those traditions relate to the characters' struggles to arrive at a more coherent sense of self should make apparent the complexity of folklore and the good deal of time, commitment, energy, and, often, pain required to return to community and to heal through folklore.

The impetus of my work had much to do with the void I found in studies already done regarding the "sense of self via return to community" theme in contemporary literature. The attention given to the role of folklore portrayed in the texts under consideration seemed slight to me. As I stated in the introduction, I don't believe we can completely grasp how a return to community facilitates a sense of self if we do not fully comprehend the folkloric work that return entails. My analysis reveals these two actions as mutually dependent and, thus, should make clear the scholar's obligation to a thorough examination of both, as well as an inspection of how the two relate to each other, for certainly they do.

One of the things I learned as a result of my work is that in regard to the search for self, the relationship between community and folklore crystallizes more completely when, in addition to these success stories, we take a look at texts that present another picture of the contemporary search for self: that of failure. James Welch's *The Death of Jim Loney* serves as an excellent example. Here, too, we have an individual who, unable to see the shape of his life clearly, embarks on a quest for self-knowledge. Like the ones studied herein, Loney's search is "ritually embraced and prescribed"—folklore engaged (P. Allen, *The Sacred Hoop* 93). What differs in this case is that Loney does not become a part of a community; he insists on remaining emotionally separated from those available to him.[6] Without community, he has no one to support his folkloric attempt to sort out his life. And without this support, he sinks deeper into a sense of futility that ultimately results in his own destruction. Loney's experience conveys the message that even if a sense of self through folklore endeavor is performed in isolation (as is often a requisite of those Native American vision quests like Loney's), for it to be successful, the sustenance of community is required. In all honesty, then, to clarify the codependency of folklore and community, works such as Welch's should be stationed alongside those of this study. Besides, doing this can only aid one in presenting a more well-rounded view of the present-day search for self—one that removes the rose-colored glasses so eagerly donned if "success stories" are all that are offered.

My students often ask me what literature, be it nineteenth or twentieth century, has to do with them. When this question arises, and it almost invariably does each semester, I refer them to the words of Kay Boyle:

> As far as the question of whether the writer can change the world [. . .] this much we know: that throughout history, so great has been the fear of the power of the writer, that books have been burned in the belief that putting the flame to the printed word also destroyed the conviction that lived in the word. (Sumrall 70)

Asking my students to examine the relationship between literary messages and book burnings brings home to them the idea that literature must surely have something to say to us and about us or silencing it by fire wouldn't be necessary. And because this discussion typically occurs at the start of the semester, they are then prepared for a study of literature that seeks to link the life of the novel with the life they are living. A folklore and literature discussion can only help fulfill this objective. Why? Because folklore is neither quaint nor antiquated. It is hands-on, hearts-in living, a way to whole survival. The authors of this study use literature to remind us of this folklore fact, placing folklore and literature on a level playing field: their work reciprocal, their value equal.

NOTES

Introduction

1. Tu Smith studies Frank Chin's *The Year of the Dragon*, Maxine Hong Kingston's *The Woman Warrior*, Alice Walker's *The Color Purple*, John Edgar Wideman's *Sent for You Yesterday*, N. Scott Momaday's *House Made of Dawn*, Leslie Marmon Silko's *Ceremony*, Tomas Rivera's [. . .] *y no se lo trago la tierra*, and Sandra Cisneros's *The House on Mango Street*. Kubitschek studies the works of such authors as Octavia Butler, Zora Neale Hurston, Paule Marshall, Nella Larsen, Gayl Jones, and Toni Morrison.

2. Jan Brunvand tells us that "the chief difficulty in defining 'folklore' more completely and scientifically is that the word has acquired varying meanings among the different scholars and writers who use it" (3). Still, he suggests that if one understands the concepts of folklore that folklorists generally hold, one can arrive at/develop a definition of folklore suitable for use in study. The definition of folklore I choose to work with follows Brunvand's, for it has, as would be expected, the first three primary qualities at its heart: (1) its content is oral (usually verbal) or custom-related or material; (2) it is traditional in form and transmission; (3) it exists in different versions (7).

3. In the interview "That Same Pain, That Same Pleasure" with Richard G. Stern, Ellison discusses what it was that made him recognize the self-affirming and defining nature of folk traditions. He tells Stern that during "fall cotton-picking season certain kids left school and went with their parents to work in the cotton fields [. . .] those trips to the cotton patch seemed to me an enviable experience because the kids came back with such wonderful stories. And it wasn't the hard work which they stressed, but the communion, the playing, the eating, the dancing and the singing. And they brought back jokes, *our* Negro jokes [. . .] and they always returned with Negro folk stories which I'd never heard before and which couldn't be found in any books I knew about. This was something to affirm and I felt there was a richness in it [. . .] what my schoolmates shared in the country and what I felt in their accounts of it—it seemed much more real than the Negro middle-class values which were taught in school [. . .] For instance, there is no place like a Negro barbershop for hearing what Negroes really think. There is more unselfconscious affirmation to be found here on a Saturday than you can find in a Negro college in a month, or so it seems to me" (*Shadow and Act* 7–9).

4. I am referring here to the texts mentioned earlier—Bonnie TuSmith's *All My Relatives* (Ann Arbor: U of Michigan P, 1994) and Missy Kubitschek's *Claiming the Heritage* (Mississippi: U of Mississippi P, 1991), as well as Jane Campbell's *Mythic Black Fiction* (Knoxville: U of Tennessee P, 1986). Although Campbell's study focuses on the romance as "the predominant mode in Black historical fiction," she, too, focuses on the character in search of self, what she terms the *questing figure* and, in many cases, ties the quest's success to a return home.

5. From Steven J. Zeitlin, Amy J. Kotkin, and Holly Cutting Baker, eds., *A Celebration of American Family Folklore: Tales and Traditions from the Smithsonian Collection* (New York: Pantheon, 1982), 8.

6. Among the theories available, this study will draw on, but is not limited to, the following: Roger D. Abrahams, "Folklore and Literature as Performance," *Journal of the Folklore Institute* 9 (1972): 75–94; Jan Harold Brunvand, *The Study of American Folklore: An Introduction* 3d ed. (New York: Norton, 1986); Alan Dundes, "The Study of Folklore in Literature and Culture: Identification and Interpretation," *Journal of American Folklore* 78 (1965): 136–38; Steven Swann Jones, introduction, *Folklore and Literature in the United States: An Annotated Bibliography of Studies of Folklore in American Literature* (New York: Garland, 1984); James Kirkland, introduction, "Connecting Folklore and Literature" (unpublished manuscript); Mary Ellen B. Lewis, "The Study of Folklore in Literature: An Expanded View," *Southern Folklore Quarterly* 40 (1976): 343–51; Bruce A. Rosenberg, *Folklore and Literature: Rival Siblings* (Knoxville: U of Tennessee P, 1991); Robert A. Georges and Michael Owen Jones, *Folkloristics: An Introduction* (Bloomington: Indiana UP, 1995); Barre Toelken, *The Dynamics of Folklore* (Boston: Houghton, 1979).

7. Dorson identifies three major pitfalls of folklore and literature studies when he writes, "Too many of these studies fail to demonstrate the presence of folklore in creative writings. They employ the concept of folklore in so fuzzy and loose a fashion that it soon loses any precise meaning. A more successful group of these analyses adequately perceives folklore in literary dress, but then fails to render any meaningful judgment about this discovery" (187).

8. In terms of elaboration and/or modification, one might refer to the studies produced subsequent to Dorson's assertions, such as Alan Dundes's "The Study of Folklore in Literature and Culture," Roger Abrahams's "Folklore and Literature as Performance," Mary Ellen B. Lewis's "The Study of Folklore and Literature: An Expanded View," and Neil Grobman's "A Schema for the Study of the Sources and Literary Simulations of Folkloric Phenomena," *Southern Folklore Quarterly* 43 (1979): 17–37.

9. Trudier Harris's *Fiction and Folklore: The Novels of Toni Morrison* (Knoxville: U of Tennessee P, 1991), and Marilyn Sanders Mobley's *Folk Roots and Mythic Wings in Sarah Orne Jewett and Toni Morrison* (Baton Rouge: Louisiana State UP, 1991) also suggest that questions regarding aesthetics are not the only ones involved

in finding folk traditions in literature. For instance, Harris's work delineates the structural and thematic relationships between African American cultural traditions and Morrison's literary adaptations and transmutations. And Mobley's work argues that both Morrison and Jewett "reclaim and affirm for fiction parts of their cultural heritage that society had begun to discard as irrelevant or marginal to the dominant national experience" (6). In other words, both Harris and Mobley do folklore and literature studies that join discussions of form with discussions of content and meaning.

10. My work, then, is part of an ongoing discussion of this theme in contemporary American literature, a discussion initiated by Bonnie TuSmith's *All My Relatives,* Jane Campbell's *Mythic Black Fiction,* and Missy Kubitschek's *Claiming the Heritage.*

11. In her study of Leslie Marmon Silko's *Ceremony,* TuSmith focuses on how storytelling as style and structure helps the text achieve its thematic objectives; that is, how storytelling offers a narrative strategy that moves "the reader from an individualist to a communal frame of mind." Although TuSmith tells us that the novel "is itself a curing ceremony for anyone who works through it," full regard is never given to the curative ceremony tradition (of which storytelling is but a part) or the relevance of the character's engagement in it. Because of this, the idea that Silko identifies the curative ceremony as a Native American folk tradition designed to facilitate and designated as facilitator of such a "journey to wholeness" is not fully developed. Campbell's and Kubitschek's studies exhibit the same limitation.

12. Mobley writes that her own approach "[. . .] can offer a new way of connecting separate strands of American culture and literary expression" (19). Kubitschek, in her study of one thematic objective of African American women writers, tells us she is concerned with the way "chronology's almost necessary focus on distinct stages and therefore definitive shifts [. . .] can obscure certain kinds of continuities" (5).

13. Where the authors are concerned, I agree with Bonnie TuSmith that any textual interpretation benefits from a consideration of the author's "scholarly statements and, to a limited extent, their biographical experiences." However, because "I am investigating what the writer is saying through the literature," I privilege the literary work (30).

14. Ethnic group as folk group, see also Jan Harold Brunvand, *The Study of American Folklore;* Elliot Oring, *Folk Groups and Folklore Genres* (Logan: Utah State UP, 1986); Robert A. Georges and Michael Owen Jones, *Folkloristics: An Introduction.*

15. In a discussion of women in folklore, "The Creator Gods: Romantic Nationalism and the Engenderment of Women in Folklore," *Feminist Theory and the Study of Folklore,* ed. Susan Tower Hollis, Linda Pershing, and M. Jane Young (Urbana: U of Illinois P, 1993), Jennifer Fox writes, "[. . .] it takes little imagination to realize that the category of gender itself is a social construct whose associations permeate our own scholarly discourses. If we are to alter existing gender-based power relations, the concept of gender must be viewed as both socially and historically contingent and politically charged" (31). Because discussions of ethnicity mirror discussions, like the one above, of gender,

the category of ethnicity can be viewed in the same way Fox views the category of gen-der. *Ethnicity* is a fairly new term and, like *gender,* constantly shifting in meaning and, subsequently, as loaded with connotation as any other descriptive term used to label and set apart groups of people according to physical characteristics, behaviors, and expecta-tions. For further discussions of this, see Elaine Showalter, ed., *The New Feminist Crit-icism: Essays on Women, Literature, and Theory* (New York: Pantheon, 1985); Alice Jardin's *Gynesis: Configurations of Woman and Modernity* (Ithaca: Cornell UP, 1985); various selections from Luce Irigaray's *Speculum of the Other Woman,* trans. Gillian C. Gill (Ithaca: Cornell UP, 1985) and Ann Garry and Marilyn Pearsall, eds., *Women, Knowledge, and Reality* (Boston: Unwin Hyman, 1989); chapter 1 of TuSmith, *All My Relatives*; David R. Colburn and George E. Pozzetta, eds., *America and the New Eth-nicity* (Port Washington: Kennikat, 1979).

16. One should note that while the folk groups delineated in the texts by Stowe and Otto, for instance, are both gender and activity based, the ethnic backgrounds of the members vary. The works of both Stowe and Otto reflect the fact that female folk traditions are shared across ethnic lines, so to speak. Moreover, both works illustrate the way in which folk groups are typically formed—that is, the members come together because of a shared interest in a tradition, not because the members share a common ethnicity, and in many cases not even because they share a common gender. Neither author conveys the idea that the tradition is solely the province of any particular ethnic descent—be it Anglo, Euramerican, or African American.

17. In order to avoid confusion, I want to address my wording here. I use the phrase "positive sense of self and place in the world" instead of, for instance, the term *identity* because I am no way positing that the novels relate the possibility of achieving a *fixed identity* through tradition immersion. Part of the value of this study comes in my historicizing the notion of identity—showing that while the idea of a fixed identity may have been available to earlier writers, it is no longer available to twentieth-century authors. In other words, the theoretical questions surrounding identity are more perti-nent to contemporary writers and their characters than they are to the authors and characters of the earlier works. Many are the theorists who refute coherency when it comes to identity. However, I believe the authors—through their texts and characters—suggest a coherent self is most assuredly possible, but much is involved before one arrives at that point. This study centers on what the texts suggest such a journey might entail. Because I have found that the concept of even a stable sense of self is met with rather rabid opposition today, I would go so far as to argue the necessity at this point in time of the American author's positive message regarding the same.

18. I take my critical lead in this chapter from such works as Rosan A. Jordon and Susan J. Kalčik, *Women's Folklore, Women's Culture* (Philadelphia: U of Pennsyl-vania P, 1985); Joan Radner, *Feminist Messages: Coding in Women's Folk Culture* (Chicago: U of Illinois P, 1993); Susan Tower Hollis et al., *Feminist Theory and the*

Study of Folklore (Urbana: U of Illinois P, 1993); and Elaine Showalter, *Sister's Choice* (Oxford: Clarendon, 1991).

19. Zitkala-Šă's legend portrayal reflects the way legends are understood and used within most cultures. A combination of fact and fiction, legends, as we see in *American Indian Stories,* serve to preserve history, transmit values, teach lessons, and identify individuals as part of the group.

20. Previously, Mena was relegated to the dusty back corners of study because both her style and content (seemingly) advanced stereotypical images of Mexican American life and culture. In *Understanding Chicano Literature,* Carl and Paula Shirley tell us that María Cristina Mena wrote "romantic, sentimental, completely ide-alized and unrealistic stories" that perpetuated "among Anglo readers a romanticized stereotype of Mexican Americans" (96). Furthermore, in his essay "The Evolution of Chicano Literature," *Three American Literatures: Essays in Chicano, Native American, and Asian American Literature,* ed. Houston A. Baker Jr. (New York: MLA, 1982), Ray-mund Parades asserts that "a braver, more perceptive writer would have confronted the life of her culture more forcefully" (85). Only through López's (re)evaluation that revealed the trickster element embedded in her fiction was Mena's work retrieved from such negative readings.

21. When it comes to studying difference, it is important to analyze the changes wrought by time upon a particular group's conceptualizations of important social institu-tions (such as we see occurs with the women's concept of marriage from Stowe's text to Otto's), especially in terms of how those changes affect one's ability to achieve selfhood. However, my central concern has to do with how the experiences surrounding the fulfill-ment of self differ *across* cultural lines and what cultural lessons can be learned when we study the specific folk tradition(s) designed and utilized to facilitate that goal.

Chapter 1. With This Needle

1. See Radner, *Feminist Messages,* 1–31; Linda Pershing, "Peace Work out of Piecework: Feminist Needlework Metaphors and the Ribbon around the Pentagon," *Feminist Theory and the Study of Folklore,* 334–36; Cecilia Macheski, ed., introduction, *Quilt Stories* (Lexington: UP of Kentucky, 1994), 1–7; Elaine Hedges and Ingrid Wendt, *In Her Own Image: Women Working in the Arts* (New York: Feminist, 1980), 1–10, 13–19.

2. Elaborating on this assertion, Showalter tells us that piecing and patchwork have "[. . .] become metaphors for a Female Aesthetic, for sisterhood, and for a politics of feminist survival. In the past two decades especially, they have been celebrated as essen-tially feminine art forms, modes of expression that emerge naturally from womanly impulses of nurturance and thrift, and that constitute a women's language unintelligible to male audiences or readers" (146).

3. Throughout this chapter, I will be using the term *needlework* in an idiosyncratic way to cover all of the crafts associated with producing textiles for household use.

4. Needlework, especially when understood in the manner indicated above, has been almost entirely the province of women in Euramerican societies. Yet both functional and recreational needlework were and still are in some traditional cultures—Native American and African, for instance—practiced by men as well. Men of the Pueblo groups, in particular, have long engaged in a variety of needlework crafts, creating items for the home, such as blankets, as well as accessories for ceremonial costumes. In addition, although it is not produced for household use, Kente, a hand-woven cloth the origins of which date back to twelfth-century Ghana, was originally done by men. As a creative outlet, quilting especially has been important for both women *and* men. Marilyn Lithgow, in *Quiltmaking and Quiltmakers* (New York: Funk & Wagnalls, 1974), writes, "The Union Soldier recuperating from wounds sustained in the Civil War and the midwestern farmer confined to the wheelchair by a physical illness discovered for themselves what generations of American women have known, that making a quilt can fulfill a deep need for personal self-expression" (5). Of course, one should understand the distinction between practicing quilting because one is physically unable to do much else and quilting or needleworking because it is, in effect, what you must do—in particular, to express and define yourself.

5. The availability of materials and the sales of mass-produced needlework products today have not kept traditional patchworkers from saving fragments or creating useful articles from scraps. Thrift and utility are still at the heart of much patchworking practiced today.

6. Showalter in "Common Threads" tells us, "Quilting was a practical and economic necessity in a country where ready-made bedding could not be easily obtained before the 1890's and where in the cold New England or prairie winter each family member might need five thick quilts" (*Sister's Choice* 148). And Marilyn Lithgow, in *Quiltmaking and Quiltmakers,* explains that as "new cloth was scarce" in America's earlier days "what cloth was available usually had to be made into new clothing." The American housewife "had two choices in making her bed coverings—she could use the contents of her scrap bag, all the precious patches of cloth that she had saved from worn-out clothing, or she could make her own cloth from home-grown flax and wool" (3).

7. Elaine Hedges and Ingrid Wendt, in *In Her Own,* explain that "throughout western history, spinning, weaving, and sewing have always been among the most basic of women's domestic tasks. Indeed, the Bible defines the ideal or 'virtuous' woman in Proverbs 31 [. . .] as she who 'seeks wool and flax, and works with willing hands [. . .] puts her hands to the distaff, and her hands hold the spindle.' A 'spinster' was originally a spinner and an essential member of every family. In fact, the Massachusetts legislature at one point in the seventeenth century decreed that each household must contain at least one spinner, so important was this work" (3).

8. When we look at the compendium of Stowe's work, we find evidence she understood the varying ways women viewed needlework. Although *The Minister's Wooing* presents a view of needlework that confirms it was more than a dreaded chore, in *The Pearl of Orr's Island* and *Oldtown Folks* Stowe portrays little girls who hate needlework and rebel against being taught to sew.

9. For abundant evidence of these patchwork design aspects, one must read, "The Patchwork Quilt" by Annette (pseudonym), in Macheski, *Quilt Stories*, 11–15; Pershing, "Peace Work out of Piecework," 334–36. For wonderful discussions of women's hidden messages via intentional flaw in technique and material, superstitions evidenced in quilts, and secret meanings ingrained in quilts, refer to Radner, *Feminist Messages*, 1–31.

10. Note that later on in the text Mrs. Simeon Brown drops out and Madame de Frontignac joins in. This change in membership is typical of folk groups; folk group membership is fluid—one can be a member of more than one folk group at one time, switch from group to group as time goes by, or drop out from folk grouping entirely. Nevertheless, because "the acceptance of traditions" by members of the group "usually implies some degree of conformity with group tastes and values" (Brunvand 40), it should not surprise us that Mrs. Simeon Brown chooses to leave the group—there is a clear line of demarcation between her views on slavery and the views of the other members.

11. The sewing technique Stowe describes Miss Prissy practicing most often is called invisible mending; the value of the work lies in its invisibility. As Jane Marcus explains in "Invisible Mending," *Between Women*, ed. Carol Ascher, Louise DeSalvo, and Sara Ruddick (Boston: Beacon, 1984), "Invisible mending is delicate, necessary, skilled labor [. . .] The measure of a woman's skill is the degree to which the work can't be seen" (388).

12. In "Quilts and Women's Culture," *In Her Own Image*, Elaine Hedges, makes a similar assertion, as does Showalter in "Common Threads," *Sister's Choice*. See also Lucy R. Lippard, "Up, Down, and Across: A New Frame for New Quilts," *The Artist and the Quilt*, ed. Charlotte Robinson (New York: Knopf, 1983).

13. We do not see Mrs. Jones's needleworking because she arrives just as the tea is laid out and the men join the party.

14. In "The Shadow Block: Female Bonding in Quilters," *Women and Performance: Journal of Feminism* 4.1 (1988–89): 6–22, Joanne Karpinski explains that such meetings were and are a means "through which women articulate for and with each other values which have been denied full expression within the culture's dominant. Exclusively female by its own choice the [quilting] enclave represents the cultural construction of difference" (18).

15. Stowe knew well what women's relationships with each other provided, as they shaped her own life to a great degree. Joan D. Hedrick covers this area of Stowe's life in "'Peaceable Fruits': The Ministry of Harriet Beecher Stowe," *American Quarterly*

40.3 (1988). In this essay, Hedrick affirms my understanding of the dynamics of women's groups when she writes, "In institution and networks set apart from male culture and public exercises of power, women were free to develop their own forms, expressions, rituals, and cosmologies" (307–8). Hedrick also refers us to the illuminating work on this subject by Carroll Smith-Rosenberg: "The Female World of Love and Ritual: Relations between Women in Nineteenth-Century America," *Signs* 1 (fall 1975): 1–29. For studies that traverse women's relationships over a greater period of time and through philosophical and psychological lenses, see Ann Garry and Marilyn Pearsall, eds., *Women, Knowledge, and Reality;* Mary Field Belenky, Blythe McVicker Clinchy, Nancy Rule Goldberger, and Jill Mattuck Tarule, eds., *Women's Ways of Knowing* (New York: Basic, 1986).

16. For further discussions centering on the dynamics of folk groups, see Toelken, *The Dynamics of Folklore;* Dundes, *Interpreting Folklore,* 1–32; Oring, *Folk Groups and Folklore Genres,* 1–44; Brunvand, *The Study of American Folklore,* 38–57.

17. For history of quilting, wonderful representation can be found in Lithgow, *Quiltmaking and Quiltmakers,* 26–63; Anderson, *Collector's Guide to Quilts,* 151–63. Whitney Otto herself relied upon and refers her readers to Thomas K. Woodward and Blanche Greenstein, *Twentieth Century Quilts, 1900–1950* (New York: Button, 1988); Pat Ferrero, Elaine Hedges, and Julie Siber, *Hearts and Hands* (San Francisco: Quilt Digest, 1987); and the works of Setsuko Segawa.

18. Referring to such writers as Marge Piercy, Joyce Carol Oates, and Adrienne Rich, Showalter tells us, "Most of the women writers adopting quilt imagery in their poems and novels, however, were not quilt-makers themselves. In contemporary American women's writing, Elaine Hedges has written, the quilt often stands for an idealized past, 'a way of bridging the gulf between domestic and artistic life that until recently women writers have found such difficulty negotiating.' Textile imagery, 'especially imagery associated with quilts, the piecing together of salvaged fragments to create a new pattern of connections, and integrated whole [. . .] provides the elements [. . .] for a new transformative vision.' This imagery is nostalgic and romantic" (*Sister's Choice* 162).

19. In *Quiltmaking and Quiltmakers,* Marilyn Lithgow explains, "the overall design of both pieced and appliqué quilts is usually divided into 'blocks' which repeat a pattern that forms a total design when the blocks are 'set' together to make the finished top. The three layers of the quilt—the top, the batting, and backing—are then 'put in' a quilting frame to hold them taut and are stitched together in a pattern already marked on the top of the quilt" (2).

20. Although it may appear as though Finn is the sole voice of this text, at the close of the novel she reveals Anna as the one who told her "everything" she wanted to know about quilting, about the women of the circle. Thus, I believe it is plausible we are meant to hear two voices collaborating to convey instructions and stories. Anna's voice underlies many of the instructions, but Finn, as student and listener, adds her voice as she questions, interprets, argues, and finally relates the information she receives.

21. "Mrs." is the way Otto refers to the mistress of the house.

22. Anna's quilt story here is based in part on the quilt story of Harriet Powers. As Cecilia Macheski asserts in *Quilt Stories,* "Whitney's novel retells the tragic story of Power's surrender of her cherished quilt to a white woman in order to make a few dollars to buy food during the Depression, but alters the ending, creating a modern daughter who reclaims the quilt from the woman who 'bought' it. The daughter asserts her right to the fabled quilt because she knows the stories that must accompany the pictures; without the stories the quilt is meaningless, a wall hanging without history or context" (5).

23. One might argue that by portraying Marianna as torn between her black and white identities, indulging in a series of affairs, and embracing what looks like an updated version of the black woman's traditional role as mammy or domestic, Otto is playing into racial stereotypes. But the fact that in the story a similar question is put to Marianna suggests to me that Otto not only anticipated such an accusation but also prepared a defense: Marianna's thoughts regarding the same. Marianna made her decision to work for Glady-Jo with little regard to stereotypes. Her choice was based on what would provide her with a greater sense of well-being, of self—the issue at the heart of the text. As problematic as Otto's falling back on a stereotype may be, we create another problem when we view as wrong Otto's presentation of a very real, albeit all-too-typical, situation. We risk missing the fact that Marianna's choice to follow a stereotype is just that—a choice.

24. In his review of the novel in *Contemporary Literary Criticism* 70 (1991), John Smith asserts "[. . .] the instructions carry a subtext: assemble and stitch a quilt as you would build and sustain a human relationship" (91). However, as I suggest throughout this part of chapter 1, the metaphor goes beyond this simple connection, for quilting is also linked to how to build and sustain the self in light of these relationships.

Chapter 2. Everybody Loves a Good Story

1. On the other hand, it becomes clear early on that John's wife finds much in the tales to be taken to heart. For her the tales are a means to understanding the community into which she has entered.

2. John is a more involved interpreter in other Chesnutt stories. As Sundquist points out in *To Wake the Nations* (Cambridge: Belknap, 1993), in Chesnutt's "Tobe's Tribulation," an Uncle Julius tale not included in *The Conjure Woman,* John, as narrator/ethnographer, comes closer than he did in *The Conjure Woman* to interpreting for us the role of black folklore in Uncle Julius's life (314). In fact, in this tale John virtually sums up for the reader Uncle Julius's folk view.

3. Isidore Okpewho, in chapter 5 of *African Oral Literature* (Bloomington: Indiana UP, 1992), discusses the social relevance of oral literature and, therefore, the

oral artist. He lists these as the four principal purposes or functions served by the oral traditions. The individual who takes on the role of oral artist, Okpewho explains, accepts responsibility for meeting these objectives.

4. Succinct and to the point, Houston Baker's definition of conjure, which appears in *Modernism and the Harlem Renaissance* (Chicago: U of Chicago P, 1987), suffices here: "*Conjure* is the transatlantic religion of diasporic and Afro-American masses in the New World. Descended from *vodun*, an African religion in which the priestess holds supreme power, conjure's name in Haiti and the Caribbean is *voodoo* [. . .] Conjure is a power of transformation that causes definitions of 'form' as fixed and comprehensible 'thing' to dissolve [. . .] *Conjure* is also known, of course, as folk medicine" (44, 46).

5. Georges's discussion of the social uses of storytelling events—"Toward an Understanding of Storytelling Events," *Journal of American Folklore* 82 (1969)—reflects Okpewho's understanding of the purposes and functions of oral traditions. As Georges explains, every storytelling event has social use, be it "to pass the time, to teach a lesson, to explain or describe some social or physical phenomenon." And participants interpret, articulate, and communicate these social uses to others (317–18). Still, it is Okpewho who identifies the storyteller (the artist) as the chief beneficiary of storytelling events, which is what Uncle Julius is on this occasion. Okpewho asserts, "Perhaps nobody enjoys this psychological release quite as much as the artists themselves; for a start, these tales of fantasy are products of their own creation or recreation. But the more interesting thing about these stories is that somewhere between the lines we see aspects of the artists' own lives reflected either directly or indirectly." Any given story reflects "[. . .] the deep-seated feelings and outlook on life of its narrator." Through story, the storyteller reveals him- or herself and controls his world (109).

6. Robert Hemenway, "The Functions of Folklore in Charles Chesnutt's *The Conjure Woman*," *Journal of the Folklore Institute* 13 (1976): 283–309.

7. The schoolhouse has special resonance. A symbol of the Reconstruction era, when the Klan was burning down schoolhouses, it stands as a reminder of a battle yet to be won.

8. Handed down as they are from generation to generation, most tales are considered "[. . .] the common property of the society" in which they are found. And, therefore, the identities of individual artists are often abdicated, as "[. . .] artists are forced to compromise themselves or suppress their personalities in the interests of their work." And yet, because "[. . .] the personality of the artist continues to emerge and is sometimes forcefully asserted against the pressure or tyranny of the tradition," one might find in a tale not only "a close correspondence between the life of the artist and the subject of his or her song or tale" but also the very presence of the artist's personality (Okpewho 34–35). The latter, especially, is what I believe we find in the tales of Uncle Julius. That is to say, incorporated into a given tale is the segment of himself he wished to reveal at the time.

9. Sylvia Lyons Render, in the introduction to *The Short Fiction of Charles W. Chesnutt* (Washington: Howard UP, 1981), also describes Uncle Julius's behavior in this instance in this manner: "He is altogether altruistic in letting his favorite, Miss Annie [. . .] keep and use his priceless rabbit foot to improve her health in 'Sis' Becky's Pickaninny'" (24).

10. In *Mythic Black Fiction*, Jane Campbell makes a similar assertion. Although her central concern is with the way in which African American authors employ romance conventions to illuminate African American history and culture, she tells us that Bradley's novel focuses "on a theme of extraordinary magnitude: the African American must acknowledge and explore the complexity of black history and culture that is symbolized in the term Afro-American. In the process, the Afro-American must reclaim fundamental aspects of his or her heritage: ancestor worship, the supernatural, and African religion and folklore" (137).

11. Jack describes Moses in relation to the stories surrounding him. His description of the formation and passage of these stories falls closely in line with Jan Harold Brunvand's explanation of legend creation and diffusion in his work *The Study of American Folklore*. Here we learn that "rumors, anecdotes, and legends alike are concerned with remarkable, even bizarre, events that allegedly happened to ordinary people in everyday situations. These reports and stories are recounted, usually in conversation, as a way of explaining strange things that occur—or are thought to have occurred—and they are passed on in order to warn or inform others about these unprovable events." Moreover, legends, like the Moses stories are "circulated in *cycles,* or groups of narratives relating to one event, person, or theme. Among these stories there may be both long, well-developed accounts and mere fragments of rumor or hearsay" (158–59).

12. George Laurence Gomme best articulates a large part of John's problem. As William A. Wilson tells us in "Folklore and History: Fact Amid the Legends," *Utah Historic Quarterly* 41 (1973): 40–58, in 1908, Gomme "began his book *Folklore as an Historical Science* with these words: 'It may be stated as a general rule that history and folklore are not considered as complimentary studies. Historians deny the validity of folklore as evidence of history, and folklorists ignore the essence of history which exists in folklore.'" Today there are, of course, many scholars who prove exceptions to this generalization—Sterling Stuckey and Lawrence Levine, for example.

13. John longs to feel as though he "knows" his father, his family, and his past. By telling his father's story, his family's story, John will become an authority on his own heritage. Yet, for a story to be told, a listener is required. And not just any listener at that. John requires an active listener, someone who is willing to participate in a storytelling event.

14. As both Uncle Julius and John do, in essence, narrate *their own* stories of slavery, it seems only fitting to me that in each case the principle audience member is

the same as that of many a slave narrative—not only white, but also female. In fact, we might even see the two texts as representative of the changes to that specific teller/audience relationship over time.

15. As we already know, Moses spent a great deal of time in his attic study perusing what John comes to find are factual bits of family history left to Moses by his grandfather, C.K. John realizes that what Moses was searching for was a complete history, the very same thing John seeks in the annals C.K. left to Moses, in the folio Moses left to John, and in the note cards and journals John left to himself, created and abandoned years ago.

16. William A. Wilson comes to this idea as well in "Folklore as History." Oral folklore, he writes, "can tell us what the people lived of." For to know only the history of, for instance, the "medicine of Utah without experiencing the struggles of those who lived it, or to know the history of settlement without feeling the mental anguish of the Dixie immigrant, or to know the history of irrigation without living the accounts of violence and bloodshed between neighbors fighting desperately for the same water—to know only these things is to know only half our history, the dehumanized half. As Theodore Blegen says, it is the folklore and the grassroots history that 'break through the crust of figures and graphs to the living realities that alone can give them significance.' The figures and graphs tell us what people did; folklore tells us what they thought and felt while they were doing it" (43–44).

17. For further discussion of the concept of speaker as author/authority, see Elizabeth Tonkin's introduction to *Narrating Our Pasts: The Social Construction of Oral History* (New York: Cambridge UP, 1992), 1–17.

18. In "The African American Historian: David Bradley's *The Chaneysville Incident*," *African American Review* 29.1 (1995): 97–107, Matthew Wilson asserts we all must understand what John is learning: "historical consciousness, leavened by the imagination, allows us all, no matter what our experience and ethnicity, to know where we all stand in the present" (97).

Chapter 3. New Footing on Ancient Ground

1. Zitkala-Šă's work does not fit easily into one literary tradition. Because the text contains a series of related autobiographical sketches, set in an identifiable American region, infused with Native American traditions, we can argue with validity that it is autobiography, that it is regionalism, that it is literary folklore. Yet, I believe, this ambiguity is telling in itself. In this text, literary traditions collaborate to reveal fragmentation, an underlying fracture that coexists with the affirmation of self, place, and cultural heritage. This ambiguity mirrors the struggle the narrator experiences throughout the text—the struggle to make a whole self out of the parts existing in two seemingly separate realms: the past and the present.

In "Trickster's Voice in the Works of Zitkala-Sä," *Tricksterism in Turn-of-the-Century American Literature*, ed. Elizabeth Ammons and Annette White-Parks (Hanover: UP of New England, 1994), Jeanne Smith writes: "While the book's title suggests they all should be considered stories, even representative 'American Indian' stories, what we find inside is an eclectic mix of autobiography, personal essay, short story, and political tract [. . .] each piece presents a different facet of the same subject. For Zitkala-Sä the personal is inseparable from the political" (51). See also Martha J. Cutter's essay "Zitkala-Sä's Autobiographical Writings," *Melus* 19.1 (1994): 31–44.

2. These aspects of traditional Native American life are discussed at length in *Lakota Society*, ed. Raymond J. DeMallie (Lincoln: U of Nebraska P, 1982) and *Lakota Belief and Ritual*, ed. Raymond J. DeMallie and Elaine A. Jahner (Lincoln: U of Nebraska P, 1982).

3. In "Zitkala-Sä's Autobiographical Writings," Martha J. Cutter asserts that Zitkala-Sä's comments at the close of this portion of the text do not reflect a "striving for wholeness, a coherent identity." Rather, her words present "a scathing indictment of a dominant ideology which forces acculturation at the expense of self" (36).

4. This story's placement in the text is important. It presents another version of the Native American's experience with spirituality—one quite different from Zitkala-Sä's own, described in the autobiographical story preceding it. In "Trickster's Voice in the Works of Zitkala-Sä," Jeanne Smith writes: "Zitkala-Sä strategically places this story just after the reprinted essay 'The Great Spirit' (originally titled 'Why I Am a Pagan'), an essay in which she explains her own spiritual views after a visit from a converted 'native preacher,' who mouthed 'most strangely the jangling phrases of a bigoted creed'" (51).

5. Certainly, the gender implications of this story are also significant. The story reverses gender roles—it is the warrior's daughter who is the hero, not her lover, who in fact fails the Indian test of masculine prowess. The significance of this may be directly related to the Lakota culture, which, despite the worship of White Buffalo Calf Woman, was more male-dominated than some other groups (e.g., the Iroquois), perhaps because it centered around the buffalo hunt. At the same time, Lakota culture, like many others, allowed exceptional women to embrace "masculine" roles. There was the tradition of the "Warrior woman" or "manly hearted woman," for instance, and the "warrior woman" type of legend makes "masculine" roles available to women (Karcher). See Raymond DeMallie, "Male and Female in Traditional Lakota Culture" and Beatrice Medicine, "'Warrior Women'—Sex Role Alternatives for Plains Women," *The Hidden Half: Studies of Plains Indian Women*, ed. Patricia Albers and Beatrice Medicine (Lanham: UP of America, 1983), for thorough discussions on these subjects. One should also note that although Tusee takes over the masculine role, she also capitalizes on the expectations of her own gender. As Jeanne Smith writes, "Because as a woman she is an observer at the victory dance rather than a participant, she can do what a man

can't. No one would suspect that an appealing young woman at the edge of the camp-fire, or a wandering old woman humming to herself, is a murderous avenger" (54). Zitkala-Ša had some awareness of and sympathy for the women's rights movement; hence, one might view this story as her way of building a bridge between Native and white women's concerns about the conceptualizations of women's roles and capabilities. See Sara Evans, *Born for Liberty: A History of Women in America* (New York: Free Press, 1989), and Ruth Spack, "Re-visioning Sioux Women: Zitkala-Ša's Revolutionary *American Indian Stories*," *Legacy* 14.1 (1997): 25–42; DeMallie, "Male and Female in Traditional Lakota Culture."

6. Jeanne Smith points out another aspect of Lakota culture conveyed through this story. She tells us, "Tusee is a powerful trickster/savior in this story. Her disguise as a bent woman with a bundle on her back echoes a Lakota trickster tale in which Iktomi [Lakota trickster] throws grass into his blanket and carries it as if it is a great burden in order to trick and catch some ducks. [. . .] Upsetting traditional role expectations, Tusee's trickster strategies save her lover's life, and by extension the honor of her people (54).

7. This story connects back to the autobiographical section of the book. In the final section, entitled "Retrospection," we learned that Zitkala-Ša experienced a kind of revelation that gave her life's work new hope and direction. In "An Indian Teacher" she says, "At last, one weary day in the schoolroom, a new idea presented itself to me. It was a new way of solving the problem of my inner self. I liked it. Thus I resigned my position as teacher; and now I am in an Eastern city, following the long course of study I have set for myself" (97–98). This "long course of study" mirrors the career choice of the young woman of the legend. As Dexter Fisher tells us in her foreword to *American Indian Stories*, "Zitkala-Ša subsumed her creative energy into a life work of progressive reform for Indians [. . .] lecturing and campaigning across the country for Indian citizenship, employment of Indians in the Bureau of Indian Affairs, equitable settlement of tribal land claims, and stabilization of laws relating to Indians [. . .] She became known to Indians and government officials alike as a persuasive public speaker and an effective, if relentless, mediator. She [. . .] found the way to use her education and skills of expression to aid her people" (xviii, xvi).

8. One might say that the woman of the legend receives the vision Zitkala-Ša alludes to in the autobiographical section of the text; a vision that tells her what she must do and so she does. The combination of their experiences practically matches George Sword's description of Lakota vision-seeking recorded in DeMallie and Jahner, *Lakota Belief and Ritual*. Swords tells us, "It is the custom of all the Lakotas to seek a vision when they are to undertake some important thing or wish for something very earnestly. A vision is something told by a *wakan* being and it is told as if in a dream." Moreover, Sword asserts, "when one seeks a vision and receives a communication he must obey as he is told to do" (84–85).

9. Blue Star's remembrance of the structure of identity reflects the essence of tribalism. As William Bevis tells us in "Native American Novels: Homing In," "the first assumption of tribalism is that the individual is completed only in relation to others, that man is a political animal (lives through a relationship to a village state), and the group which must complete his 'being' is organized in some meaningful way. That meaning, not just land, is what has been lost" (587). Bevis's essay appears in *Recovering the Word: Essays on Native American Literature*, ed. Brian Swann and Arnold Krupat (Berkeley: U of California P, 1987).

10. Bevis sees the tribal "being" as having "three components: society, past, and place. The 'society' of the tribe is not just company; it is law." And it is the customs, ritual, and practices of law that "bind people together into more than a population" (586).

11. In "Native American Literatures and the Canon," Patricia Okker tells us that regardless of Zitkala-Ša's presence in many American literature anthologies, few scholars have dealt with her work in depth (89). That this is the case becomes apparent even when one peruses the critical collections dedicated exclusively to Native American literature. Although their number is ever increasing, few do more than wave a hand at Zitkala-Ša's contribution to that body of creativity. Perhaps this is because her work, as I mentioned in the first part of this chapter, does not fit easily into one literary genre. Or maybe it is this combined with (1) the fact that her "formal principles" are often considered "European and print-derived," and (2) the scholar's tendency to posit the dawn of Native American literature post–Zitkala-Ša that accounts for her virtual absence from studies in Native American Literature (Swain and Krupat 6–7). Whatever the case may be, omitting Zitkala-Ša means blinding readers to a legacy.

Many critical collections focused on Native American literature make only cursory mention of Zitkala-Ša. See *Recovering the Word: Essays on Native American Literature*, *Critical Perspectives on Native American Fiction*, ed. Richard F. Fleck (Washington: Three Continents, 1993); *New Voices in Native American Literary Criticism*, ed. Arnold Krupat (Washington: Smithsonian, 1993); Charles E. Larson, *American Indian Fiction* (Albuquerque: U of New Mexico P, 1978); *Studies in American Indian Literature*, ed. Paula Gunn Allen (New York: MLA, 1983); Andrew Wiget, *Critical Essays on Native American Literature* (Boston: Hall, 1985).

12. Although not my immediate concern in this study, much work has been done on the structure of this novel as it relates to thematics. See David Moore, "Myth, History, and Identity in Silko and Young Bear: Postcolonial Praxis," Krupat, *New Voices in Native American Literary Criticism*; Valerie Harvey, "Navajo Sandpainting in *Ceremony*," Fleck, *Critical Perspectives on Native American Fiction*; and Larson, *American Indian Fiction*.

13. The story of Ck'o'yo magic, which breaks in on the text as Tayo comes to this realization, tells of two brothers, Ma'see'wi and Ou'yu'ye'wi, duped by a new magic into neglecting their duties to the mother corn altar. As the whole community

eventually fooled into laziness as well, the mother, Nau'tsity'i, grows angry and leaves the community, taking with her all things that provided sustenance to the people. They are left with only the new magic, which, in the end, offers them nothing but diversion.

14. The story of the greenbottle fly was told to a younger Tayo after Josiah caught him in the act of killing flies because his teacher told him they were diseased and, therefore, dangerous. In the story, an extension of an earlier one, it is the green-bottle fly who goes to ask forgiveness for the people, whose mother has left them to starve because they withdrew their attention from the old ways and, thus, from her. After Josiah finished the story, Tayo feared what would happen as a result of his slaughter. Josiah's response indicates to Tayo that mistakes will be made, but what matters is that something is learned in the process: "I think it will be okay [. . .] None of them were greenbottle flies—only some of his cousins. People make mistakes. The flies know that. That's how the greenbottle fly first came around anyway. To help the people who had made some mistakes [. . .] just remember the story"(101–2).

15. In order that he may come to terms with himself and his world, Silko has Tayo participate in a specific Native American tradition—the ceremony. She has him engage in this tradition because, as Kathleen Margaret Dugan tells us in *The Vision Quest of The Plains Indians: Its Spiritual Significance* (Lewiston: Edwin Mellen, 1985), Native Americans viewed ceremonies as a way "to communicate with the One Above, and implore, in an extremely effective manner, the help needed to survive and prosper. In concept and practice Indian ceremonials gave form to the chaos of life. Varying in structure from the simple and personal to the extraordinarily complex tribal rituals, such as the Sun Dance, these ceremonies served many functions. On the simplest level, they helped build up the person by integrating his inner self. On the most complex, they gathered the people together and harmonized them with each other, with the community, and exteriorly, with the universe [. . .] In itself, ceremony had a highly instructive role. Together with the time-honored legends recounted by campfires, it helped to perpetuate the traditional values [. . .] in a distinct way for each tribe, since the number and type of rituals differed from tribe to tribe. In myths, the Indian from childhood witnessed the retelling of the people's heritage. The sacred rituals dramatized and explained it. Eventually he was able by participation to feel his place in it, since rituals contributed in a powerful way to the establishment of personal identity and indicated direction in life by showing what one had to do to preserve this way of life for future generations. Participation also inculcated a sense of the extent to which religious response was necessary, for by involving the total person, it called every human power into service" (84–86).

16. As William Oandasan writes in "A Familiar Love Component of Love in Ceremony," *Critical Perspectives on Native American Fiction*, ed. Richard F. Fleck, "Betonie informs Tayo [. . .] that there are intricately delicate harmonies and balance to maintain—this is to suggest, within each person, community, the earth and the sky. But Betonie also adds to this statement that these principles—for example, reciprocity, equilibrium, and

simultaneity—are always shifting so that the people, their ceremonies and stories, and existence itself must also change accordingly, or else they will become static and thereby become eventually extinct. Betonie furthers tells the story of the primordial meeting between witches from all parts of the world, when an arch sorcerer unleashed through a story (a curse?) the division and destruction of the earth. Betonie reminds Tayo of the false separation of white people and people of color, the closing of open land into fenced land, the destruction of natural life and resources by mechanized devices and forces, etc." (241).

17. I use the term *tribal individual* here to indicate Native American thinking on individualism and identity, a Native American understanding of what it means to "be." In his essay "Native American Novels: Homing In," William Bevis explains that in Native American thought there is "a tribal rather than an individual definition of 'being.'" In light of that, identity "is not a matter of finding 'one's self,' but of finding a 'self' that is transpersonal and includes a society, a past, and a place. To be separated from that transpersonal time and space is to lose identity. [. . .] That an individual exists is not contested, and Native American life and novels present all the variety of personality expected in our species; but the individual alone has no meaning [. . .] Individuality is not even the scene of success or failure; it is nothing" (590–91).

18. Although throughout this study I argue that going home is but a part of characters' journeys to selfhood, it is, nonetheless, an essential part of that journey. As we saw in *The Chaneysville Incident*, for example, place is extremely relevant to the success of John's search for self. And that place is also significant to Tayo's ceremony is made apparent in this section of the story. As Robert Nelson writes in *Place and Vision: The Function of Landscape in Native American Fiction* (New York: Lang, 1993), although Tayo's life and "the life of the People is out of harmony with the place where they happen to be," it is, nevertheless, "the same place, and the same people; but the *relationship* between them has fallen out of balance." A new relationship to place is needed for harmony to be restored between the people and the land, among the people themselves, and within Tayo. And as Silko shows us in the novel, this requires a ceremony, a cultural tradition designed to bring Tayo and his people "back into harmony with the world they happen to be living in [. . .] Tayo must re-visit the land itself in order to reestablish contact with the power of healing that he may find there" (13–15).

19. For a thorough discussion of Navajo sandpainting and its use and relevance in Silko's work, see Valerie Harvey's "Navajo Sandpainting in *Ceremony*." Harvey asserts, "Within Navajo Indian culture, sandpainting or 'dry painting' is an involved ceremonial ritual used mainly for healing purposes. An integral part of the Navajo religious tradition, a sandpainting is created out of natural elements by a tribal medicine man with the intended purpose of restoring the spiritual, emotional, physical, and psychological health of an individual. Believed to be greater than the 'white man's' medicine, and lasting anywhere from one to nine days in duration, a sandpainting ceremony becomes a vehicle through which an individual finds his or her way back to health by becoming united, once again, with the wholeness and balance of the physical and spiritual world. [. . .] The

symbols and objects used in the sandpainting that Betonie makes are bear footprints, rainbows, mountains, prayersticks, hoops, and prayer; all part of the symbolic significance of the white-corn sandpainting" (257).

The ceremony Betonie and Tayo engage in, Shamoon Zamir argues, both reflects Silko's dependence upon and marks her departure from Native American culture. See Zamir's essay "Literature in 'National Sacrifice Area': Leslie Silko's *Ceremony*," *New Voices in Native American Literary Criticism* (Washington: Smithsonian, 1993).

20. I mean to use the terms *otherworldly* and *entrancing* as Paula Gunn Allen would have them used: "without the hypersentimental side effects implied" by those terms. That is, I do not mean them to indicate some kind of childish magicalness experienced by Tayo through the structural devices of ceremony in which Betonie engages him. Rather, these terms are meant to refer to the "hypnotic state of consciousness" Tayo discovers, which, as Allen tells us, is the "aim of ceremony." I make this distinction because I want to avoid what Allen sees as "the failure of folklorists to comprehend the true metaphysical and psychic nature of structural devices such as ceremonial repetition [. . .] a result of the projection of one set of cultural assumptions onto another culture's customs and literatures [. . .] The twin assumptions that repetition serves to quiet childish psychological needs and to assure participants in a ceremony that they are exerting control over external phenomena—getting something they want badly—are projections. The participants do indeed believe that they can exert control over natural phenomena, but not because they have childishly repeated some syllables. Rather, they assume that all reality is internal in some sense, that the dichotomy of the isolate individual versus the 'out there' only appears to exist, and that ceremonial observance can help them transcend this delusion and achieve union with the All-Spirit. From a position of unity within this larger Self, the ceremony can bring about certain results, such as healing one who is ill, ensuring that natural events move in their accustomed way, or bringing prosperity to the tribe. [. . .] The tribal person perceives things, not as inert, but as viable and alive, and he or she knows that living things are subject to processes of growth and change as necessary components of their aliveness. Since all that exists is alive and since all that is alive must grow and change, all existence can be manipulated under certain conditions and according to certain laws. These conditions and laws, called 'ritual' and 'magic' in the West, are known to American Indians variously. The Sioux refer to them as 'walking in the sacred manner,' the Navajo as 'standing in the center of the world,' and the Pomo as 'having a tradition.' There are as many ways of referring to this phenomenon as there are tribes" (*Studies* 14–17).

21. There we are told that stories are the essence of life, "they are all we have [. . .] You don't have anything if you don't have the stories" (2). Thus, Rachel Stein writes, in *Shifting the Ground: American Women Writers' Revisions of Nature, Gender, and Race* (Charlottesville: UP of Virginia, 1997), we should view Tayo's ceremony as a "reconstruction of traditional stories that reassert the spiritual union of tribe and natural world [. . .] In an essay entitled 'Landscape, History, and the Pueblo Imagination,' Silko explains

that in Laguna tradition stories are the means of creating a collective culture in which humans and their natural surroundings are bound together in a meaningful relation [. . .] Silko observes that the tribe forms and reforms itself as a social entity through stories; in Laguna culture the transmission of stories is a collective project in which all members of the tribe participate. [. . .] Every tribe member learns portions of the traditional oral stories for recitation and transmission and learns to view his or her own history as a strand within the web of traditional, family, and personal stories. This web of stories binds the tribe into a collective in which the well-being of each member is a communal concern and in which the members fulfill what Allen calls 'complementary' male/female roles within generally egalitarian and participatory social structures. The stories also bind the tribe into the context of the larger natural world" (116–17).

22. From an American Indian viewpoint, Paula Gunn Allen explains in her work *The Sacred Hoop,* "We are the land, and the land is mother to us all. [. . .] We are the land [. . .] that is the fundamental idea that permeates American Indian life; the land (Mother) and the people (mothers) are the same. [. . .] The earth is the source and the being of the people, and we are equally the being of the earth. The land is not really a place, separate from ourselves, where we act out the drama of our isolate destinies. [. . .] We must not conceive of the earth as an ever-dead other that supplies us with a sense of ego identity by virtue of our contrast to its perceived non-being. Rather for American Indians, like Betonie, the earth *is* being, as all creatures are also being: aware, palpable, intelligent, alive. [. . .] Tayo's illness is a result of separation from the ancient unity of person, ceremony, and land, and his healing is a result of his recognition of this unity. [. . .] The healing of Tayo and the land results from the reunification of land and person. Tayo is healed when he understands in magical (mystical) and loving ways, that his being is within and outside him, that it includes his mother, Night Swan, Ts'eh, Josiah, the spotted cattle, winter, hope, love, and the starry universe of Betonie's ceremony" (119–20).

23. In "An Act of Attention: Event Structure in *Ceremony*," *Critical Essays on Native American Literature,* ed. Andrew Wiget (Boston: Hall, 1985), Elaine Jahner discusses Tayo's experience as an emerging as well and urges us, as readers, to relate his culturally specific experience to our own. And this is an important point, for authors who thematically incorporate their group's folklore into their texts do so to teach us about their culture, and to help us actually learn from their example. As Jahner tells us, "Tayo's participating in the sunrise event is both convergence and emergence. Past understandings of the meaning of experiences converge and permit emergence to new levels of comprehension, new parts of the story and new aspects of the ceremonies. Events are boundary experiences marking stages of life for the protagonist. They also mark stages of the story for the reader who can experience their impact by relating to their significance as primary human experiences that are at one and the same time, acts of recognition and experiences of renewal of energies. As recognition, event implies pattern, form that is enduring yet specific as to time and place. As experience, it implies conscious participation in the dynamic energies that generate and perpetuate life and

form. Both the pattern and the experience are, by their very nature, culturally specific; and it is at this level that a reader must bring his or her own cultural experiences into relation with those of the protagonist" (239–40).

24. Of the relevance of this female figure, Robert M. Nelson writes in *Place and Vision*, "All who study the novel agree that the figure of Ts'eh plays a crucial role in this ceremony [. . .] The efficacy of this ceremony depends on the precise relationship that Tayo establishes with the figure Ts'eh. The entity whom Tayo encounters is, clearly, to be understood as a 'spirit of place,' a more-than-human being who represents the land's own life, who knows How Things Work and who is willing to share this knowledge with the People. The People must acknowledge her existence and find a way to see her for what she is, a way to make a place for her in their conceptual map of the world and the forces at work there" (15). In terms of Laguna culture and Tayo's specific ceremony, Rachel Stein asserts, in *Shifting the Ground*, "Ts'eh is a sacred shapeshifter, in the tradition of spirit beings such as Buffalo Man and Sun Man, who appear in the traditional Laguna stories that Silko collected in *Storyteller* and that she discussed in the essay 'Landscape' [. . .] Such shapeshifters convey spiritual knowledge to the tribe by momentarily assuming human shape in order to form unions with tribespeople. The nature gods and goddesses act as lovers and teachers, offering their human partners sacred knowledge and sacred items that aid the entire tribe. Thus, these relationships epitomize the Laguna belief in the reciprocal spiritual kinship of human and nature, the belief, discussed above, that the Laguna *became* a people when they articulated a partnership relationship to the surrounding landscape" (134).

25. A tribal sense of being entails knowing that an individual's life cannot be fulfilled unless the relationships among all beings of the universe are also fulfilled. As Paula Gunn Allen explains, tribal life acknowledges "the essential harmony of all things," sees "all things as being of equal value in the scheme of things, denying the opposition, dualism, and isolation (separateness) that characterize non-Indian thought" (*Studies* 4–5).

26. In "The Feminine Landscape of Leslie Marmon Silko's *Ceremony*," Paula Gunn Allen asserts, "For Tayo, wholeness consists of sowing plants and nurturing them, caring for the spotted cattle, and especially knowing that he belongs exactly where he is, that he is and always has been home. [. . .] He is able at last to take his normal place in the life of the Laguna, a place that is characterized by nurturing, caring for life, behaving like a good mother" (*Studies* 132–33).

Chapter 4. What I Learn from You Goes with Me on the Journey

1. In "The Vaginal Serpent and Other Themes from Mexican-American Women's Lore," *Women's Folklore, Women's Culture*, ed. Rosan A. Jordan and Susan J. Kalčik (Philadelphia: U of Pennsylvania P, 1985), Jordon urges us to view Mexican-

American women's folklore as a "source of information for examining how Mexican American women actually view their culturally assigned roles and how they respond to cultural pressures" shaping individual behavior (26).

2. In "Chicana Literature from a Chicana Feminist Perspective," *Chicana Creativity and Criticism: Charting New Frontiers in American Literature,* ed. María Herrera-Sobek and Helena María Viramontes (Houston: Arte Público, 1988), Yvonne Yarbro-Bejarano tells us that the experience of the Chicana writer deriving "literary authority from the oral tradition of her community, which in turn empowers her to commit her stories to writing [. . .] has been traditionally excluded from literary representation"(141). However, this is not only precisely the experience Mena's own writing represents in this instance, but also just the experience brought to life by the women of her story via the relationship they share.

3. Mena was "commissioned by *Century* specifically to write stories about Mexican life." Given the fact that her work often followed, as López tells us, "xenophobic essays [. . .] such as W. Morgan Shuster's 'The Mexican Menace,'" such a surface reading would fit in well with *Century Magazine*'s implied requirement that Mena present what might be termed a "pretty picture" of Mexican culture (27).

4. For an insightful discussion of Aztec creation myths, see Frances Toor, *A Treasury of Mexican Folkways* (New York: Crown, 1952).

5. According to the myth, after the death of Coatlicue's warrior husband, Coatlicue sought solace in her religion and found it by engaging in related rituals meant to bring spiritual comfort and release. We are told by *mamagrande* via the narrator, "'Daily, when the afternoon falls, Coatlicue burns incense in the temple to the god of her ancestors, at the feet of whose image her beloved Camatzin had deposited a thousand times the laurels of his victories in the hunt and in war. Religion is the consolation unique in these afflictions. When cries the soul, only one balsam exists to cure the wound. Pray, souls that cry, if you wish that your pains be diminished'" (48).

6. I use the term *storytelling* as an umbrella term, for myth telling, taletelling, legend telling, etc. are all forms of storytelling. The point is not the type of narrative, but the act of narrating.

7. See Ralph Ellison's *Shadow and Act,* as well as the introduction to this study, where I discuss Ellison's experience and his comments regarding it.

8. Ellison made it clear that while writing may have been his vehicle to self, folklore could be someone else's. Along the same lines, I say "for instance" here to indicate that the tradition of storytelling is just one of the folkloric ways a connection to the past and its peoples can be made. As the other works of this study indicate, there are other folklore traditions—many of them culturally specific traditions, like the ceremony Tayo engages in—utilized for the same purpose. And as Fernández, the second author studied in this chapter, shows us in her work, within her own cultural community alone, a multitude of traditions have been designed and are practiced for the centering and defining benefits they provide.

9. See Roger D. Abrahams, "Folklore and Literature as Performance," and Mary Ellen B. Lewis, "The Study of Folklore in Literature." Both discuss folklore as performance and provide additional references to other folklore and performance analyses.

10. As Edith Hamilton tells us in *Mythology* (Boston: Little, 1942), "the real interest of myths is that they lead us back to a time when the world was young and people had a connection with the earth, with trees and seas and flowers and hills, unlike anything we ourselves can feel. When the stories were being shaped, we are given to understand, little distinction had as yet been made between the real and the unreal" (3). And, as Jan Harold Brunvand writes in *The Study of American Folklore*, myths "may be defined as 'traditional prose narratives, which, in the society in which they are told, are considered to be truthful accounts of what happened in the remote past.' Typically, they deal with the activities of gods and demigods, the creation of the world and its inhabitants, and the origins of religious rituals. Whenever myths purport to explain such matters as origin of geographic features, animal traits, rites, taboos, and customs, they are known as *explanatory* or *etiological* narratives" (136).

11. The narrator's experience with the languages available to her anticipates contemporary theory on the subject, the majority of which supports the idea that language plays a central role in the search for self-definition. As Gloria Anzaldua asserts in *Borderlands/La Frontera: The New Mestiza* (San Francisco: Spinsters/Aunt Lute, 1987), "Ethnic Identity is twin skin to linguistic identity—I am my language" (58). Through her narrator's struggle to find a language through which she can articulate herself, Mena does what Ada Savin, in "A Bridge over the Americas: Mexican American Literature," *Bilingual Review* 20.2 (1995), tells us contemporary writers Lorna Dee Cervantes and Sandra Cisneros do in their works: subject both English and Spanish "to a process of decentralization that goes hand in hand with the repositioning of the writer's self vis-à-vis her two cultural poles: Mexican and American" (122–27). Moreover, what comes out of her repositioning is similar as well, "a form of hybrid, a language that amalgamates the two systems, thus annihilating the alleged but commonly accepted binary opposition" (123). And yet, although the narrator's turn to "Spanish bears the mark of cultural estrangement, of painful loss," as is apparent in much contemporary writing, the comments Mena has her make regarding this turn not only indicate a preference but also represent an affirmation.

12. Nenita uses the term *ritual* when she refers to her experiences with these combined traditions. Family traditions, such as these, are those "forms of expression and behavior, generated by and perpetuated among the members of a family, which grow out of, celebrate, or otherwise reflect the identity of the family as a group and of individuals within the family as members of that group" (B. Allen 1).

13. Speaking of folklore content, Barbara Allen tells us that family stories, for instance, "often focus on the exploits of individual members, emphasizing their identities as unique and independent personalities; yet those individuals are also given relational

Notes to Pages 143–45

labels, such as Grandmother Rogers or Cousin Pat, placing them precisely in the network of family relationships." Often, different kinds of family traditions are used in combination to serve simultaneously these separate, but interrelated, identities (4).

14. In "'Woof!' A Word on Women's Roles in Family Storytelling," *Women's Folklore, Women's Culture,* ed. Jordon and Kalčik, 149–62, Karen Baldwin tells us, "The body of narratives common and private to any community of kin is a composite and dynamic whole. Its constituent elements [. . .] are both changing and interchangeable. No one person in the family is the ultimate source of the group's oral history, its poems, tales, and proverbs. Many people must be heard to tell their 'two bits' before the whole begins to make sense. And the performance of the whole body of narratives has as many social centers as there are kitchens and parlors, side yards, and front stoops for hearing out the family yarn spinners and oral historians. The family draws its narratives from many sources and tells its story with many voices, and the ways in which family tellers change and interchange their portions of the whole are importantly collaborative" (151). Baldwin's essay focuses on the storytelling techniques of her own family members— specifically, but not limited to, the female family members. What she shares with us of the dynamics of their storytelling mirrors what the aunts do here in *Intaglio.*

15. Here again it is the essence of the tradition that matters. In *A Treasury of Mexican Folkways,* Frances Toor tells us that Mexicans used, among other things, traditional folk dancing "to dramatize what they wished to teach" (316). Although Andrea is more a "modern" dancer than a folk dancer, she puts her dance to use for the same reasons folk dancers have in the past and still do today. In *The Study of American Folklore,* Brunvand tells us that "dances and dramas began in ritual and developed into entertainment. [. . .] 'The dance,' wrote Curt Sachs, historian of the subject, 'is the mother of the arts.' In its basic form of a rhythmic, stylized pattern of individual or group movement performed with or without music in response to a religious or creative urge, dance has existed in every known culture, including the most primitive and it occurs even among animals. From the movements of dancing, Sachs suggested, were derived the other means of artistic expression, all of which eventually drifted away from the close involvement with worship and the cycle of life to their current connections largely with self-expression and entertainment" (351). Andrea uses dance for both its age-old "folk" purpose and its more contemporary; for her, dance is about the cycle of life as well as about expressing the self and entertaining others. Brunvand also asserts that Native Americans, immigrant groups—such the Mexican American group that peoples *Intaglio*—and dance companies are probably where we will find our most valuable information on the role of dance in the lives of individuals and communities today.

16. See Toor, *A Treasury of Mexican Folkways,* 39–51.

17. Such creation and expression of self through the processes of a craft calls to mind what Michael Owens Jones, in "The Concept of 'Aesthetic' in the Traditional Arts," *Western Folklore* 30 (1971): 77–104, has to say about approaching folk art with its

processes in mind. He writes: "To treat any work of art as simply an object, without regard for the *processes* of production and consumption, is to fail to understand the meaning for the art or the reasons for the formal, material, and expressive qualities that it exhibits." Pershing concurs with Owens on this matter in "Peace Work out of Piecework," 1–31.

18. Filomena is religious in the traditional sense to be sure, but what is important here is Filomena's dedication to and use of what is understood as "folk religion." Brunvand explains: "Many people, perhaps most, engage in some aspects of folk religion, which comprises, in Don Yoder's words, 'views and practices of religion that exist among the people apart from and alongside the strictly theological and liturgical forms of the official religion.' These traditional unofficial religious attitudes and actions may range in complexity from simple aspects of prayer, veneration of religious objects, blessings, faith-promoting stories, and the like, up to elaborate folk-religious organizations such as the voodoo practiced in New Orleans, which derives from Haiti, and the Southern snake-handling cults, which take their inspiration from the literal interpretation of Biblical practices" (314).

19. Fernández's presentation of this tradition provides proof of Turner's assertion that "home altars and their makers can be looked upon as a source for further understanding the role Mexican American women play in facilitating human relationship and interrelationship in the context of the family and the community." See Turner, "Mexican American Home Altars: Towards Their Interpretation," *Aztlan* 13.1–2 (1982): 309–11.

20. Complex and elaborate, Day of the Dead rituals are described and discussed at length—and in regard to particularities of differing communities—in Toor, *A Treasury of Mexican Folkways,* 236–44. And his illuminating discussion of the practices of the Tarascans on the island of Janitzio mirrors Nenita's description of her experience almost to the letter (243–44).

21. Flowers for the dead.

22. In "The Vaginal Serpent and Other Themes from Mexican-American Women's Lore," Jordan explains the differing behavioral expectations of men and women within Hispanic communities: "Within the family, the husband/father's authority is seen as absolute. The wife/mother's role is characterized by self-sacrifice, service to the needs of others, and nurturance. Her activities are narrowly confined to home and family, and mothering—bearing and raising children—is seen as her primary function. For men, sexual relations outside marriage are permitted or even encouraged, and fathering children (legitimate or illegitimate) is considered proof of virility. Training for these adult roles begins in childhood, as girls are given much less freedom than boys and are expected to help with housework and child care. As adolescents, girls are watched over carefully to ensure their sexual purity, while boys are encouraged to begin developing sexual prowess, which is thought to be proof of masculinity" (26).

23. To a great degree, these women are described as faith healers. As Brunvand explains, "'Faith healers,' semiprofessional folk specialists in traditional medicine, usually

employ a combination of personal and religious power, sometimes in combination with certain herbs or nostrums. Their concepts of diseases and cures may reflect popular writings on medicine of many decades earlier, and they generally also display folk attitudes held by their particular regional or ethnic group. For instance, the Mexican-American *curanderos* may be called upon to treat *mal puesto* (afflictions involving magic or witchcraft) or *males natural* (natural diseases, unknown among Anglo-Americans and not treated by physicians) such as *empacho* (a form of indigestion), *mal ojo* (evil eye), *susto* (fright sickness), and *caída de la mollera* (fallen fontanel)" (310).

24. Long considered simply domestic duties—i.e., housework—cooking and the forms of needlework mentioned here can, thanks to the joint venture of feminist scholarship and folklore studies, now be understood as valuable performative folk traditions, perhaps falling under one of the following headings: Occupational Folklore, Family Folklore, or Folk Crafts, the term I use to refer to the household traditions passed on to Zulema in the novel. See Judith Levin, "Why Folklorists Should Study Housework," *Feminist Theory and the Study of Folklore* (Urbana: U of Illinois P, 1985).

Conclusion

1. We tend to think of industrialized living as complicated, which it certainly is. But so, too, is living according to traditions handed down through generations. The problem is that industrialized living often means a movement toward the formal instruction of those things traditionally learned through folklore and considered a part of everyday life: music, morals, manners, stories, myths, etc. Still, it is not as though the two never meet. They do, and perhaps more so now than ever before. In "The Folkness of the Non-Folk," *Folklore and Society,* ed. Bruce Jackson (Hatboro: Folklore Associates, 1966), Charles Seeger's thirty-year-old comment still applies: "You can't kill a culture [. . .] You can suppress it, cripple it, acculturate it and its principal traditions. But its continuity and creativity are built into the very bodies of its carriers. Sooner or later a revival sets in. We can see the operation of both these factors in full swing in our own day. It is not only scholarship and business enterprise that launched the folklore revival movement in the United States. It was equally an initiative of the people in general 'on the hoof,' as it were—especially young people. It was a rebellion against a wrong direction taken by former generations. An attempt to re-capture a *Kulturgut* that was supposedly scuttled but had kept on floating in out-of-the-way places. What is actually being done is what folklore always has done: recreating whatever comes its way. Except that this has had to be done by most urbanites after a gap of a century or so, instead of at the breast or soon after, everything is going according to folk-Hoyle. The revival moment is, essentially, the folkness held in common by the folk and the supposedly non-folk alike coming to the surface in the cities, re-asserting itself in spite of—indeed, because of—three generations' efforts to suppress it. Functionally viewed, it is a reascent of folkness

within the non-folk (which was supposed to not have any) coupled with the surviving folkness of the folk, whose sole property it was supposed to be" (3–4).

2. I agree with Alan Dundes that "an individual's sense of identity changes throughout the life cycle [. . .] An individual may and will maintain different identities at the same time" (*Folklore Matters* 12, 21). Thus, as I did in the introduction's discussion of identity, let me once again clarify my use of terms. The term *whole* refers to the coherency of self the characters achieve through their folklore engagement; likewise, the term *connected* refers to the lasting and essential sense of union the characters form with the members of the folk groups they have entered into or returned to. As I have shown in my analysis of the texts, the characters learn through both example and personal practice that folklore provides a way for them to make sense of the various identities they have taken on or have allowed to be imposed upon them.

3. Other folk groups have been portrayed using the oral tradition for these purposes as well. See Amy Tan, *The Joy Luck Club* (Asian-American); Lee Smith, *Oral History* (southeastern Anglo-American); and the short stories of Stuart Dybek (Polish-American), for instance.

4. See James Ruppert, "Dialogism and Mediation in Leslie Marmon Silko's *Ceremony,*" *Explicator* 51.2 (winter 1993): 129–34.

5. To name a few: N. Scott Momaday, *The Way to Rainy Mountain;* Lee Smith, *Oral History;* Amy Tan, *The Joy Luck Club;* Toni Morrison, *The Song of Solomon;* Paule Marshall, *Praisesong for the Widow;* John Wideman, *Sent for You Yesterday.*

6. In "Whose Dream Is This Anyway?" *The Sacred Hoop* (Boston: Beacon, 1992), Paula Gunn Allen identifies the various communities of which Loney could have been a part: "the small town community he lives in, the Indian community his mother came from, the Catholic community he was raised by, even the men's community of ex-basketball stars and their onetime fans" (93).

WORKS CITED

Allen, Barbara. "Family Traditions and Personal Identity." *Kentucky Folklore Record* 28.1–2 (1982): 1–5.

Allen, Paula Gunn, ed. *Studies in American Indian Literature.* New York: MLA, 1983.

————. *The Sacred Hoop: Recovering the Feminine in American Indian Traditions.* Boston: Beacon, 1992.

Anderson, Suzy McLennan. *Collector's Guide to Quilts.* Radnor: Wallace, 1991.

Anzaldua, Gloria. *Borderlands/La Frontera: The New Mestiza.* San Francisco: Spinsters/Aunt Lute, 1987.

Baez, Joan American. *The Quotable Woman.* Philadelphia: Running Press, 1991.

Baker, Houston. *Modernism and the Harlem Renaissance.* Chicago: U of Chicago P, 1987.

Baldwin, Karen. "'Woof!' A Word on Women's Roles in Family Storytelling." *Women's Folklore, Women's Culture.* Ed. Rosan A. Jordan and Susan J. Kalčik. Philadelphia: U of Pennsylvania P, 1985. 149–62.

Bauman, Richard. *Story, Performance, and Event.* New York: Cambridge UP, 1986.

Bellow, Saul. *Seize the Day: Seven Contemporary Short Novels.* Ed. Charles Clerc and Louis Leiter. 3d ed. New York: Harper, 1982.

Bevis, William. "Native American Novels: Homing In." *Recovering the Words: Essays on Native American Literature.* Ed. Brian Swann and Arnold Krupat. Berkeley: U of California P, 1987. 580–620.

Blassingame, John W. *The Slave Community.* New York: Oxford UP, 1972.

Bradley, David. *The Chaneysville Incident.* New York: Harper, 1981.

————. Personal interview. 13 Sept. 1993.

Brunvand, Jan Harold. *The Study of American Folklore: An Introduction.* 3d ed. New York: Norton, 1986.

Campbell, Jane. *Mythic Black Fiction: The Transformation of History.* Knoxville: U of Tennessee P, 1986.

Chesnutt, Charles. *The Conjure Woman.* Ann Arbor: U of Michigan P, 1969.

Coffin, Tristram P. *Our Living Traditions.* New York: Basic, 1968.

Cooke, Michael G. *Afro-American Literature in the Twentieth Century.* New Haven: Yale UP, 1984.

Cutter, Martha J. "Zitkala-Ša's Autobiographical Writings." *Melus* 19.1 (1994): 31–44.

DeMallie, Raymond J., ed. *Lakota Society.* Lincoln: U of Nebraska P, 1982.

DeMallie, Raymond J., and Elaine A. Jahner, eds. *Lakota Belief and Ritual.* Lincoln: U of Nebraska P, 1982.

Dorson, Richard. "The Identification of Folklore in American Literature." *Journal of American Folklore* 70 (1957): 186–209.

Dugan, Kathleen. *The Vision Quest of the Plains Indians: Its Spiritual Significance.* Lewiston: Edwin Mellen, 1995.

Dundes, Alan. "Defining Identity through Folklore." *Identity: Personal and Socio-Cultural: A Symposium.* Ed. Anita Jacobson-Widding. Uppsala, Sweden: U of Uppsala, 1983. 235–61. Rpt. in *Folklore Matters.* Knoxville: U of Tennessee P, 1989.

———. *Folklore Matters.* Knoxville: U of Tennessee P, 1989.

———. *The Study of Folklore.* Englewood Cliffs, N.J.: Prentice Hall, 1965.

Eisen, Armand. *Believing in Ourselves 1997 Calendar.* Kansas City, MO: Andrews and McMeel, 1996.

Ellison, Ralph. *Invisible Man.* New York: Random, 1952.

———. *Shadow and Act.* New York: Random, 1953.

Farnsworth, Robert M. Introduction. *The Conjure Woman.* By Charles W. Chesnutt. Ann Arbor: U of Michigan P, 1986. v–xix.

Fernández, Roberta. *Intaglio: A Novel in Six Stories.* Houston: Arte Público, 1990.

Fisher, Dexter. Foreword. *American Indian Stories.* By Zitkala-Sä. Lincoln: U of Nebraska P, 1985. v–xx.

Fox, Jennifer. "The Creator Gods: Romantic Nationalism and the Engenderment of Women in Folklore." *Feminist Theory and the Study of Folklore.* Ed. Susan Tower Hollis, Linda Pershing, and M. Jane Young. Urbana: U of Illinois P, 1993.

George, Robert A. "Toward an Understanding of Storytelling Events." *Journal of American Folklore* 82 (1969): 313–28.

Georges, Robert A., and Michael Owen Jones. *Folkloristics: An Introduction.* Bloomington: Indiana UP, 1995.

Hamilton, Edith. *Mythology.* Boston: Little, 1942.

Harris, Trudier. *Fiction and Folklore: The Novels of Toni Morrison.* Knoxville: U of Tennessee P, 1991.

Harvey, Valerie. "Navajo Sandpainting in *Ceremony.*" *Critical Perspectives on Native American Fiction.* Ed. Richard F. Fleck. Washington: Three Continents, 1993. 256–62.

Hedges, Elaine. "Quilts and Women's Culture." *In Her Own Image: Women Working in the Arts.* Eds. Elaine Hedges and Ingrid Wendt. New York: Feminist, 1980. 13–19.

Hedges, Elaine, and Ingrid Wendt, eds. *In Her Own Image: Women Working in the Arts.* New York: Feminist, 1980.

Hedrick, Joan D. "'Peaceable Fruits': The Ministry of Harriet Beecher Stowe." *American Quarterly* 40.3 (1988): 307–32.

Hemenway, Robert. "The Functions of Folklore in Charles Chesnutt's *The Conjure Woman*." *Journal of the Folklore Institute* 13 (1976): 283–309.

Holstein, Jonathan. *American Pieced Quilts.* New York: Viking, 1973.

Jahner, Elaine. "An Act of Attention: Event Structure in *Ceremony*." *Critical Essays on Native American Literature.* Ed. Andrew Wiget. Boston: Hall, 1985. 238–45.

Jones, Michael Owens. "The Concept of 'Aesthetic' in the Traditional Arts." *Western Folklore* 30 (1971): 77–104.

Jones, Steven Swann. Introduction. *Folklore and Literature in the United States: An Annotated Bibliography of Studies of Folklore in American Literature.* New York: Garland, 1984.

Jordon, Rosan A. "The Vaginal Serpent and Other Themes from Mexican-American Women's Lore." *Women's Folklore, Women's Culture.* Ed. Rosan A. Jordan and Susan J. Kalčik. Philadelphia: U of Pennsylvania P, 1985. 26–44.

Karcher, Carolyn. Letter to the author. 21 Mar. 1998.

Karpinski, Joanne. "The Shadow Block: Female Bonding in Quilters." *Women and Performance: Journal of Feminism* 4.1 (1988–89): 6–22.

Kirkland, James. Introduction. "Connecting Folklore and Literature." Unpublished Manuscript.

Kubitschek, Missy Dehn. *Claiming the Heritage: African American Women's Novels and History.* Mississippi: U of Mississippi P, 1991.

Lauter, Paul, et al., eds. *The Heath Anthology of American Literature.* 2d ed. 2 vols. Lexington: Heath, 1994.

Levin, Judith. "Why Folklorists Should Study Housework." *Feminist Theory and the Study of Folklore.* Ed. Susan Tower Hollis, Linda Pershing, and M. Jane Young. Urbana: U of Illinois P, 1993. 285–96.

Lippard, Lucy R. "Up, Down, and Across: A New Frame for New Quilts." *The Artist and the Quilt.* Ed. Charlotte Robinson. New York: Knopf, 1983.

Lithgow, Marilyn. *Quiltmaking and Quiltmakers.* New York: Funk & Wagnalls, 1974.

López, Tiffany Anne. "María Cristina Mena: Turn-of-the-Century La Malinche and Other Tales of Cultural (Re) Construction." *Tricksterism in Turn-of-the-Century American Literature.* Ed. Elizabeth Ammons and Annette White-Parks. Hanover: UP of New England, 1994. 21–45.

Macheski, Cecilia. ed. *Quilt Stories.* Lexington: UP of Kentucky, 1994.

Marcus, Jane. "Invisible Mending." *Between Women.* Ed. Carol Ascher, Louise DeSalvo, and Sara Ruddick. Boston: Beacon, 1984.

McCorkle, Jill. Review of *How to Make an American Quilt* by Whitney Otto. *New York Times Book Review,* 24 Mar. 1991, 10.

McLennan Anderson, Suzy. *Collector's Guide to Quilts.* Radnor: Wallace, 1991.

Mena, María Cristina. "The Birth of the God of War." *Century Magazine* 88 (1914): 45–49.

Mobley, Marilyn Sanders. *Folk Roots and Mythic Wings in Sarah Orne Jewett and Toni Morrison.* Baton Rouge: Louisiana State UP, 1991.

Momaday, N. Scott. *The Way to Rainy Mountain.* Albuquerque: U of New Mexico P, 1969.

Nelson, Robert. *Place and Vision: The Function of Landscape in Native American Fiction.* New York: Lang, 1993.

Noda, Kesay E. "Growing Up Asian in America." *Seventy-five Readings Plus.* Ed. Santi V. Buscemi and Charlotte Smith. 4th ed. Boston: McGraw, 1998.

Oandasan, William. "A Familiar Love Component of Love in *Ceremony.*" *Critical Perspectives on Native American Fiction.* Ed. Richard F. Fleck. Washington: Three Continents, 1993.

Okker, Patricia. "Native American Literatures and the Canon." *American Realism and the Canon.* Ed. Tom Quirk and Gary Scharnhorst. Newark: U of Delaware P, 1994. 87–100.

Okpewho, Isidore. *African Oral Literature.* Bloomington: Indiana UP, 1992.

Oring, Elliot. *Folk Groups and Folklore Genres.* Logan: Utah State UP, 1986.

Otto, Whitney. *How to Make an American Quilt.* New York: Ballantine, 1991.

Parades, Américo. "Folklore, lo Mexicano and Proverbs." *Aztlan* 13 (1982):1–11.

Parades, Raymund. "The Evolution of Chicano Literature." *Three American Literatures: Essays in Chicano, Native American, and Asian American Literature.* Ed. Houston A. Baker Jr. New York: MLA, 1982. 33–79.

Pavlic, Edward. "Syndetic Redemption: Above-Underground *Emergence* in David Bradley's *The Chaneysville Incident.*" *African American Review* 30.2 (1996): 165–84.

Pershing, Linda. "Peace Work out of Piecework: Feminist Needlework Metaphors and the Ribbon around the Pentagon." *Feminist Theory and the Study of Folklore.* Ed. Susan Tower Hollis, Linda Pershing, and M. Jane Young. Urbana: U of Illinois P, 1993. 334–36.

Pryse, Marjorie, and Hortense J. Spillers, eds. *Conjuring: Black Women, Fiction, and Literary Tradition.* Bloomington: Indiana UP, 1985.

Radner, Joan Newlon. *Feminist Messages: Coding in Women's Folk Culture.* Urbana: U of Illinois P, 1993. 1–31.

Render, Sylvia Lyons, ed. *The Short Fiction of Charles W. Chesnutt.* Washington: Howard UP, 1981.

Roach, Susan. "The Kinship Quilt: An Ethnographic Semiotic Analysis of a Quilting Bee." *Women's Folklore, Women's Culture.* Ed. Rosan A. Jordan and Susan J. Kalčik. Philadelphia: U of Pennsylvania P, 1985. 54–64.

Roth, Philip. *Goodbye, Columbus. Seven Contemporary Short Novels.* Ed. Charles Clerc and Louis Leiter. 3d ed. New York: Harper, 1982.

Ruppert, James. "Dialogism and Mediation in Leslie Marmon Silko's *Ceremony.*" *Explicator* 51:2 (winter 1993): 129–34.

Savin, Ada. "A Bridge over the Americas: Mexican American Literature." *Bilingual Review* 20:2 (1995): 122–27.

Schorer, Mark. *William Blake.* New York: Holt, 1948.

Schrager, Samuel. "What Is Social in Oral History?" *International Journal of Oral History* 4 (1983): 76–98.

Seeger, Charles. "The Folkness of the Non-Folk." *Folklore and Society.* Ed. Bruce Jackson. Hatboro: Folklore, 1966.

Shirley, Carl R., and Paula W. Shirley. *Understanding Chicano Literature.* Columbia: U of South Carolina P, 1988.

Showalter, Elaine. *Sister's Choice: Tradition and Change in American Women's Writing.* Oxford: Clarendon, 1991.

Silko, Leslie Marmon. *Ceremony.* New York: Penguin, 1977.

Smith, Jeanne. "Trickster's Voice in the Works of Zitkala-Sä." *Tricksterism in Turn-of-the-Century American Literature.* Ed. Elizabeth Ammons and Annette White-Parks. Hanover: UP of New England, 1994.

Stahl, Sandra Dolby. *Literary Folkloristics and the Personal Narrative.* Bloomington: Indiana UP, 1989.

———. "Personal Experience Stories." *A Handbook of American Folklore.* Ed. Richard M. Dorson. Bloomington: Indiana UP, 1983.

Stein, Rachel. *Shifting Ground: American Women Writers' Revisions of Nature, Gender, and Race.* Charlottesville: UP of Virginia, 1997.

Stowe, Harriet Beecher. *The Minister's Wooing.* Cambridge: Riverside, 1896.

Sumrall, Amber Coverdale, ed. *Write to the Heart: Wit and Wisdom of Women Writers.* Freedom, CA: Crossing, 1992.

Sundquist, Eric J. *To Wake the Nations.* Cambridge: Belknap, 1993. 271–454.

Toelken, Barre. *The Dynamics of Folklore.* Boston: Houghton, 1979.

Tonkin, Elizabeth. *Narrating Our Pasts.* New York: Cambridge, 1992.

Toor, Frances. *A Treasury of Mexican Folklore.* New York: Crown, 1952.

Turner, Kay. "Mexican American Home Altars: Towards Their Interpretation." *Aztlan* 13.1–2 (1982): 309–26.

TuSmith, Bonnie. *All My Relatives: Community in Contemporary Ethnic American Literatures.* Ann Arbor: U of Michigan P, 1994.

Updike, John. *Rabbit, Run.* New York: Fawcett, 1960.

Welch, James. *The Death of Jim Loney.* New York: Penguin, 1979.

Wooster, Ann-Sargent. *Quiltmaking: A Modern Approach to a Traditional Craft.* New York: Galahad, 1972.

Yarbro-Bejarano, Yvonne. "Chicana Literature from a Chicana Feminist Perspective." *Chicana Creativity and Criticism: Charting New Frontiers in American Literature.* Ed. María Herrera-Sobek and Helena María Viramontes. Houston: Arte Public, 1988.

Zeitlin, Steven J., Amy J. Kotkin, and Holly Cutting Baker, eds. *A Celebration of American Family Folklore: Tales and Traditions from the Smithsonian Collection.* New York: Pantheon, 1982.

Zitkala-Šă (Gertrude Bonnin). *American Indian Stories.* Lincoln: U of Nebraska P, 1985.

INDEX

acculturation, xxi, 100, 102, 106, 179
achievement of self, xiv, 160
agency, xi
Allen, Barbara, "Family Traditions and
    Personal Identity," 141
Allen, Paula Gunn, *Studies in American
    Indian Literature* and *The Sacred
    Hoop*, 116–28 passim
American Indian Stories, discussion of,
    100–16; folk traditions in, 101; legends
    in, 101, 109–16; ritual, ritualized liv-
    ing, as means to self in, 101, 112;
    sense of self, notion of self, under-
    standing of self in, 100, 102–3, 105,
    109, 114–15; storytelling in, 102
Anderson, Suzy McLennan, *Collector's
    Guide to Quilts*, 13
author/authority, speaker as, 96–97, 178

Baker, Houston, *Modernism and the
    Harlem Renaissance*, 64
Bauman, Richard, *Story, Performance,
    and Event*, xvi, 132–34
Bellow, Saul, *Seize the Day*, ix
Bevis, William, "Native American Nov-
    els: Homing In," 116
"The Birth of the God of War," discus-
    sion of, 130–40; folk traditions in,
    140; legends in, 136; myth in, 131–37;
    role of storytelling in, 130–40; sense
    of self in, 131, 134, 140; storytelling
    event in, 132–34
black folklife, traditions. *See* folk traditions
Blassingame, John, *The Slave Commu-
    nity*, 63
Bradley, David, xv, xvii, xx; *The
    Chaneysville Incident*, 82, 100, 117,
    133–34, 163

Brunvand, Jan, *The Study of American
    Folklore*, defining folklore, xi–xii, 167

Ceremony, discussion of, 116–28; folk
    traditions in, 116–18; legends in,
    121, 124; myth, mythic tradition in,
    122–23; ritual as means to self in,
    116–22, 125; sense of self in, 116–17;
    storytelling in, 121
ceremony, as folk tradition, means to
    self, in *Ceremony*, 116–28
The Chaneysville Incident, discussion
    of, 82–98; legends in, 84–87, 95; oral
    tradition as means to self in, 82–83,
    87, 95–98; ritual in, 88–89; role of
    storytelling in, 82–98; sense of self
    in, 65, 81; storytelling event in,
    86–87
Chesnutt, Charles, xvii, xx, 60, 86, 131,
    161, 175–77; *The Conjure Woman*,
    60, 92, 98
conjure, defined, 176; in *The Conjure
    Woman*, 60–82 passim
The Conjure Woman, discussion of,
    60–82; folk traditions in, 63; issues of
    slavery in, 60–82; legends in, 63; oral
    tradition in, 60–61, 76, 81; role of
    slave folktale in, 62–65; sense of self
    in, 65, 67; storytelling event in,
    66–67; storytelling tradition as
    means to self in, 60–82 passim;
    taletelling in, 77, 81
creative self-expression. *See* self-
    expression
cultural community, x, xv, 140, 162, 187;
    female, xxiii, 7, 140, 152; *see also* folk
    group
cultural group. *See* folk group

199

cultural tradition. *See* folk tradition(s)

dance tradition, as means to self, 189; in *Intaglio, A Novel in Six Stories*, 140–44
Dorson, Richard, "The Identification of Folklore in American Literature," xiv
Dundes, Alan, *Folklore Matters*, defining identity, xii

Ellison, Ralph, search for self, ix–xiii, 134, 167; *Invisible Man*, ix–x; *Shadow and Act*, x, xii, 167, 187
ethnic group. *See* folk group

female community. *See* folk group
female traditions, crafts (folk, cultural), as means to self, xix–xx, xxiii; in *How to Make an American Quilt*, 25–58 passim; in *Intaglio, A Novel in Six Stories*, 140–57 passim; in *The Minister's Wooing*, 2–25 passim
Fernández, Roberta, xv, xvii, xxiii, 131, 140, 187, 190; *Intaglio, A Novel in Six Stories*, 140, 189
folk aesthetic, xiv, xxi
folk culture, xv, xix, 58, 67; *see also* folk traditions
folk group, defined, vs. gender and ethnicity, xvii–xix, xxiii, 169–70, 173–74, 192; in *How to Make an American Quilt*, 27–28; in *The Minister's Wooing*, 3, 7, 16–19, 23
folk religion, defined, 190
folk religious beliefs, practices, as means to self, in *Intaglio, A Novel is Six Stories*, 146–52
folk tradition(s), discussion of, as means to self, xii–xxiv, 161, 167, 169, 170, 191; in *American Indian Stories*, 101; in "The Birth of the God of War," 140; in *Ceremony*, 116–18; in *The Conjure Woman*, 63; in *Intaglio, A Novel in Six Stories*, 140, 148, 154–55; in *The Minister's Wooing*, 2–3; performance centered approaches to, 2–3; *see also* dance,

folk religion, legends, myth, mythic ceremony, needleworking, storytelling
folklore, as means to self, xii–xxiv; as personal resource, xii; cultural context of, xi–xii; defined, xi–xii; female cultural traditions as, 2–3; performance centered approach to, 2–3, 168; studies of, xxiv
folklore in literature, use of, x–xxiv
folkloric activity, work, 23–24, 149, 164
folktale teller, xx, 64; *see also* storyteller

gender and ethnicity, discussion of, xvii–xix
Georges, Robert A., *Folkloristics: An Introduction*, xii

Hedges, Elaine, "Quilts and Women's Culture," 4
Holstein, Jonathan, *American Pieced Quilts*, 4
How to Make an American Quilt, discussion of, 25–58; female traditions (folk, cultural) as means to self, 25–58 passim; folk group in, 27–28; needlework traditions, as means to self, 25–58 passim; quilt, quilting as narrative structure, mode of living, 26–27, 28–58; slavery in, 49–50; storytelling in, 57

individual wellness, discussion of, xiv–xxiv
Intaglio, A Novel in Six Stories, dance as means to self in, 140–44; discussion of, 140–57; family folklore in, 141–42; folk religious beliefs in, 146–52; folk traditions as means to self in, 140, 148, 154–55; needlework traditions as means to self in, 144–46; ritual as means to self in, 140–43, 146–52, 156; sense of self in, 150; storytelling in, as means to self, 140–44, 155–57

Jahner, Elaine, "An Act of Attention: Event Structure in *Ceremony*," 122–23

Jones, Michael Owen, "The Concept of 'Aesthetic' in the Traditional Arts," xii
journey to know, discussion of , xix–xxiv
journey to self. *See* journey to know

Karpinski, Joanne, "The Shadow Block: Female Bonding in Quilters," 19
Kubitschek, Missy, *Claiming the Heritage: African American Women's Novels and History*, x, 168–69

legend(s), discussion of, as means to self, xxi, 171, 177–80, 182, 187; in *American Indian Stories*, 101, 109–16; in "The Birth of the God of War," 136; in *Ceremony*, 121, 124; in *The Chaneysville Incident*, 84–87, 95; in *The Conjure Woman*, 63
Lippard, Lucy, "Up, Down, and Across: A New Frame for New Quilts," 5
Lithgow, Marilyn, *Quiltmaking and Quiltmakers*, 4
López, Tiffany Ana, "María Cristina Mena: Turn-of-the-Century La Malinche and Other Tales of Cultural (Re) Construction," xxii–xxiii; 150, 171

Mena, María Cristina, xvii, xxii–xxiii,130–40, 157, 161, 171, 187–88; "The Birth of the God of War," 130
The Minister's Wooing, discussion of, 2–25; female traditions (folk, cultural) as means to self, 2–25 passim; folk group in, 3, 7, 16–19, 23; folk traditions, performance centered approach, 2–3; needlework traditions as means to self, 2–25 passim; quilting tradition as narrative structure in, 5–7; quilting traditions as mode of living, quilting bees, 13–17; ritual, 21; sense of self, 20, 22–23; slavery, issues of, 13–14; storytelling in, 6
multicultural, multicultural studies, x, xvi
myth, mythic ceremony, mythology, as means to self, xxi–xxii, 161, 181–82,

187–88, 191; in *Ceremony*, 122–23; in "The Birth of the God of War," 131–37

needlework traditions, as means to self, xix–xx; in *How to Make an American Quilt*, 25–58; in *Intaglio, A Novel in Six Stories*, 140, 144–46; in *The Minister's Wooing*, 2–25
Noda, Kesay E., "Growing Up Asian in America," 162

Okpewho, Isidore, *African Oral Literature*, 81
oral tradition, oral storyteller, as means to self, xx, 161, 176, 187, 192; in *The Chaneysville Incident*, 82–83, 87, 95–98; in *The Conjure Woman*, 60–61, 76, 81; *see also* storytelling tradition
Oring, Elliot, *Folk Groups and Folklore Genres*, 137–38
Otto, Whitney, xv, xvii, xix–xx, 144, 152, 160–63, 170–71, 174–75; *How to Make an American Quilt*, 25, 162

Parades, Américo, "Folklore, lo Mexicano and Proverbs," 134
patchwork, piecework. *See* needlework traditions; *see also* quilting
Pershing, Linda, "Peace Work out of Piecework: Feminist Needlework Metaphors and the Ribbon around the Pentagon," 2, 19

quilting, quilting traditions as narrative structure, mode of living/self-defining tool, in *How to Make an American Quilt*, 26–27, 28–58; in *The Minister's Wooing*, 5–7 passim; *see also* needlework traditions

ritual, ritualized living, as means to self, xxii, 164, 174, 179–80, 182–84, 187–90; in *American Indian Stories*, 101, 112; in *Ceremony*, 116–22, 125; in *The Chaneysville Incident*, 88–89; in *Intaglio, A Novel in Six Stories*,

ritual, *cont.*
  140–43, 146–52, 156; in *The Minister's Wooing*, 21
Roth, Philip, *Goodbye, Columbus*, ix

search for self, discussion of, ix–xxiv
self-definition. *See* sense of self
self-expression, 49, 67
sense of self, notion of self, self-definition, understanding of self, discussion of, xvii–xxiv, 161–65; in *American Indian Stories*, 100, 102–3, 105, 109, 114–15; in "The Birth of the God of War," 131, 134, 140; in *Ceremony*, 116–17; in *The Chaneysville Incident*, 65, 81; in *The Conjure Woman*, 65, 67; in *Intaglio, A Novel in Six Stories*, 150; in *The Minister's Wooing*, 20, 22–23
Showalter, Elaine, *Sister's Choice: Tradition and Change in American Women's Writing*, 2–5, 27
Silko, Leslie Marmon, xv, xvii, xxi–xxii, 100, 116, 150, 161–62, 167–69, 180–86; *Ceremony*, 116, 163
slave folktale, role of, in *The Conjure Woman*, 62–65
slavery, issues of, in *The Conjure Woman*, 60–82; in *How to Make an American Quilt*, 49–50; in *The Minister's Wooing*, 13–14
Stahl, Sandra Dolby, "Personal Experience Stories," *Literary Folkloristics and the Personal Narrative*, 60–61, 71
storyteller, storytelling tradition, as means to self, xii–xiii, xx–xxiii, 161–65, 169, 176, 187, 189; in *American Indian Stories*, 102; in "The Birth of the God of War," 130–40; in *Ceremony*, 121; in *The Chaneysville Incident*, 82–98; in *The Conjure*

Woman, 60–82; in *How to Make an American Quilt*, 57; in *Intaglio, A Novel in Six Stories*, 140–44, 155–57; in *The Minister's Wooing*, 6
storytelling event, moment, taletelling session, 176–78; in "The Birth of the God of War," 132–34; in *The Chaneysville Incident*, 86–87; in *The Conjure Woman*, 66–67
Stowe, Harriet Beecher, xvii, xix, 2, 26, 30, 58, 144, 152, 160–61; *The Minister's Wooing*, 2, 58, 60, 144, 171–74
Sundquist, Eric, *To Wake the Nations*, 63
survival folkways, 83, 86

taletelling moment, session, xx; in *The Conjure Woman*, 77, 81
Toelken, Barre, *The Dynamics of Folklore*, defining folklore, xi; folk group, xvii
Tonkin, Elizabeth, *Narrating Our Pasts*, 96
trickster, tricksterism, xxii–xxiii, 171, 179–80
Turner, Kay, "Mexican American Home Altars: Towards Their Interpretation," 147
TuSmith, Bonnie, *All My Relatives*, x, 168–69

Updike, John, *Rabbit, Run*, ix

Welch, James, *The Death of Jim Loney*, 164
women's folklore, 2, 26, 155, 170, 186–87, 189; *see also* folk culture

Zitkala-Šă, xviii, xx–xxi, 100, 116, 120–21, 124, 161, 171, 178, 181; *American Indian Stories*, 100, 128, 180

Literary Legacies, Folklore Foundations was designed and typeset on a Macintosh computer system using QuarkXPress software. The text and chapter openings are set in New Caledonia. This book was designed by Bill Adams, typeset by Kimberly Scarbrough, and manufactured by Thomson-Shore, Inc. The paper used in this book is designed for an effective life of at least three hundred years.